MORE
IF YOU'VE GOT IT
FIVE PLAYS FROM THEATER OOBLECK

Dave Buchen
Jeffrey Dorchen
David Isaacson
Mickle Maher
Danny Thompson

Hope and Nonthings
Chicago

Ugly's First World copyright © 1989 by Jeffrey Dorchen
Necessity copyright © 1998 by Danny Thompson
Innocence and Other Vices copyright © 2002 by Dave Buchen
Letter Purloined copyright © 2006 by David Isaacson
There Is a Happiness That Morning Is copyright © 2011 by Mickle Maher

ISBN 978-0-9815643-2-6
First Edition, July 2012
Printed in the United States of America

CONTENTS

PREFACE

Sometime around the winter of 1988–89, Bob Fisher and I drove north from Hyde Park to see a play at Cabaret Voltaire, a bar/performance space on the outskirts of Wicker Park. Word was that a new theater company from Detroit or Michigan or someplace had set up shop in the bar's back room, and what they had going was unlike anything anyone had ever seen before. Bob and I were in a theater company of our own at the time—an improv-based group trying to find its way out of Hyde Park and into the larger Chicago theater scene—so we were curious to see what all the fuss was about.

From the outside, Cabaret Voltaire seemed blank and lifeless—one nondescript building among the other dull, industrial structures around it. But inside, the place was hopping. This was an urban roadhouse of sorts, apparently, an art-freak speakeasy, hard to find and all the more enticing because of it. Out back, in what had once been a storage room or boiler room or some such, was the ramshackle, junk-house space created by Theater Oobleck to put on their plays.

The show we'd come to see was Jeff Dorchen's *The Slow and Painful Death of Sam Shepard*, a fictionalized account of the famous playwright's rise from backwoods Arkansas to pop-culture icon/sellout, and the family that spawned him. It was, as promised, like nothing I'd ever seen before. Sloppy, sprawling, insane, literary, hilarious, lowbrow, highbrow, unpredictable, and supremely theatrical. The one indelible image I carry from the performance is of a hunched-over Randy Herman (as Tom Wolfe) applying yet more Wite-Out to the whitewashed suit of a lanky Mickle Maher (as Sam Shepard) with the hopes of keeping Shepard looking as Wolfe-esque as possible. All this played out before a standing-room crowd hanging on every word of this brilliant new play. What's more, the company that created it was something altogether unto itself—a new voice defining a new way to think about and respond to the world. Theater, it seemed, didn't have to be respectable or adult or sexy or be written by someone dead or famous to earn its keep. Theater could be wild and anarchic and fun. It didn't have to have a director, an approach Oobleck was famous for, and it didn't have to be expensive. At Oobleck, you could see a show for a few dollars—or for free if you were broke.

That spring, Bob and I moved to the north side and, along with the other members of our ensemble, began creating plays of our own. Around that time, someone explained to me that the typical storefront company tends to last about seven years. People emerge from their 20s to find that they need to make money, or move to Los Angeles or New York (which I did), or raise children (which I also did), or try something new. Theater is hard. Running a small, off-Loop company that can't promise money or audiences or press but can promise the proverbial blood, sweat, and tears is nearly impossible. Life intervenes. This was true for my company which, though glorious while it lasted, effectively closed shop some five years after moving north. But Theater Oobleck, with some notable dry spells, has been creating theater every bit as thrilling, baffling, enlightening, and exhilarating as *The Slow and Painful Death of Sam Shepard* for nearly a quarter of a century. Over the years, I was lucky to be able to see a few of these shows and even perform in one, as Montgomery Clift in David Isaacson's *The Making of Freud*. For my money, there is no other theater company in America that has so consistently created original, excellent, principled theater—and their longevity and commitment are a testament to that fact.

Greg Kotis
Brooklyn, 2012

INTRODUCTION

Ann Arbor, Michigan. Fall 1984. A hand-scrawled flier on the wall of the Residential College announced auditions for a group of short plays. Show up anytime between noon and 2 p.m., it read. I arrived around 12:30 and found two guys sitting on a table, talking. I was there for the auditions. "Sorry, too late. We already handed out all the parts to our friends. If you want to perform, go write a play."

That was different. No more parts; go make your own.

My quickly assembled one-act would be included in this collection of short plays, titled *Joanna's Fine Foods*, mounted by Streetlight Theater Company. Streetlight was the brainchild of high school friends Jeff Dorchen and Danny Thompson. Dorchen says that, after high school, they had the idea of performing plays under streetlights on the corner near Dorchen's home in suburban Detroit. In college, says Thompson, he and Dorchen were sitting on an Ann Arbor curb one beautiful night, weary of submitting scripts to different campus theater companies—so they decided to start their own, naming the company Streetlight because they were sitting under one. One Streetlight motto: "Plays for people who don't have time to do plays."

These early one-acts were never actually performed under a streetlight, but they were short. Until Mickle Maher's full-length *King! Cow and his Helpers*, that is, staged in the Residential College cafeteria in 1984. Maher's was also the first play that did away with the director. Instead each scene had its own "facilitator," and Maher wrote an "author's tantrum" that was passed out with the program, calling for the end of directors.

The decision to eliminate the director was a political one. Many of the founding Streetlight members considered themselves card-carrying anarchists—the kind of anarchists that had done their intellectual homework and knew that anarchy was not synonymous with chaos and destruction but rather that it was a call to self-responsibility. As one can imagine, this no-director experiment presented some new challenges. As Maher recalls, 28 years later:

> *The decision to do without a director of course led to everyone being a little less up on their lines than they might've been. Dress rehearsal was a disaster. We ran the play—it was blechh—and sat down in our circle for the communal note session. And here it was, just like in the movies, the lowest point, where the hero is beaten and bloody and thrown to the mat and she's accidentally drunk poison and the music's stopped and it's not even raining and so forth—it felt just like that, when David Isaacson said (before anyone could give a useless note on the terrible rehearsal), "OK. We're going to take a ten-minute break.*

Then we're going to come back in here and run it again." And there was no discussion, no counter, no grousing—we just did it. Because not to would result in something too terrible to contemplate: a show below a standard we hadn't even really set for ourselves yet. We did two runs the night before opening, and on opening we were still sloppy and free range, but we killed it and it was the first time I understood what ensemble meant, the chemicals involved, the juice.

This doing without a director would become a cornerstone of Streetlight's working method, and was more fully realized with Thompson's 1985 play *El Presidente Is Not Himself Tomorrow*, when the idea of facilitators was sent packing, too. Instead, there were "outside eyes." At the end of a scene, the cast members would sit in a circle and deliver notes to each other. These were sometimes unruly, mind-numbingly contentious sessions. We spent hundreds of hours giving notes over the course of a single production. But for both performers and playwrights, the benefits were immense.

Consensus building within the outside eye process was all but an impossibility, so with Maher's *King! Cow*, the rule of "actor's prerogative" was born. Meaning, the actor gathers all notes from outside eyes and then decides which ones to take. In the end, the actor can even decide whether or not to change a line.

El Presidente was also an experiment in group rewriting. A rough version of the play was read and hours turned into days of painful hashing. This method is now more the stuff of crazy legend than some utopian ideal. But in the early days, some actors enjoyed their prerogatives, as did Dorchen in Isaacson's *Three Who Dared* (1988) when he decided to enter yelling the line, "Hey, Ezra Pound is lighting his farts on the front lawn!"

With the decision to eschew directors, another rule was born: the playwright must perform in the play as well. If the playwright was not in the play, as had happened with some of the early one-acts, the playwright could tacitly take on the role of director. Even though the decision to abolish the director had been an anarchist one, those of us who still wanted to exercise our electoral vote also understood the advantages of forfeiting the notion of a singular or unified vision. As Thompson says: "A mess of opinions suits theater. The eyes of a hundred audience members are rarely served by a single note giver. Sure, it's an easier system, but it's freakishly distrustful of everyone else involved, including the audience."

In 1988, Streetlight Theater Company moved to Chicago only to find there was another group named Streetlight. Many new names were considered—including Feather Throat Theater, Bug Fight Theater, The Obscene Plagiarists, and Theater Big—but it was Theater Oobleck, derived from Dr. Seuss' sticky green goo that falls from the sky and threatens the kingdom, that, after hours and hours of debate, was eventually chosen.

Oobleck has called Chicago home ever since. Over the past quarter century, a variety of participants have dedicated themselves to the group's rigorous working method and the promise of little remuneration. It was in Chicago that Oobleck firmly adopted its pricing policy of a suggested donation, followed by the tag line, "More if you've got it, free if you're broke." No audience member was denied access, regardless of his or her ability to pay. Unless, of course, the theater was full, which many times, as the group gained notoriety, it was.

Staged in 1989, Jeff Dorchen's *Ugly's First World*, the earliest work in this collection, rose out of the dawn of Oobleck. Dorchen had recently returned from a two-month solo trip to Morocco. Emotionally powerful, the trip provided vivid dreams, such as Lord Greystoke transforming into Tarzan, some of which became scenes in *Ugly*. Says Dorchen:

> *I thought it was really important to speak about postmodernism in an apocalyptic way, with music and comedy and commentary on capitalist imperialism. T.S. Eliot's Christianity annoyed me, especially as we in the U.S. had been severely smacked around by the Reagan "Morning In America" bullshit, which I thought was very Christian but little did I know how much worse it could get, as we discovered under W. Bush. Aleister Crowley seemed a great foil to that nonsense, and that he and Eliot were contemporaries seemed significant.*

In 1999, ten years following its Oobleck production, *Ugly's First World* was mounted at the Actors' Gang in Los Angeles. Produced by Mark Seldis, this version was directed by Bill Cusack, who had performed in Oobleck's 1989 production of Robin Harutunian's *In Cheap Shoes*. Cusack managed to cast a Dorchen doppelganger, Christopher Gerson, as the eponymous, lead zombie named Ugly. For the L.A. production, Dorchen heavily trimmed *Ugly's First World*, but the original, shaggy version is presented in this volume.

As company members' writing skills increased so did their skills as performers. And because playwrights continued to cast that remarkably consistent, yet slowly evolving, group of friends, an ensemble developed an identifiable and idiosyncratic style. Danny Thompson is one Oobleck playwright who writes parts with particular actors in mind. For his play, *Necessity*, first performed in 1998, he wrote the part of Thomas Edison with an eye on "that ball of fire" actor-carpenter-now restaurateur Ben Schneider. For Thompson's own role, he fashioned O.T., a "magical idiot" sidekick for Edison in the form of a backwoods *Forrest Gump/Slingblade* guy. In Thompson's irreverent tale, Edison is both an escaped convict and a mass murderer. Albert Schweitzer is on the chain gang, too. Says Thompson today:

> *I distrust heroes. I think the biggest con ever perpetrated on Americans was not pulled off by P.T. Barnum, who never expected anyone to*

believe him, but by Edison, who never believed anyone wouldn't. We may never know Edison's real story due to a lifetime of embellishments and lies. Lately, I'm having difficulty walking into a bookstore because of the mountains and mountains of Steve Jobs books on tables. I truly fear for us if we start trying to raise a generation of Steve Jobses. We're not even mistaking the captain for the ship anymore—we're mistaking the admiral for the fleet.

A similar distrust of heroes infuses Dave Buchen's *Innocence and Other Vices* (2002). Buchen joined Oobleck when it moved to Chicago in 1988. He went along to the first meeting "because that was what all my friends were doing." At the time, he was drawn to Oobleck for its political leanings. In fact, it took him a few years to realize that theater was a passion for him. But following that discovery, Buchen became a core member of the group, both as a performer and as a playwright.

He had been toying with the idea of writing a play about Luis and Isolina Ferré, a kind of "odd couple" brother and sister from one of Puerto Rico's richest and most powerful families, when the Kenneth Lay/Enron scandal hit. Buchen says:

> *In my memory, the reaction to the crimes of Enron was one of OH DEAR ME! How could this have ever happened? We used to be such an innocent country, now look at us; we have been sullied by these crimes. And it seems that this loss of national innocence happens quite regularly in the U.S. With Watergate we lost our innocence. The Vietnam War was the end of our innocence. The assassination of Kennedy ...*

Since Streetlight's beginning, David Isaacson has been a pivotal figure. And during the years when Oobleck risked disbanding as core members kept leaving Chicago, Isaacson kept hold of Oobleck's ropes and, on a number occasions, thwarted its disappearance. Throughout, he has written sprawling yet precise historically, politically, and theoretically informed opuses ("opera" is actually the plural of opus, and Isaacson's plays are operas of sorts, minus the music, minus the singing).

With its modular and permutative structure, *Letter Purloined* (2006) is a nod to Chicago's Neo-Futurists. Says Isaacson, "I wanted to write something where: a) the actors did not know what order the play would be in on that night, and b) where each order materially affected the plot and meaning of the play." True to Isaacson form, the play enlists a spectacular variety of sources—from Shakespeare to Kofi Annan to Derrida—and the variable structure allows the audience to witness the play being reorganized each night, a conceit that reveals something important about the mechanics of narrative and the nondirectorial imperative of Oobleck. Chance, in this play, becomes a sort of outside eye. With its original and stellar cast, including Colm O'Reilly in an astounding performance as Cassio, *Letter Purloined* was remounted as part of the 2006 New York International Fringe Festival.

Mickle Maher's *There Is a Happiness That Morning Is* (2011) is the most recent Oobleck play to be produced. Maher set out to write a play about sex and love and from the beginning he had the inimitable Diana Slickman in mind for the part of Ellen. After an early staged reading at the Goodman Theater and perfectly "nice" feedback, Maher knew something wasn't working—so he rewrote the play in rhymed verse.

The pastoral college setting for the play was inspired by Maher's time studying at Bennington in the mid-1990s. "It was always astounding to see people's dramas play out against such a backdrop of splendor," he says. "It made them both more dramatic and ridiculous at the same time. That was always in my mind."

In *Happiness*, Maher committed an Oobleck no-no. He did not perform in his own play. In fact, there have been a number of Maher plays produced by Oobleck in the last few years missing Maher as a performer. But don't worry, he will not become Oobleck's first director, nor would he want that. Maher is a prolific playwright and his plays are finding their way to stages across the country and in Europe. The Catastrophic Theatre's Houston production of *There Is a Happiness That Morning Is* opened soon after the first Oobleck run closed.

It is our hope that these original works, incubated within a close-knit, ever-shifting community with a history stretching nearly three decades and a very idiosyncratic working method, will have readers. Perhaps you will read them aloud. If you so choose, you will perform them. You will use a director or you will not. Or maybe, if there are no more parts because other people's friends have taken them all, these plays will inspire you to write your own.

Terri Kapsalis
Chicago, 2012

Danny Thompson's graphic for *Ugly's First World*,
made at two a.m. on the floor of a copy shop

Ugly's First World
by Jeffrey Dorchen

Ugly's First World was first performed in 1989 by Theater Oobleck at Theater Oobleck in Chicago, with the following cast:

Victim	Barbara Thorne
Cruel	Richard Boike
Stupid	Randy Herman
Ugly	Jeffrey Dorchen
Crowley	Mickle Maher
Ligeia	Terri Kapsalis
T.S. Eliot	Danny E. Thompson
Lord Greystoke	Randy Herman
Jane Clayton	Lisa Black
Ssamad	David Isaacson
Anna	Barbara Thorne
Jurgen	Dave Buchen
Mina	Robin Harutunian
Jesus	Dave Buchen

In a subsequent remount, the part of Mina was played by Wylie Goodman.

Original songs and music by Jeffrey Dorchen
Logo design by Danny E. Thompson

Acknowledgements
I would like to acknowledge all the Ooblecks whose gags I lifted; Micky, Stefan, Atti and Thomas, whom I met in Agadir, for the rashasha, I hope you all made it across the border; Del Close for the correct pronunciation of "Crowley;" Professor L____, in O____, whose name was changed to protect his innocence; Paul Castella for his pancultural wisdom.

Special thanks
To David Freiman for importing himself from NYC for the remount, Sharon Klein, Annette and Martin Greiner, Laura Saaf, Curious Theater Branch, the Outside Eyes, and again, Theater Oobleck, without whom this play would have been an unfinished novel written by a bitter, lonely person.

A NOTE FROM THE PLAYWRIGHT

Ugly's First World is about memory—fragmented and dissolving—and about hopes and desires. The main characters all seek drastic changes in their political and spiritual environments which they hope will turn them into happy people, or at least resolve some burdensome conflict within them. The fact that some of them achieve their goals is what makes this play farce. I wrote about an apocalyptic metaphysical shift because I don't believe I will ever witness one, and I wrote about it in a farcical way because I believe that without such a shift I will remain a prisoner of my misguided, boring life, forever overreacting to the annoyances of a society so petty, miserable, and spiritually hollow that even sensible people can often understand my dissatisfaction with it. The members of Theater Oobleck, who all have their own crotchets against our doomed culture, brought this play to life in their miraculous collective way, without a director. I don't want to imply that everyone in Oobleck is a misfit, but I certainly feel like one, and the fact that they could be so adept at bringing such a ridiculous person's voice to the stage so entertainingly leaves me admiring them as much as it makes me wonder why they didn't have any better way to occupy themselves.

The people I consider my colleagues and friends are very creative, lovable people, but they lack that quality of good citizenship that would motivate them to make significant contributions that would benefit the republic or create virtue among the landed aristocracy. Still, I believe there is an eccentric deity in some back alley of the cosmos who is tallying up our questionable achievements in a book of his favorite things, and we will all join him in a drafty, dilapidated Heaven where pesticide-free avocados are always ripe, we never get colds, records never scratch, movies are always free, the water pressure is always adequate, and my taste buds will grow back. We will all have a variety of useful sex organs and we will be stunningly attractive. The twenty-four-hour library will serve cider and greasy, crunchy doughnuts. The cops will all wear high heels and fall down a lot.

This play was written from the depths of my heartbreak and despair, so I hope you will approach it with an appropriate lack of maturity. Succumb to its dumbness. Handle it as you would a silly thing.

CHARACTERS

Victim
Cruel
Stupid
Ugly
Crowley
Ligeia
T.S. Eliot
Lord Greystoke
Jane Clayton
Ssamad
Anna
Jurgen
Mina
Jesus

Set: The only permanent set piece is the garbage collage/barrier, behind which characters appear or disappear as if on a puppet stage. It should be low enough on the downstage side to be easily vaulted over, and high enough upstage to conceal a crouching actor. It appears in all exterior Gotham City scenes; otherwise it is concealed behind curtains.

Acting style: My suggestion—and the way it worked for us—is that the zombies are slapstick cartoons, although their comic violence can and should lapse into a darker style as it becomes redundant. Apparently, having been in Hell causes one to talk like a Bowery Boy. The scenes in Eliot's apartment are stark and absurd, until he is saved, whereupon he and Cruel adopt a nineteenth-century presentational style of histrionics. The scenes in Morocco should be as realistic as possible after Jane leaves her husband, as Ssamad has told her he's taking her to the "real world." Even when there are linguistic and visual lapses into farce or unreality, as when the zombies appear as Moroccans in the cafe, or in internal monologues, a cinematically "real" style of acting helped us set these scenes apart from the lunacy of Gotham. When Tarzan returns, he brings with him the farcical qualities, destroying the Moroccan "world."

Accents: The symbol "@" indicates that a character is speaking with an accent, but it is not used consistently, under the assumption that common sense and actors' prerogative will come into play. In general, all Moroccans speak without accents when speaking in Riffi or Arabic, and Jurgen speaks without an accent when speaking in German. Choices should be strong enough to give the audience a sense of which language is being spoken, even on lines where the language isn't indicated before the line. Incidentally, those language disclaimers, set off before a line by a colon, are meant to be spoken. If a line is written: "Jurgen. In English: Hello there." The actor should say: "In English: Hello there."—the disclaimers being part of the dialogue. They are used with even less consistency than the "@." We spoke them in character, but without accents, even when the following line was in a language we normally spoke with an accent. Some disclaimers can be dropped or more added according to actors' prerogative, as long as clarity and rhythm aren't sacrificed. Ssamad has a thicker accent in German than in English.

Music: The music in this play is all performed by the zombies. They are musical zombies. They sing. They dance around and hit each other with things. Three very talented people should play them. A piano should be near or on the edge of the stage. One of the actors playing a zombie should be able to play it. Cruel should be able to play the ukulele. Ugly should be able to play the guitar without making too many mistakes. If you don't know any people who can do these things, maybe you can move to another town and meet some.

Props: To do this play you will need: Limbs, glasses of tea, entrails, a teapot, vomit, omelets, assorted trash, some cups, a knife, a candle lantern, a lighter, some string, coroner's things, a china teacup, A telephone, a wine sack, ink pad, a small coin, an index card, a dead rat, airline tickets, a hand mirror, a phone directory, a feather, a peach, a saucer, a ukulele, a grail, a neck brace, some rope, a letter from hell, a magic carpet, a sign that reads "IN ARABIC: APPLAUD THE BUFFOON," a guitar made from a human torso, a washbowl full of bloody water [optional], a 20 dirham bill, a Berber banjo, a photo of Ligeia in a standup frame, a briefcase full of torture devices, a book called *Aleister Crowley Versus T.S. Eliot: A mythical debate, by Jane Clayton, Lady Graystoke.*

ACT ONE

SCENE 1

Lights up, gloomy, on Victim, picking through the trash in an alley in Gotham City. She turns to the audience, gags, and vomits.

VICTIM

I'm ahead of my time and look at me, ain't it sad? Goddam Jesus gonna come back an' I'll put glass up his ass. Heaven's rippin' me off. Heaven's gonna follow me. I'm gonna kill God for doin' this to me. This guy gets a hard-on when he sees castration graffiti. This lady wants to get raped by Cary Grant, thinks she'll like it. They both tear the skin on themselves and make their sexes bleed. They smell like shit an' they hate themselves. They got pus all over 'em, biggest pimples I ever saw, pimple THIS BIG in their faces. You think Jesus is gonna fuck THEM? You gonna fuck 'em? All they want is to get fucked. You gonna fuck 'em when they're so ugly? You gonna fuck 'em ugly or you gonna try to make you think they're pretty like you think garbage is pretty? You should fuck 'em an' think they're ugly!

Jesus loves poor people, but he never fucked no ugly lepers. Lepers just wanna get laid. Jesus won't even call 'em on the phone. He wants to know what's the big deal. He's so pretty he gets his dick sucked whenever he wants it.

We're gettin' robbed! Everybody's goin' t' Hell. King Arthur went to fuckin' Hell cuz he didn't get no fair trial. Can't get no fair trial from God. You think God's gonna fuck you if you're ugly? I'm ahead of my time. You think I'm goin' t' heaven? Fuck you! I'm goin' t' Hell, don't tell me no more lies about that shit. I don't even have no food t' eat. Everything's cumin' outta me so I can't eat nothin' but myself. I threw up my lungs and my stomach and Jesus made me eat 'em.

[She scoops some puke off the ground and eats it.]

You think you're helping me? You think you're helpin' Africa? You can't do shit if you can't fuck no ugly lepers. You fuck a leper an' call her up next day. If you cry cuz she won't see ya no more an' she wants t' know what's the big deal, then you done somethin'. When you softskin apes suck their pimples any time they want, an' you cry cuz they don't love ya, then you can help Africa. You can't do shit. If you can't satisfy no fat ugly stupid cruel suicide your revolution is bullshit. You kill yerself cuz some leper don't love you, then you got a revolution. I'm ahead of my time, you think Jesus is gonna stick his tongue in my ass?

[Victim turns to root in garbage once more. Cruel the zombie appears behind garbage collage.]

CRUEL
NO MORE ROOM IN HELL!

[*Victim runs to where Stupid the zombie appears.*]

STUPID
NO MORE ROOM IN HELL!

[*Victim runs to where Ugly, hideously scabbed zombie, appears.*]

UGLY
NO MORE ROOM IN HELL! Ya scum-a-the-Earth bitch!

[*Lazzi of the chase, ending up with the zombies alone on stage.*]

UGLY
NAAAAH! She got away! Somebody better make me happy real quick, or I'll do somethin' horrible!

STUPID
Maybe she didn't get away. Maybe I ate her an' fuhgot.

UGLY
Ooo, you'd do that, too. If you did I'd hafta have Cruel here suck yer eyes out.

CRUEL
An' I'd oughta do it, too.

STUPID
Well, OK.

[*He offers his face to Cruel, who slowly brings his puckered lips toward Stupid's eyes. Ugly spots Victim peeking up from behind the garbage collage.*]

UGLY
There she is!

[*The Zombies dive after her behind the collage. Screams, growls. Severed limbs come flying onstage from the garbage. Lazzi of tug-of-war with entrails, etc. Stupid and Cruel climb back onstage over the collage; each picks up a limb and gnaws on it. Guitar strumming begins behind garbage. Stupid and Cruel begin a little step with the limbs as their ol' bamboos. They sing backup as Ugly emerges from behind the collage strumming a guitar made from Victim's limbless torso. They sing, "Living In the Kingdom Come."*]

"Living in the Kingdom Come"
(For three zombies, two severed limbs, and torso)

BACKUP
Living in the Kingdom Come

UGLY
I have returned from

BACKUP
Living in the Kingdom Come

UGLY
Living in a world where the hope for change was
Meager if not nil
I was not happy with the Death that I was living
I was not happy
So when my chance came I made my break
And I escaped from Jesus Christ who had enslaved me

BACKUP
Living in the Kingdom Come

UGLY
I was not happy

BACKUP
Living in the Kingdom Come

UGLY
Living in a world where my memories plagued me
Throughout the Eternal Night
I was not happy with the life I'd left behind me
I was not happy
And so I've come back to set things straight
And get revenge on all those fuckers who betrayed me

BACKUP
Living in the Kingdom Come

UGLY
I'll kick their asses

BACKUP
Down to the Kingdom Come

UGLY
I'll send them packing

BACKUP
Down to the Kingdom Come

[*The song ends.*]

UGLY
Ah, yes—revenge, my chummmmmmmmmmy rectal cankers.

CRUEL
YOUR revenge.

UGLY
That's right, ass-suck, MY revenge. Since I am the only one of us with any memory of his past life on Earth, you two have been allowed to tag along only as slaves at the beck and call of my monomaniacal revenge. Har har! And you despise me for it.

STUPID
Hey, dat's right! Fuck diss shit, I'm goin' home.

UGLY
Ah, but you are also completely in my power, almost.

STUPID
Oh yeah. I fuhgot.

UGLY
And you worship me! For it was I who dug our fuckin' escape tunnel up outta the overcrowded prison of Hell. It was I who cried out against the wicked Yahweh an' his snivelin' little brat an' the senile Holy Spook, an' to Allah an' Hoo-hah an' any other fuckin' fat-ass deity I cry defiantly, "Let my people go!" Not dat I care, I just like to cause trouble. An' as the tunnel widens, an' the lightbulbs are screwed in an' the wheelchair lift installed, the Defiant Dead of Hell shall spill out onto the wretched Earth like steaming blood from the spout of a harpooned whale!

CRUEL
Yeah, we worship you now, but when this is over we're gonna unwrap you like a onion.

UGLY
Ooo, I'm shakin'. Look. [*He shakes his hand in front of Cruel's face, then slaps him.*] What makes you think it's ever gonna be over? My vengeance shall live forever, for I am ugly and evil and eternally undead. Nyah ha ha!

9

But what ho! Some dude cometh.

CRUEL
[*Drawing a knife.*] Lemme go make a few slits in 'im before we tear 'im t' shreds an' eat 'im, all righ—Whoa!

[*They all cringe against an unseen force.*]

CRUEL
Shit! Sumpin' weird about dat guy.

STUPID
He makes me feel creepy ... Yuk!

[*Stupid and Cruel exit hurriedly.*]

UGLY
[*Standing his ground.*] Hey, come back, dummies. Yer s'posed t' feel creepy. Yer creeps! [*He cringes, stands his ground.*] I ain't afraid of no mortal man.

[*He cringes, increasing in disgust and fear until he is a quivering mass. Crowley enters. He begins to tidy up the stage.*]

CROWLEY
Hello, there.

UGLY
Don' hit me!

CROWLEY
Now why would I hit you? For making this mess? Oh, no no no, you're just a fun-loving animated corpse. Just out for a good time. I take it there's no more room in Hell?

UGLY
Who wants t' know?

CROWLEY
No one wants to know, of course. We've been robbed of that passion, like all others. No, the mass of men would surely rather stand on queues all day long, vacantly scraping their brains from their nostrils in the service of common sense than catch a glimpse of the terrible truth that could wake a putrefied gent such as yourself out of his infernal bed to dance on the echoing floor of the abandoned ballroom that is the Earth.

UGLY
What are you babblin'?

10

CROWLEY
I speak, of course, of the decay of the three worlds: Heaven, Earth, and the
Third World, Hell.

UGLY
"And the Third World, Hell." Listen, Chuckles, I done my time in Hell, an'
lemme tell ya somethin', you Earth guys got it easy.

CROWLEY
What do you mean? We're passionately bankrupt.

UGLY
Gosh, passionately bankrupt. An' here I am feelin' sorry for myself.

CROWLEY
Keep a civil tongue in your head! [*He swiftly claps his hand on Ugly's skull
and clutches it viciously.*] You feel that? You feel pain? Relish it, it's the only
passion left us on this moribund sphere. There it goes! Up into Heaven,
right into God's greedy little purse. Heaven's been leeching off our passions
for ages now.

UGLY
God damn, man, what is that stink cumin' offa you?

[*Crowley kicks him to the ground.*]

UGLY
OW! Motherfucker, you hurted me.

CROWLEY
Is there any love anymore? Any joy? No, it's all been stolen from us. Every
stillbirth, every pratfall, every fascist regime is just God's vain attempt to
squeeze more passion from us. But haha! The joke's on him! We've made
ourselves boring. That'll show him!

UGLY
Look who yer lecturin' on the injustice of it all, Pretty Boy. Will ya lookit
me?

CROWLEY
With God's help we've made this a bleak, grey world. And Heaven feels
the shortage, very sharply, I assure you. The economy of Heaven has never
been worse. The streets of gold have degraded to rusty iron. The harps
have withered to broken banjos. The demolished hull of Helios' chariot
lies abandoned in a vacant lot. Grimy faced cherubim hustle the streets in
rags. Unemployed saints lie passed-out drunk in doorways in puddles of
their own saintly vomit.

UGLY
Aw, my heart bleeds for 'em.

CROWLEY
Shut up, Filth.

UGLY
Ugly. The name's Ugly.

CROWLEY
Is it? How archetypal. A name pregnant with semiotic contiguity. If I heard that a zombie named Ugly had escaped Hell I would certainly be led to assume that something apocalyptic was afoot. In this case of course, I would have been sadly deceived.

UGLY
Yeah, fuck you too.

CROWLEY
You do not deserve the noble name of Ugly. And I will call you Filth until you do. Now, crawl away, Filth, before I crush you. And remember: the economy of Heaven could completely collapse any day. When that happens you could do worse than be on the good side of someone like me.

UGLY
The only good side of you's gonna be yer big fat byootocks retreatin' the hell outta my sight—all right, all right, I'm goin' already.

[*He skulks off.*]

CROWLEY
What pathetic scum. Who shall pay for the creation of dregs such as he? Surely Heaven is responsible, to a degree, but let's not let humanity off so easily. The malaise of modernity has tightened its grip on us all. Who is to blame? Who are the reckless ones who've all but destroyed the human capacity to feel, in the most essential sense of the word? Oh, I could point fingers. I could, for example, point at T.S. Eliot, in whose living room I now stand, into whose home you are about to become inert specters, pretending, according to the strictures of viewing theatrical realism, that you don't exist. How very exciting for you. And so what good to point the accusatory digit at T.S. Eliot when I could chop off my finger and toss it among you and more than likely it would land pointing at some other comatose carcass? But don't take such harsh words to heart. True Moderns never take anything to heart.

[*Crowley has set the next scene during his speech. He exits.*]

12

SCENE 2

T.S. Eliot's apartment in Gotham City. Table and two chairs. A telephone. Files and X-ray slides. Eliot enters with Ligeia, leading her by the arm.

LIGEIA

[*Pleasantly enough.*] Only winter's jealous embrace clings with such frigid fear as this hand on my arm.

ELIOT

[*Removing his hand from her arm.*] What? What does that mean? Winter? Winter has an embrace, you say? Someone is jealous of winter? Winter is jealous of you?

LIGEIA

Winter is jealous —

ELIOT

Winter is jealous? What? [*He is very confused.*] Be quiet! You want to cause trouble, right? You want to be a nuisance. [*He takes off his coat, jacket, tie and shirt during the following, leaving his undershirt on.*] I am taking off my coat. I am taking off my jacket. I am taking off my tie. I am taking off my shirt. I am leaving my undershirt on. What are you staring at? Are you thinking about winter again? Stop! It's warm in here. Take off your coat.

LIGEIA

What?

ELIOT

[*Tugging her lapel.*] Your coat. Take it off.

LIGEIA

[*Removing her coat and letting it fall to the floor.*] It falls away. Like the skin of a snake.

ELIOT

[*Picking up the coat.*] Like a coat. [*He drapes it over the back of one of the chairs.*] Like a coat! Like a coat! What are you staring at? I am correct. A coat is a coat! What do you want from me? [*He huffs angrily, goes to the phone and dials.*] I am calling your mother with the aid of this telephone.

LIGEIA

Mother? The storm that sired a tempest in a teapot? The chicken salad that laid a scrambled egg?

ELIOT

I'm trying to concentrate. A salad laid an egg? Is this some dream you had? I can't understand your words. Are you trying to tell a joke? Or are you hungry? I'll give you some cereal after I—Annabelle? Hello. This is obviously your brother Thomas. Listen to me, Anna. Anna, don't cry. Instead, come to my apartment. Yes, leave your place right now and come here. Now I have no more to say. I'll hang up. [*He hangs up. To Ligeia:*] Sit on the horizontal part of that chair. [*She sits. He sits in the other.*] I will now ask you a question, and you will answer it as clearly—please—as CLEARLY as you possibly can: Are you Ligeia Usher?

LIGEIA

[*Apprehensively.*] Do you have a volcano in your brain?

ELIOT

No. You have failed. I will try asking something different: what is the first thing you remember?

LIGEIA

Wrapped in twisting velvet, a galaxy. I fell. A poisonous crab was dislodged from my back by the fumbling hands of plummeting. Groomed, sleek and panting, arrival. The safety of midnight. The silver moon and the iron river. Happy birthday. Looking up from the animal feet of the four-legged, towering night.

ELIOT

Very well. We will try something entirely different. I will speak, and, if you want that cereal I mentioned, you will listen. Carefully: My name is T.S. Eliot. I am a famous poet, although lately I have been mentally incapable of writing. Or perhaps the problem is with my emotions. I don't know. In any case, I have had to give up poetry and take this position—[*He thinks about the word "position" and examines that of his body.*]—this JOB as the coroner of Gotham City, so I know very well the following facts: Three nights ago my niece, Ligeia Usher, failed to return home to the apartment she shared with her mother. At six minutes past seven o'clock the next morning her corpse was discovered in a vacant lot. Ligeia's torso had been forced open from inside the chest cavity. Originating in the heart, the force grew and broke through the rib cage, rending a vertical fissure from here [*Indicating his collarbone.*] to here [*Indicating his crotch.*].

LIGEIA

Like a coat!

ELIOT

That is the wrong response to a question I have not asked. I am sorry to disappoint you if you thought you were being clever. Had I asked the question, the answer would have been: "Like a human body that had been forced open from inside." Or, more accurately: "Like one hundred twenty-five such bodies." For in the past three days exactly one hundred twenty-five corpses have been found, all mutilated in the same manner, and all belonging, in the sense that a corpse belongs to the person whose intangible essence once inhabited it, all belonging to the same person: my niece, Ligeia. You may now open your mouth, but please leave it open and do not say anything.

[*Ligeia opens her mouth. Eliot examines her teeth, then some X-ray slides.*]

ELIOT
Thank you. Close your mouth, please.

LIGEIA
Rinse, spit, this won't hurt a bit.

ELIOT
I recall that writing songs and poems was something you were fond of ... IS something you ARE fond of ... but now is not the time for such activities. Please give me your hand.

[*Ligeia complies. Eliot produces an ink pad and an index card and takes her fingerprints. He compares them with another set.*]

LIGEIA
Have you fingered me yet, my pianist of the skin?

ELIOT
I am not your pianist of the skin!

LIGEIA
You hold the candle to the egg.

ELIOT
I do no such thing! No more insults, no more telling jokes! Dissemble no more! You are Ligeia Usher!

LIGEIA
[*Momentarily in pain.*] AH!

ELIOT
Your behavior has been inexcusable. Your mother and I have been alternately frantic and existentially puzzled. Leaving home without notifying us of your whereabouts. Cluttering up the streets with your one hundred and twenty-five deaths.

LIGEIA
Then you scramble the wrong egg! The egg that has hatched is the chicken to be counted! AAAAH!

15

ELIOT
Enough about eggs. Enough about candles and pianos and volcanos and spitting in teapots. You will now explain your actions, and afterwards I will give you some cereal.

LIGEIA
[*Pressing her hands to her solar plexus.*] AH! ... AAAAH!

ELIOT
That is a very dramatic representation of what I'm certain is genuine hunger, but the eating of the cereal will follow the explaining of the actions.

[*Ligeia's mouth contorts in silent agony. She flails frantically at her chest.*]

ELIOT
NOW what? You're itchy? Or are you dancing? Do you want the cereal or don't you? Explain!

[*Blackout. Sound of a scream and the ripping of flesh and clothing.*]

SCENE 3

Auditorium at Mohammed V University in Rabat, Morocco. John Clayton, Lord Greystoke, is delivering the commencement address. Jane Clayton, Lady Greystoke, and the Greystokes' Moroccan chauffeur, Ssamad, are in attendance, watching from seats that can later serve as the car.

GREYSTOKE
... and so on, and so forth, et cetera, et al, ad hoc, ad hominum, ad infinitum, blah, blah, blah.

[*Ssamad holds up sign: "IN ARABIC: APPLAUD THE BUFFOON"; sound of wild applause.*]

GREYSTOKE
And now some final parting words: To all outward appearances it must seem to have been a pleasure for me, John Clayton, Lord Greystoke, to serve here at Mohammed V University in Rabat, Morocco, as Professor of French and English Literature, just as it must have seemed, on superficial inspection, to have been a pleasure for my wife, Jane Clayton, Lady Greystoke, to tag along doing aimless, fruitless research.

JANE
[*Aside.*] Yes, what a smashing time we appear to have had. I've never shat so much in my life.

[*A murmur ripples through the audience: "Tarzan is coming! Tarzan is coming!"*]

GREYSTOKE
Silence! Who said that? Tarzan is NOT coming! Understand? Tarzan is NOT coming! Thank you. To continue: You've all been marvelous students, to the untrained eye. The passion with which you study European languages and literature could almost convince one that you didn't hold us in carefully disguised contempt.

JANE
[*Aside.*] Yes, it's very sneaky of you.

[*Murmurs: "Tarzan is coming."*]

GREYSTOKE
I said leave it out! Tarzan is MY alter ego. I say whether he comes or not. Thank you. To continue: But all good things, and even things that only seem good, must come to an end. Ramadan, the month of daytime fasting, begins tomorrow, and the wife and I are getting out of this Third World Hell. But Lady Greystoke and I will certainly be thinking of you as we sip our Darjeeling out at Greystoke Manor, remembering what a smashing time we would have seemed to have been having to the eyes of some uninsightful third party. Lastly I will just remind you that Tarzan is NOT coming, despite rumors you may have heard to the contrary. Thank you.

[*Ssamad holds up the "applause" sign again; wild applause. Jane crosses to Lord Greystoke. Ssamad follows.*]

JANE
Wonderful speech, darling. You gave voice to my sentiments exactly.

GREYSTOKE
Well, why shouldn't I? You've been bludgeoning my eardrums with those sentiments since the day we got here.

JANE
Yes, of course.

GREYSTOKE
Do you have the tickets, Ssamad?

SSAMAD
@ Yes, Sir John. Your airplane is leaving from Casablanca from now three hours.

GREYSTOKE
Good! Where the Hell is Cheetah with the luggage? Well, Ssamad, I must say that certainly only someone with the sensitivity of a potato could imagine that you have been of invaluable service to us and that we will miss you enormously.

SSAMAD
@ Thank you, Sir.

GREYSTOKE
Blast it's hot in here! Let me take off this bloody tie.

JANE
Oh, John, is it really true? Will we really be back in our own little English country garden by tomorrow morning, so that I may once again rot away the empty hours staring off into familiar surroundings?

GREYSTOKE
I promise you, my love. Damn, this jacket is strangling me!

[*Lord Greystoke removes his jacket and begins unbuttoning his shirt. Ssamad goes to help him, and slyly stuffs each article of clothing down the front of his dirty menial's jumpsuit.*]

SSAMAD
@ Let me help you, Sir.

JANE
At last! I must be dreaming! Oh pinch me, Dearest. Pinch me and say that Tarzan will never come again.

GREYSTOKE
Dammit, I said he wasn't coming! And don't worry, I shall soon be pinching you long into the night.

JANE
Yes, pinch me, Dearest. Pinch me to the quick. Make me feel something. I thought I could feel something here, but it's just no good. I haven't broken through my congenital numbness since my very memorable attack of appendicitis a good many years ago. But—Dearest, you mustn't disrobe here in the auditorium! We must set an example to the wogs!

GREYSTOKE
But I'm burning up! I'm hot and itchy, I tell you!

[*His shirt off, Lord Greystoke drops his trousers, revealing a loincloth. He beats his chest and gives the horrifying roar of the bull gorilla.*]

18

JANE
Oh no! John, you promised!

GREYSTOKE
Who am John? I and I Tarzan.

JANE
I hate you. Go away, you're ruining everything.

GREYSTOKE
We livin' in Babylon, mahn.

JANE
No we're not.

GREYSTOKE
You ahn me, womahn, we go to deep desert, in deep Africa, ahn out-Muslim dese Muslims. Smoke no kif, no ganja, no spliff. We show dat Jah people be dee freshest. Eat only camel dung, drink only our own urine.

SSAMAD
@ What about the tickets?

[*Lord Greystoke takes the tickets from Ssamad and tears them up.*]

JANE
That does it. John, if you're in there, I'm leaving you.

[*Lord Greystoke tries to appeal to her with the whimperings of a wounded ape. She remains cold. He takes her hand and pets himself with it, whimpering. In response to her steadfast rigidity he regains his dignity.*]

GREYSTOKE
Den I go widout you, womahn. Ciao ... ahn Jah love.

[*He exits. Jane stomps out to the car. Ssamad holds the door open for her, then goes around and gets into the driver's seat.*]

SSAMAD
@ Where we going, Lady?

JANE
Ssamad, don't call me "Lady."

SSAMAD
@ But you are wife of Lord. That make you Lady.

JANE
But I'm the wife of the King of the Jungle. That makes me Your Majesty.

SSAMAD
@ No. Sheena is Queen of Jungle. Lion is King. Tarzan is Lord of Jungle. That still make you Lady.

JANE
Well, call me something else, we're divorced!

SSAMAD
@ Where we going?

JANE
I don't know. What does one do after leaving one's husband?

SSAMAD
@ In Morocco woman don't leave her husband. But I think someone tells me that in America woman open shop to sell pottery and begins to fucking other woman.

JANE
Ssamad!

SSAMAD
@ It's true, I think someone tell me this.

JANE
Oh, what am I to do? I haven't felt connected with life at all, not since my awful and wonderful attack of appendicitis a number of years back. I had a fever so severe that all my senses became painfully acute. The slightest sound caused intense anguish. And in the midst of the fever, I had a dream. Two figures confront one another on a featureless plain. One is the poet T.S. Eliot, the other an eccentric sorcerer named Aleister Crowley. With a wave of his hand Crowley transforms Eliot into a frog and proceeds to crucify him upon a peach tree, and jam a peach into his mouth. Eliot is destroyed. But from the ruins of his amphibious corpse there springs a magnificently beautiful crystal city. This strange dream obsessed me. I wrote a book! I wasn't even aware of having written it until the publisher sent me the first edition. "What a marvelous book I've written," I said to myself. You see, my illness had passed, and with it all memory of intensity and obsession. Who was this passionate woman who'd written this book recording the triumph of ancient magic over modern despair? And this Aleister Crowley who inspired her, how envious I am of his unfettered lunacy. Have you ever heard of Crowley, Ssamad?

20

SSAMAD
@ No, but I have heard of T.S. Eliot. "Musing on the King my brother's wreck, and the King my father's death befo—"

JANE
—Oh, don't quote him to me. It makes my stomach hurt. And reminds me of my own numbness. I want to feel alive again. [*Pause.*] So I ask you, Ssamad, where will you take me?

SSAMAD
[*A heretofore unrevealed tone of grim self-assurance appearing in his voice.*] @ If we go where I want I will call you, not "Lady," but "Fish-and-chips," so you will get used to it.

JANE
Fish and chips?

SSAMAD
@ You will get used to it. [*He steps on the gas and they both jerk back with inertia.*] I will tell you in the language of the Moroccan guide: I shaou you, Fish-and-chips, I shaou you real Morocco not like Casa not like Marrakesh wit' so many hahssles diss iss goot mahns goot pipples harr. We make like diss for you bikuss you goot laidy. I knaou you, you frendt. I shaou you goot tings for you, aounly you.

JANE
And are they good people, Ssamad?

SSAMAD
@ Sure. Goot pipples. But Maroque is business. They know how to take care of themselves, make tourism work for them. Goot pipples, goot business.

JANE
[*Noticing unfamiliar terrain.*] Where are we going?

SSAMAD
@ You want intense experience?

JANE
Yes, oh yes.

SSAMAD
@ Then why don't you go with Tarzan?

JANE
Oh, Tarzan! Wherever I go with him he always has to prove his superiority

21

over everything. He doesn't want to connect with life, he wants mastery over it. Last year he burned down the carriage house just to prove his disdain for transportation. And once in the Himalayas he opened a pub just so he could beat all the Sherpas at darts.

SSAMAD
@ Why does he talk like a reggae guy?

JANE
It's an affectation.

SSAMAD
@ If he goes to the desert the rebels will kick his ass. That's where I take you, to the real world.

JANE
Are you a rebel, Ssamad?

SSAMAD
@ No, Fish-and-chips, communist. The only one in the whole country.

JANE
[*After some thought.*] What are the rebels, then?

SSAMAD
@ I do not know any rebels. I want to meet them. King Hassan gives much propaganda about them so I would like to meet them. But me, I am the only communist in the whole country. Very dangerous. I am very brave. The police catched me once, they tortured me. I show you the scars, dents in my chest like deep fingerprints in clay.

[*An old Berber woman crosses in front of the car. Ssamad slams on the brakes. She makes an angry gesture as she toddles off.*]

SSAMAD
@ But I do it for my people. Even though they think they are happy because of the tourists. You see, people like you and Tarzan, to us you are like ... like legends. Fairytales. When you come here it is like magic. Your world to us is like a land of fairytales. But one day the First World economy will ... [*To himself, without an accent as if groping in Arabic for the English equivalent.*] completely collapse ... [*With accent again, having found the word.*] ... fall down. Then no more tourists. Things will get bad and then the people will ask me. We will overthrow King Hassan, kick out religion of Islam, kick out the French, the Germans. Divide up the wealth. Lots of money here. No reason to have poor people here. You know? [*He looks back; Jane has fallen asleep.*] Sure, dream dreams, legendary Fish-and-chips. When you wake up I shaou you real world. I shaou you, Fish-

and-chips, you goot laidy, you frendt.

[*Blackout.*]

SCENE 4

T.S. Eliot's place. Eliot sits alone at the table. He calls to someone off.

ELIOT
I believe you have examined that corpse for a sufficient period of time. Please walk into this room now. [*Ligeia enters with a hand mirror.*] Please sit on the horizontal part of that chair. I feel certain that, having examined the fingerprints, skull X-rays, and your own reflection, and compared the telling features of yourself with those of the corpse in the adjacent room, you will agree that she and yourself are virtually identical.

LIGEIA
Well, the difference between a living human being and a dead body is a little bit significant, but—

ELIOT
Oh, you want to nitpick. Yes, you emerged from her body, and not vice versa. If you want to attack my postulate on those grounds I will have to accuse you of trying to make trouble.

LIGEIA
Oh, no. It's a fine postulate. I don't want any trouble. In any case, the more important distinction is that she is number 126 and I am number 127.

ELIOT
Number 127?

LIGEIA
Yes, number 127. Indivisible. Lucid. Prime.

ELIOT
Lucid? Yes, at least I can understand you. Not like the other one. All she could talk about was eggs. She was very confused. I'm glad she's dead.

LIGEIA
Well, the next prime number in the series won't arrive till number 131, so, if you value clarity, you'd better make use of me while you can.

ELIOT
I'm trying! But you keep speaking of other things. You are number 127, but in a series of what? And you speak as if you are going somewhere.

Where? And, yes, 127, a prime number, I will trust you about that for now. But what do these enigmas signify? I am trying to tell you something in order to receive a specific response. Listen. "Coroner's report; conclusion of autopsy: In the space of ten minutes, if time can be said to occupy space, a human fetus developed spontaneously within the left auricle of the heart and grew to full adulthood." That adult, incidentally, is you.

LIGEIA
I see, but—

ELIOT
I have listed the cause of death as "spontaneous accelerated cardio-ectopic pregnancy." My own term.

LIGEIA
It's ... very descriptive.

ELIOT
So now what do you have to say?

LIGEIA
Well, a long time ago, when the universe was young —

ELIOT
Stop! No no no! You will confine your comments to how you died. I mean, how you were reborn. That is, how you emerged from yourself through a rupture of tissue from the collarbone to the pubic symphysis.

LIGEIA
But you just told me.

ELIOT
But it's impossible. I mean, improbable.

LIGEIA
"There are more things in Heaven and Earth, Horatio —"

ELIOT
I am not Horatio!

LIGEIA
It's literature, T.S. Eliot. Haven't you ever heard of it?

ELIOT
No! I mean, yes! Oh ... I don't remember. Now you're mocking me. Isn't literature something that is read and written? Yes! I am correct! Literature is printed in ink on the pages of books. It does not emerge from the human

mouth in the form of noises.

LIGEIA
Oh dear. How pitiful. We've deserted you, left you a hollow man, headpiece filled with straw. Alas!

ELIOT
Please don't quote me, it makes my stomach hurt.

LIGEIA
You want to know what happened to your niece, but if I tried to tell you —

ELIOT
You are my niece!

LIGEIA
In a way. But I am also numbers one through 127 in the series. We are all present. I am merely the most recent, and therefore the most dominant, aspect. We act as exponents. I am Ligeia to the 127th power, so to speak.

ELIOT
That's not so bad. It's math. I don't understand it, but at least it's math. Continue.

LIGEIA
A long time ago this universe ran like a well-oiled machine. You on Earth created us out of your passions, desires, pains, and loves, and once created we fed on them and built from them the beautiful city of Heaven. And men and women continued to struggle on Earth while we maintained our city on the energy, created by those struggles, that rose up to us. But you became clever, learning how to ease your struggles. For example, your domestication of plants and animals was a particularly severe blow to our economy. Luckily, as we thought at the time, the enterprising young Yahweh conceived of feudalism, which, while it couldn't recreate in you the thrill of the tribal hunt or the bucolic joy of gathering food in the wild, did manage to induce enough misery to compensate for the loss of those more crystalline emotions. When passion ruled on Earth, Heaven could adorn itself with jewels. Pain is merely bricks and mortar. But Yahweh assured us that these austerity measures would be only temporary.

Meanwhile, stiff-necked people that you are, you stubbornly continued to try to improve your lot. So Yahweh sent down capitalism and systematic unemployment to taint the fruits of your technological progress, and sexual plagues to confound your attempts at clarifying your morality. Soon He began to get less and less return on His investments, but was, shall I say, ill-disposed to give up the power we had so foolishly abdicated to His financial expertise. Meanwhile, Yahweh had been working on a secret project: Hell. From what we'd heard, Hell was a sort of quarantined gulag where pain could be produced very cheaply. We were concerned, of course, but he assured us that only souls that had been excessively passionless on Earth would be sent there. So, we turned a blind eye toward it. That is, until it we discovered that Yahweh had secretly been deporting longstanding human residents of Heaven to his infernal slave camp.

ELIOT
This isn't math. I thought you were going to talk about math.

LIGEIA
What came to be called the Ex Post Facto Damnation Affair had been shrouded in the secrecy Yahweh had jealously cloaked around Him and His office. Too late we awoke to the fact that we were living in a dictatorship. Our legitimate protests were met with incommensurately vicious retaliation on the part Yahweh, who now ordered that He simply be called "God." Some of us disappeared. In the night they'd come for you, and in the morning you'd be found in a dumpster outside the Pearly Gates with your wings chopped off and your halo shoved down your throat! Our only hope was escape. And angels can only escape Heaven through the heart of the world's greatest poet, that gem, hidden among the living, your niece, Ligeia Usher, who has until now kept her genius a secret from you. [*Pause.*] And so, here we are. [*She pats herself.*] Safe, for the moment. Well, not all of us. Not yet.

ELIOT
[*Pause, then grimly.*] I'm very disappointed, Ligeia, that you would contrive such an elaborate hoax solely to insult your poetically impotent Uncle Thomas. You know how sensitive I am about it. But you never did like me, did you?

LIGEIA
How sad it is to find you thus incapable of believing an angel standing before you. Soon even memory itself will be too ephemeral for you to grasp. How sad. I'm sure whatever terrible confrontation lies ahead would have interested you greatly at an earlier time in your life.

ELIOT
I would send you away, but in the interest of science I must discover the truth. I suppose I'd better resort to torture.

[*Anna enters and sees Ligeia.*]

ANNA
What? ... WHAT? ... WHAT ARE YOU DOING TO ME? WHAT ARE YOU TRYING TO DO TO ME?!

ELIOT
Anna! Please become calm.

ANNA
[*Softly.*] Why?

ELIOT
Anna, this is your daughter ... the one we've seen so many times, recently, scandalously displaying her entrails to the public under the pretext of being dead.

ANNA
[*After a pause.*] I see. [*She sighs, goes to Ligeia.*] Well, the important thing is that you're all right. Don't worry dear, mama's here, you're safe now. Oh, you poor thing, you must be so confused. But you're alive now. Not dead. Do you understand the difference? Do you think you can stay this way for a while? Would you like to talk to someone? A counselor, a therapist?

ELIOT
Anna —

ANNA
Someone to reassure you of your position among the living, to quiet with insightful words the restlessness of your soul. Life is not so precarious as you seem to think. You needn't die without warning, it's just a delusion. Perhaps, with the correct medication, or shock treatments ... but you must be hungry. Your uncle will make us breakfast. Thomas, don't just stand there thinking about forensic medicine, go whip up some eggs.

ELIOT
Never!

ANNA
Thomas, the girl's been 125 corpses for the last three days. She must be starving.

ELIOT
A hundred and twenty-six.

ANNA
What?

ELIOT
Anna, your daughter has ... we have been deceived. I want you to go into the adjacent room. There is an object there which will demonstrate to you just how outlandishly Ligeia is willing to act in order to disrupt, to insult ... that is, to desecrate, to ... to ...

27

ANNA
Thomas, you're raving.

ELIOT
That is correct.

ANNA
I'm sure I can come up with a more reasonable interpretation—

ELIOT
Then go. Do so. Please.

[*Anna exits to the next room. She screams. Eliot gives a snort of vindication. Anna returns.*]

ANNA
You two. ... I can see that. ... You ... abominable ... goodbye.

ELIOT
Wait, Anna.

ANNA
This is a problem. You two need to solve this very serious problem and I will not be hit by any more ... stray bullets.

ELIOT
There are no bullets, Anna. It's very simple. This one came out of that one. It's called spontaneous accelerated cardio-ectopic pregnancy.

ANNA
Is that supposed to make me feel better? I understand, Ligeia. This is a cry for help. Thomas, she always looked up to you. If you hadn't given up poetry to become the city coroner Ligeia would never have had to set people on fire and become 126 corpses by giving birth to herself just to get our attention.

ELIOT
Set people on fire?

ANNA
Enough. I'm going home. I'll see you tomorrow. In the meantime you two will heal all these wounds between you. Do you understand? I will not be victimized anymore! I demand healing! Do you hear me? Healing of wounds! Tonight! While I sleep! Goodnight! [*She exits.*]

LIGEIA
"While I was fishing in the dull canal

28

On a winter evening round behind the gashouse
Musing on the king my brother's wreck
And on the king my father's death before him —"

ELIOT
I said don't quote me!

LIGEIA
You are the Fisher King of your poem, Eliot. Fishing in a wasteland. The kingdom dying. Who can rejuvenate you? Where is the innocent? Who will bring the dying, impotent king his grail?

ELIOT
I'm going to sleep. [*Exits.*]

LIGEIA
AH! Oh, the next one coming through. I'll go outside. Poor Eliot. The least I can do is not get more blood on the floor.

[*She exits. Blackout, scream, and the ripping of flesh.*]

SCENE 5
An alley in Gotham City. Ugly paces. Cruel plays with a dead rat and a cigarette lighter. Stupid sits on the garbage collage, reading aloud from the phone directory.

STUPID
Boswell, James.

UGLY
Nope.

STUPID
Boswell, Jane.

UGLY
Nope.

STUPID
Boswell, Jane again.

UGLY
No again.

STUPID
Huh. Boswell, Jane again.

UGLY
Skip t' a new one.

STUPID
Boswell, Janice.

UGLY
[*Confused at first, as Stupid has pronounced the last syllable "ice."*] Nope.

CRUEL
I think we can assume dat Boswell don't ring a bell.

STUPID
Shuddup!

UGLY
Cruel's right, Stupid. Skip t' a new last name.

STUPID
Boswick, A.

UGLY
Nope.

STUPID
Huh. Boswick, A. again.

CRUEL
Enough, already! What kinda revenge are we gonna get if you can't even remember who did what to ya?

UGLY
Jus' gimme some time. Duh fog is liftin'.

CRUEL
But diss is gonna take forever.

UGLY
We have forever, asshole.

STUPID
Hey, look, you guyses. Maybe it'd go faster if we used diss skinnier book I found.

UGLY
Don' be a idjit.

STUPID
But I hafta. [*He leafs through the book.*] Look, dere's pitchers in it.

UGLY
Throw it way an' get back t' work.

STUPID
But it's a real puuuuuuurty one.

UGLY
[*Grudgingly looking at the picture; aside.*] Holy cow! Sumpin' about diss pitcher is makin' me have a flashback!

[*Sounds of a demonic chorus. Stupid and Cruel reel off in the swirling light change of Ugly's flashback.*]

UGLY
[*On his knees.*] Ligeia! Ligeia!

ELIOT
[*Appearing.*] Go away!

UGLY
Ligeia!

ELIOT
This is a warning. My sister called me with the aid of her telephone to tell me that you might be on your way. I, in turn, called the police with the use of a similar machine. If you don't want to be arrested for harassing my niece, then you must go away now.

UGLY
Ligeia!

[*The police, played by Cruel and Stupid, each grab an arm.*]

ELIOT
She doesn't want to see you, Johnny. She hates you.

UGLY
Let me go!

ELIOT
Goodnight. [*He disappears.*]

UGLY
Let me go! Let me go!

[*The flashback is over. Ugly struggles against Stupid and Cruel.*]

UGLY
Lemme go! Lemme go, ya idiots!

CRUEL
[*Letting go.*] All right! Jeez, you were goin' mitty!

STUPID
You have duh right to remain silent. Anyting you say —

UGLY
Let go a' me, Stupid. [*He jerks his arm away.*]

STUPID
[*Indignant.*] Dat's my name, don't put too much starch in it.

UGLY
[*Retrieving the slender book and opening it.*] Ya mean don't wear it out.

STUPID
Yeah! an' don't wear it wid anyting plaid!

UGLY
Stupid, do me a favor.

STUPID
Whut?

UGLY
Kiss my knee.

STUPID
Aw, did you hoited yooseff on you little kneenie weenie?

[*Ugly has reclined with his knee raised, leafing through the book. Stupid goes down to kiss Ugly's raised knee, and Cruel is about to give the back of Stupid's head a hard whack with the phone book, when suddenly Stupid and Cruel jerk to attention, like dogs pricking up their ears. Stupid and Cruel exit quickly. Ugly remains absorbed in the book.*]

UGLY
"Ah, yes, T.S. Eliot. In your so-called poem, 'The Wasteland,' you cast yourself as the Fisher King, limp, parched, dying in a dying landscape.

32

Ancient magic cannot save you, and as witness you call your own soggy and erroneous Tarot, wielded by a chintzy fortune teller."

[*Crowley enters. Ugly is absorbed in reading, but scratches and massages himself in annoyance on his Crowleyward side.*]

UGLY
"But though you may be the king of twentieth-century poetry, you, yourself, T.S. Eliot, are the plague that infects you and your kingdom. It is not magic that is powerless, but you and the century you've dragged down with you."

[*Ugly finally notices the origin of his skin irritation in the presence of Crowley.*]

CROWLEY
Please continue. I'm enjoying it. [*Pause.*] READ ON!

UGLY
"My good man, when you published this 'Wasteland' of yours I was on the island of Sicily, systematizing all the world's magic and science into one great Book of Law. I scaled the Himalayas, snorted cocaine and heroin, scandalized my native England and attained the title of Magus 9th and 2nd degrees in the Hermetic Order of the Golden Dawn!"

CROWLEY
[*Swooping in, snatching the book away, and out again.*] That's enough.

UGLY
How rude!

CROWLEY
[*Examining the book.*] Your necropolitan accent was beginning to vex me.

UGLY
An' yer a dick.

CROWLEY
You will cease the prattle. Hmmm ... this is fantastic! *Aleister Crowley vs. T.S. Eliot: a mythical debate by Jane Clayton, Lady Greystoke.* What are you doing with this?

UGLY
Rediscoverin' my bitter past with the help of a pitcher in dere of T.S. Eliot. An' now, if ya'll excuse me—

33

CROWLEY
Like photos, do you? Take a look at this one. [*He shows a page to Ugly.*]

UGLY
YAAAH! Oh, hey, dat's you. What're you doin' in dere?

CROWLEY
I am Aleister Crowley.

UGLY
Oh, yeah? Well, if you're him, what're you doin' here? The book says he's in Sicily.

CROWLEY
I was. Until Mussolini and his fascists threw me out. Right after Eliot published "The Wasteland," I might add. A year to the day.

UGLY
Dat s'posed t' be significant?

CROWLEY
So you're interested in Eliot, are you? Well, listen to this little tidbit I found on a scrap of newspaper: something, "corpses of" someone ... "T.S. Eliot, former Poet Laureate of Gotham City, who gave up poetry to become the city coroner ..." Amazing, isn't it?

UGLY
No.

CROWLEY
Ah, shall I tell you a tale? The tale of the Fisher King, whose lands became barren and whose body withered with the land, but who was saved by the sacrifice of an innocent named Parsifal? What happened to them, the dying King and his innocent savior? Why, they were reborn as the dying King Arthur and the innocent Sir Percival, who saved his liege by bringing him the Holy Grail. Though not in Thomas Mallory's later, more cynical ver —

UGLY
Get t' the point. I got some revenge t' organize. What's diss all got t' do wid T.S. Eliot?

CROWLEY
T.S. Eliot is the seminal poet of this century. As such, it was his job to be passionate, to create passion. And what is passion?

34

UGLY

Oh ... yeah, I remember. Passion is, like, the money of Heaven, and God's like the President dat needs all yer money.

CROWLEY

Yes, God's an investor. He invests in Eliot, Eliot is a washout. God swallows a loss. Financial disaster in Heaven. God scrambles, reinvests in Hell —

UGLY

Slave labor, low overhead.

CROWLEY

Yes! An extremely supply-side move. It's not going to sit well with most of the angels, I'm sure. Angels are notoriously liberal.

UGLY

All right, I'm grapsin' diss. But Eliot's a Fisherking Arthur cuzza why? Cuz God won't give him grants t' write poetry no more?

CROWLEY

Oh, it's just a metaphor, really. Of course, in the numinous realm, metaphors do tend to take on lives of their own. Witness Eliot: the wasted king wasting away in his wasteland. Forsaken by God. But Eliot's ruin may be God's as well. If the time were ripe, I'd need only to amass my delegation and await my chance. This Jane Clayton could be useful. How I would love to meet her. I have so few sympathizers, what with the Italian Fascists and all of England reviling me as the Antichrist. But all that will change, one day, yes, and soon, I can feel it!

UGLY

Don't count yer chickens yet ... Al. What if diss Sir Merciful guy brings Eliot a cup of Holy Braille?

CROWLEY

You know, I once cured a descendant of King Arthur, a certain Lord Pendragon who was addicted to heroin.

UGLY

Oh! Well isn't dat inneresting?

CROWLEY

But the King Arthur in Eliot can never be saved. Only an innocent could bring Eliot his grail. And thanks in part to him and as he himself would tell you, innocents are few and far between these days.

UGLY

You got dat right. But ... Al ... alla dese teeoretical notions is really so unnecessary. Eliot's gonna get his cuz I'm gonna give it to him.

CROWLEY
The theoretical notions, Filth, are not unnecessary, but have in fact predicted what has come to pass! It is your revenge that is unnecessary!

UGLY
My revenge is not unnecessary! How will my vengeance be avenged without revenge?

CROWLEY
But Eliot's already destroyed!

UGLY
Yeah, if he thinks he's destroyed now, wait'll I —

CROWLEY
But, Filth, the events in Heaven —

UGLY
Goddammit my name is not Filth it is Ugly and do not talk to me about Heaven because Heaven don't got nothin' t' do wid me! I'm talkin' reality!

CROWLEY
I'm sorry, Ugly ...

UGLY
Y'know what yer problem is, Al? Yer a thinker. I'm a doer. Hey, ya called me Ugly.

CROWLEY
That's right.

UGLY
I guess you wanna be my friend or sumpin', huh?

CROWLEY
Yes, Ugly, I would like to keep on speaking terms with you.

UGLY
OK, den gimme some money. [*Pause.*] Five bucks.

[*Crowley reluctantly draws money from his pocket, holds it out, and Ugly gingerly snatches it away, then turns to go.*]

UGLY
Thanks sucker.

CROWLEY
[*Sweetly.*] Oh, Ugly ...?

UGLY
[*Returning, equally sweet.*] Yeeees, Mistuh Cromwell?

CROWLEY
Crowley. So, we have an alliance, however tentative?

UGLY
Heck, Al, we're friends for life. Whatever you say, Al. Bye, Al!

[*He goes. Lights fade on an inscrutable Crowley.*]

SCENE 6

Campground on the Atlantic in Morocco. Interior of tent, Jane alone, wearing Ssamad's jumpsuit.

JANE
Ssamad and I never made it to the desert. We were pulled over by two policemen on a moped who told us that our car looked very like the one they had misplaced a few days earlier. We all had a jolly laugh about that, and then the two policemen threw their moped into our car and drove away. We began to hitchhike, and were soon given a ride by a German hashish smuggler named Jurgen to this campground by the ocean. We have spent the last three weeks here living in Jurgen's Berber tent and smoking his hashish. I am extraordinarily bored here. Ssamad and Jurgen have fallen in love, and Ssamad has ceased to be a source of entertainment for me. I sleep in Jurgen's Ford caravan to avoid being kept awake by the noise of their passion, although it no longer causes such painful longing for the Ape Man as it did at first. Now it only annoys me. Everything annoys me. The sea, the erratic hours of the little shop on the edge of the campground, the angry little man in the shed near the entrance who takes our money each day, the filthy hole over which I must squat for an hour each morning squeezing out painful yellow puddings. The fact that we never leave this campsite. I wonder what Crowley would have done in this situation. He would never allow himself to arrive in such a situation. This annoys me.

[*Ssamad enters, wearing Lord Greystoke's tux.*]

SSAMAD
@ Hey, Fish-and-chips, you have cigarette, I make joint.

JANE
I don't want any hashish, Ssamad. It makes me restless and irritable.

SSAMAD
@ Poor Fish-and-chips. Everything is so bad with no more rich Tarzan and no more servants. I make tea. Good mint tea for Fish-and-chips.

JANE
Your Moroccan tea tastes like toothpaste. Can't you send Jurgen out in the caravan for some black tea? Where is he?

SSAMAD
@ He is outside. Making a surprise for you. You will like it.

JANE
A surprise? You mean he's learned to speak English beyond the level of a three-year-old?

SSAMAD
@ No, it's a real surprise. Give me sixty dirhams.

JANE
What for?

SSAMAD
@ For surprise!

JANE
Your asking me for money is no surprise.

SSAMAD
@ Ah! There is your white English imperialist racism coming up again.

JANE
I am not racist. Everyone annoys me equally.

SSAMAD
@ Yes, you think I am a primitive woggie. Like an animal. That is why you are not shocked that I fuck a man. It is charming to you, like your little Pekinese fucking your shoe. Hoo ho! Look at the little brown faggot!

JANE
All right! Here's sixty dirhams. What does shock me, Ssamad, is that a sober communist like yourself is such a romantic.

SSAMAD
@ Not a romantic. That's for you. I am in true love.

JANE
He's going to leave, Ssamad. He's just a tourist, like me.

SSAMAD
@ No, you are not a tourist. You are my friend. And Jurgen, he speaks bad English and I speak bad German. We cannot understand the other one, and that is true love. He is a communist also.

JANE
No, Ssamad, he is just a hippie. It's an easy mistake to make.
SSAMAD
@ He loves this country.

[Jurgen enters with teapot and Mina.]

JURGEN
@ Surprise already!

JANE
You've bought me a slave?

SSAMAD
@ No, funny Fish-and-chips. This is Mina. She is from the Rif Mountains, Berber like me. From Bab Taza like me. She works in the market. Jurgen found her and she makes us rashasha.

JANE
What is rashasha?

SSAMAD
@ Opium tea. You will like it.

JANE
I will like it. You always say that.

SSAMAD
@ It's true! You will!

JURGEN
@ I'm making cups to find for rashasha putting in to drink.

JANE
Idiot.

JURGEN
[*To Ssamad.*] In German: What did she say? She called me a name. All I'm trying to do is be nice.

SSAMAD
@ In German: No she is very happy. In English: Sun is going down, time to smoke and have a party!

MINA
In Arabic: Do you have sixty dirhams?

SSAMAD
In Riffi: Speak to me in Riffi. Here's sixty. You'll give me twenty later, right?
MINA
In Riffi: Yes. You're a good boy. So good you'll take only fifteen from a poor lady who really needs the money, right?

SSAMAD
In Arabic: Sheesh. All right.

MINA
In Riffi: Speak in Riffi. We're from the same village. I know your mother.

SSAMAD
In Riffi: A lot of good it does me to have connections with other poor people.

JANE
Does she speak French?

MINA
Oui.

SSAMAD
@ No.

JANE
English then?

MINA
Oui.

SSAMAD
@ No.

MINA
What did she say?

SSAMAD
She said she wants to look at your carpets later.

MINA
Make her buy something and I'll give you twenty percent.

SSAMAD
Thirty.

MINA
I remember the day you were born. What a red little face, what a —

SSAMAD
All right, twenty.

MINA
Such a good boy.

JANE
What are you two saying to each other?

SSAMAD
@ Talking about our village.

JANE
Are Berbers very different than Arabs? Do they still do pagan things? Magic?

SSAMAD
@ Oh, sure. Different from Arabs. Arabs have all the money. Berbers live in the mountains and eat human meat and make human sacrifices. Don't ask silly tourist questions about magic, drink your tea.

JANE
I am, it's awful.

JURGEN
@ You're wanting more sugar now for drink it?

JANE
Dammit, learn the bloody king's tongue, you baby-eating Hun.

SSAMAD
@ In English: Why do you have to make trouble with him? He's trying to be nice.

JANE
Bloody knackwurst.

JURGEN
In German: What did she say about me?

SSAMAD
@ In German: She says she likes German food much. In English: Why don't you learn German so you can insult him better?

JANE
Sure. Learn German. "I will like it." I'm surrounded by cannibals! [*Gags.*] I'm poisoned. I'm going to be ill. [*She exits.*]

JURGEN
In German: Is she going to puke?

SSAMAD
@ Huh?

JURGEN
Throw up. Vomit? [*He acts it out.*]

SSAMAD
@ In German: Yes, vomit. She will like it.

JURGEN
Whatever. [*He lights up a hash joint.*] Mensh. That rashasha's good. I have to lie down.

MINA
In Riffi: Are you taking the caucasian prostitute to the Rif to see God?

SSAMAD
Hahahaha! That's a good one! See God! Lotta tourists fall for that?

MINA
It's not a scam. People are saying that God is in the Rif and soon he'll lead the Berbers against the Arabs.

SSAMAD
What? You're crazy!

MINA
Hey, have some respect. It's true. Everyone knows about it. Ask in the market.

SSAMAD
Allah is in the Rif?

MINA

Not Allah. A new god for Berbers. Really. King Hassan is afraid of him. You can get arrested just for talking about it.

SSAMAD

Hassan is afraid—no, you're a crazy old woman.

MINA

Look at this letter from my brother, smartass.

SSAMAD

[*Examining letter.*] I don't believe it! This could cause a civil war!

JURGEN

[*Delirious.*] @ In English: I will like it. You will like it. He will like it. She will like it. We will like it. They will—

[*Jane runs back in.*]

JANE

I vomited!

JURGEN

I vomit, you vomit, he vomit, she vomit ...

JANE

[*Eagerly pouring more rashasha.*] Visions! I've had visions! Imminent spectacle! The square root of negative one! The fisherking rejuvenated! Oh my god how wonderful my god, my god, my god. [*She drinks more tea.*] Delicious! Heathen swine! Fill my grail! I am reborn.

SSAMAD

@ In English: You want to go to the Rif? Big Messiah there! Magic. You will like it.

JANE

Magic? Yes! I knew it! You just found out about a Messiah?

SSAMAD

@ Yes. I am interested also. In German: Jurgen. You want to go to the Rif?

JURGEN

Sure. I've almost smoked this whole kilo. I have to go there to buy some more shit.

JANE

What does he say?

SSAMAD
@ We leave tomorrow.

JANE
I knew it! I wished it. Any wish you make while vomiting comes true.

MINA
In Riffi: I want to go to the Rif. I'm sick of it here. Will you make the smelly German born of questionable parentage give me a ride?

SSAMAD
In Riffi: I think I can work it out. @ In German: Can we leave tomorrow?

JURGEN
@ Fuck ja! Bergestuffe or bust.

SSAMAD
In Riffi: We leave tomorrow.

MINA
Thanks. You're such a good boy.

JANE
A Messiah! Yes, I am poised on the crest of a wave rolling toward the shore of a new world.

SSAMAD
I am poised on the brink of a revolution. I can taste it!

JANE
Fellow cannibals! Drink up this blood of the stars! The heavens await our next move. Let us all vomit as one. I am alive again. The cards of the forbidden tarot of Aleister Crowley dance before my eyes! The planets ring like alarms to waken the dead! The winter of the soul is over. April is here!

[*Blackout.*]

SCENE 7
Gotham City, night. Garbage/collage. Anna, alone, out of breath, enters.

ANNA
Something's after me. A monster! An anxiety, a monstrous anxiety, an imminent knowledge, a revelation in escrow, lurking in the shadows. A potential suspicion that the world is a lot more grotesque and painful than I could ever have imagined. A horrible monster lurking at the edge of

my sight. It ... it's here! In the garbage! [*With trepidation she brings her gaze behind her to peer over the collage/barrier.*] AAAH! Oh, it's only you, Ligeia. Oh no, not again. Ligeia, you have to learn to exercise your attention span. You can't keep going from alive to dead and back again like this. You have to concentrate on one or the other, or you'll never really excel at either one.

[*Crowley enters.*]

CROWLEY
Nice weather for giving oneself a good tongue-lashing, isn't it, Madam?

ANNA
Excuse me, you rude man, I was talking to my daughter.

CROWLEY
Your daughter! [*Peers over garbage.*] Oh, yes. Been handled a bit roughly, hasn't she?

ANNA
It's not the first time.

CROWLEY
No? Experienced slasher, are you?

ANNA
I beg your pardon?

CROWLEY
Slit women from throat to cervix quite often, do you?

ANNA
Certainly not!

CROWLEY
But you said this wasn't the first time.

ANNA
No, this is in fact the 127th time I've seen my daughter in this awful condition.

CROWLEY
I see. You suffer from multiple personalities.

ANNA
The only personality I'm suffering from is yours! Have you no sympathy for the mother of a juvenile delinquent? Look at that ribcage! Shattered.

45

Exploded from the inside. The 127th time. Is that any way for an intelligent young woman, a gifted poet, who's had every advantage in life, to behave?

CROWLEY
[*Who has been peering intently behind garbage.*] Certainly not, madam ... I see what you mean ... hmm ... yes ... exploded ... a poet, you say?

ANNA
Well, I may be her mother, but I don't think I'm bragging when I say that she is the most brilliant poet of this or any century.

CROWLEY
Hmm. You may be right. This is very interesting. Madam, did you know that your daughter is a victim of spontaneous accelerated cardio-ectopic pregnancy?

ANNA
Yes, I ... what are you doing? Stop poking around in there! Get out of here you necrophiliac pervert!

CROWLEY
What? Oh, yes, madam, necrophiliac, as you say, madam. Goodnight, madam. [*He exits.*]

ANNA
Oh, god. Cardio-ectopic pregnancy. How could you, Ligeia? I wasn't a good enough mother to you, you have to give birth to yourself? Oh, this is too much! To be rejected so completely as your mother. First you outgrow me emotionally and now, biologically. Yes, I'm not myself. My body is no longer that of a mother. Do I even have a body? With my motherhood denied, what body have I left? The body of a woman. Yes, a woman's body, and the desires of a woman. A woman alone. I embrace these desires, I embrace my loneliness. I'm so lonely. My vagina itches like a huge mosquito bite.

STUPID
[*Entering.*] NO MORE ROOM IN HELL!

ANNA
[*Running to him and embracing him.*] Oh, sir! Please help me. I'm so very lonely. So vulnerable and unstable tonight. Please tell me you feel the same.

STUPID
Gee, I guess I am lonely. I can't find my friends anywhere. An' what makes me feel even lonelier is dat even if I do find 'em, they'll just be mean to me an' beat me up. But yer nice. Yer soft, like a rabbit.

ANNA
Please put your thousand-pound penis inside me.

STUPID
Sorry, it fell off while I was dead. Or maybe somethin' ate it.

ANNA
Just put your hand there then.

[*He does.*]

STUPID
Wow! Diss is just like the inside of a split-open rabbit. Smooshin' around in its guts!

ANNA
I love you.

STUPID
I love you too.

ANNA
Come with me.

[*She leads him off. Ugly enters, followed by Crowley.*]

UGLY
Leave me alone, will ya? When I said we could be friends, I didn't think you'd get so clingy.

CROWLEY
Did you hear what I said?

UGLY
Yeah, I heard ya, ya said, "God's a dickless fatass."

CROWLEY
Fascist dictator, not dickless fatass. Fascist dictator.

UGLY
Look, ya don't hafta badmouth him to me, I hate his guts plenty. But ya gotta go now cuz I gotta meet up with my pals, an' if they see you with me, they'll run away.

CROWLEY
God has become the fascist dictator of Heaven, and the angels are escaping. I'm certain they mean to overthrow him from outside.

UGLY
D'you get enough sleep?

CROWLEY
The angels can only escape Heaven through the heart of the world's greatest poet. And I've seen the body of the person through whom they're escaping to Earth. [*Sound of ripping flesh and a scream.*] There! Another angel has arrived!

UGLY
No sir. Dat, my man, was one of my people, released from their bonds a' slavery, takin' a big bite outta the human race. Eatin' people, as is their nature.

CROWLEY
I'm telling you, the angels are forming an angelic partisan resistance against the Almighty. This is your chance, as they say on Wall Street, to "get in on the ground floor."

UGLY
The ground floor of Heaven, huh? Seems like I been dealt dat deal before.

CROWLEY
Don't you even want to hear my offer?

UGLY
No. Cuz I don't like you. You gimme the willies. On top of which you follow me around alla time, which I don't like, especially now at diss moment in time when I am on the verge of enactin' my revenge, now dat I have fully recalled who I was before I died an' what shit was done to me an' who dunnit. I need Stupid and Cruel right now, not you!

CROWLEY
Of course you need me. The world needs me. I'm going to change the world. I'll find Jane Clayton, she'll help me. She understands, she believes, it's all in the book, she captured my voice perfectly. Together we'll make the world safe for people like me. People with radical ideas. People ahead of their time. I'm ahead of my time! I deserve a break! Today!

UGLY
Kin I have my book back?

CROWLEY
NO! I never want to hear my words come out of your mouth again. It was a nauseating experience. My words pouring forth from your gorge like vomit!

48

UGLY
Listen, yer foolin' yerself if ya think you kin change anyting. If the angels got a plan of their own nuttin' you kin do kin change it. Angels don't give a shit about you or me. I oughta know.

CROWLEY
You know nothing! I am close friends with Ashtaroth, one of the greatest angels. Haven't been able to get in touch with her through the usual channels, though. God must be blocking ethereal transmissions. But the girl! Yes, the poet through whom the angels are escaping. Ashtaroth is sure to be among them. I must protect her till she comes through. She's in great danger what with all these zombies rising from their graves. I must find her and trail her ... like a shadow! [He exits.]

UGLY
Haha! They'll get to her before you do, Al. You can't stop the angels and you can't stop the zombies. An' you can't stop me or my vengeance. Cuz yer just some guy. All you kin do is walk around an' talk a lot an' wave yer arms around.

[Stupid is thrown on from offstage. Cruel comes on after him.]

CRUEL
Look what the cat dragged in.

UGLY
Where ya been, Stupid?

CRUEL
[Grabbing Stupid by the hair, then disgustedly wiping the hair grease from his hands.] Where ya been, Stupid?

STUPID
I dunno.

CRUEL
What's this little curly hair under yer fingernail? [He takes it and smells it.] Smells like pussy.

UGLY
[Tasting it.] Tastes like pussy. You been gettin' some pussy t'night?

STUPID
Rabbit.

UGLY
Listen, Stupid, do me a favor. See dat little spot on the ground dere?

STUPID
[*With nose to ground and butt in air.*] What little spot?

[*Cruel kicks his ass. Stupid topples over.*]

STUPID
OW! Why do I always do everything you tell me to?

UGLY
Cuz yer Stupid. Now listen up. I got it all pieced together. Before I died my name was Johnny Spider. My girlfriend's name was … aw, Hell. Let's sing it. Exposition always sounds better to music.

[*He gives them sheet music. They go to their instruments, one of which should be a piano.*]

UGLY
Has love gotcha down? Has every new toothpaste and deodorant failed you? Ever considered the possibility dat ya might just be too ugly t' fall in love? Or datcher just too big of an asshole? Sure ya have. Well now dere is an answer: Instead of sittin' home feelin' lonely an' rejected, get out dere wid a chainsaw an' take it out on somebody!

[*The three zombies perform "Ligeia and Johnny."*]

UGLY
Ligeia and Johnny were lovers
Oh lordy how dey could love
Crazy an' happy an' horny
Tight as a fist in a glove

CHORUS
He was her man, but she set him on fire.

UGLY
Johnny was fixin' his Harley
Ligeia was foolin' around
Playful as Satan on Monday
She found a lighter lyin' dere on the ground

CHORUS
He was her man, but she set him on fire.

UGLY
Clickety-flick went the lighter
Ignito-kaboom went the air
Johnny went up like a scarecrow
From his toenails to his hair

50

CHORUS
He was her man, but she set him on fire.

UGLY
Johnny got outta the sickhouse
Leaned on his bad baby's bell
Her uncle, ol' T.S. Eliot
Had 'im locked in a prison cell
CHORUS
He was her man, but she set him on fire.

UGLY
Johnny was ugly an' evil
Johnny was morbid an' mean
Johnny took a jailhouse clothesline
An' swung from a ceiling beam

CHORUS
He was her man, but she set him on fire.

UGLY
Johnny is back from the dead now
Gonna give Ligeia an fright
Skull fulla smoke an' a mouthfulla teeth
He's gonna eat some pussy tonight

CHORUS and **UGLY**
He was her man, but she set him on fire
He was her man, but she sent him to hell
He was her man, but he's back from the grave!

UGLY
[*Speaking as the other two vamp.*] Yes, ladies and gentlemen, it's the old story: burned by love. Why did she do it? I dunno. Why wouldn't she see Johnny, I mean me, after I got outta the hospital? I don't know an' I don't care. Cuz I ain't Johnny no more. I'm Ugly now, an' I'm here for one ting an' one ting only: revenge, amen. Revenge! Amen!

[*Blackout.*]

ACT TWO

SCENE 1

Outdoor cafe in the Place Djemma el Fna, Marrakesh. Mina, Jane, Ssamad at table.

JANE
[*Sipping rashasha from a china teacup.*] The difference between the pure psychotic and the pure prophet is that every now and then the prophet will recognize in herself the symptoms of psychosis. But as recognizing oneself as a psychotic tends to cause one to question the validity of one's revelations, the aspiring prophet is well-advised to take a large dose of opium upon waking, repeating the dosage continually throughout the day, with another large dose before retiring for the night.

SSAMAD
Jurgen's caravan broke down here in Marrakesh. We've been waiting a week for it to be repaired. "It'll be ready tomorrow, if Allah wills it. In three days, if Allah wills it. Before the end of Ramadan, if Allah wills it." Ramadan ended yesterday. Apparently Allah is still waiting for foreign auto parts to arrive.

JANE
As I wander through the labyrinth of Marrakesh's medina, packed tight as it is with market stalls and beggars and street musicians, a maze-like map of a new city constructs itself behind my eyes. A city watched over by a new God. I know that my destiny is interwoven with that of this new God. I am ready at any time to leave for the Rif Mountains.

SSAMAD
I hear more and more talk of the new Berber god, Barraka. Tension between Arabs and Berbers is heating up. I'm afraid that if the car isn't repaired soon, it might be too dangerous for me to go to the Rif. King Hassan is trying to restrict travel there. With luck we'll leave before Jane has spent all her money on opium pods and has none left to pay bakshish to the soldiers at the roadblocks.

JANE
For the past week I've barely spoken with the others. But tonight we are dining at a cafe in the Djemma el Fna, the large, crowded square that is the gateway to the medina, in celebration of the end of Ramadan. So I shall have to speak on earthly terms with these mortals who are unaware of their own divine internal sparks. But I am confident of my ability to negotiate this worldly world, though a thousand angels shriek in my skull. [*She sits.*] Ssamad, whether you like it or not, the arena of myth is an actual place where real events happen. And furthermore, historical decisions are often made based on those events. King Hassan himself is quaking in his

pointy slippers at the provocation of this new god.

SSAMAD
[*Sitting.*] @ Fairytales and legends don't change history.

JANE
Who do you think had more influence on history, Jesus Christ or Julius Caesar?

SSAMAD
@ Karl Marx. Jesus is a made-up story. You wish the world to be beautiful like the stories. But it is not. [*Referring to Mina.*] This woman here is a tired old woman who wants only to go back to her village and be with her family.

JANE
She wants to see the new God!

SSAMAD
@ She wants to be happy in this ugly world. So she tries to catch the beautiful stories. The way all Moroccans want something from the beautiful tourists. Only something, a small piece of the fairytale in their pockets.

JANE
She is a potentially divine being whose inner self is seeking to reunite with its divine nature.

SSAMAD
@ Do you get enough sleep?

MINA
In Riffi: What are you two talking about?

SSAMAD
We both like you very much.

MINA
Oh, that's so nice.

[*Jurgen enters, sits down.*]

JURGEN
@ Dey make it goot now, de car.

JANE
It's fixed?

JURGEN
@ Ja! It's all make it fixed. Fuck out. Goot.

MINA
What did he say?

SSAMAD
We leave tomorrow.

MINA
Oh good!

JURGEN
In German: We leave tomorrow.

SSAMAD
@ Good.

JANE
What did he say?

SSAMAD
@ We leave tomorrow.

JANE
Good. A toast, everyone!

[*She pours herself more tea from a leather wine sack. A Moroccan street musician has come up behind Jane playing a Berber banjo. He is played by Cruel.*]

MUSICIAN
[*Regarding the wine sack.*] @ Where you buy diss?

JANE
Go away. Imshee.

MUSICIAN
I trade. For guitar.

JANE
[*Disturbed by his pallor.*] Laa. Laa. Imshee.

MUSICIAN
@ Thank you. [*He leaves.*]

JANE
Did he look strange to you?

SSAMAD
@ Like normal.

JANE
He looked like a corpse risen from the dead.

SSAMAD
@ Fish-and-chips, you drink too much rashasha. [*He reaches for her cup.*]

JANE
[*Protective of her drug.*] Leave off!

SSAMAD
@ It makes you crazy, I can see it.

JANE
Just fuck off, Ssamad.

JURGEN
In German. I think she drinks too much rashasha.

SSAMAD
@ I said so already.

JURGEN
Oh.

[*A Moroccan boy, in ratty clothes, has appeared at the table near Jane. He is played by Stupid.*]

BOY
Un dirham, Madame. [*He sticks out his hand.*]

JANE
[*Disturbed, again, by the zombie look.*] Laa laa.

BOY
Pour manger. [*He rubs his empty belly.*]

JANE
Laa laa. Imshee.

[*The Waiter, played by Ugly, arrives at the table.*]

55

WAITER
Qu'est-ce que vous voudriez?

JANE
Qu'est-ce que vous av—[*Speechless on seeing his hideousness.*]

WAITER
@ You are English? Fish-and-chips! You laheek haggis?

JANE
What?

WAITER
@ You laheek to it haggis? You it him? Haggis?

JANE
Why—haggis?—yes I do, as a matter of fact.

WAITER
@ Special tonight: haggis!

JANE
I'll have haggis, then.

SSAMAD
In Arabic: What's haggis?

WAITER
[*Re: Jane.*] In Arabic: Does she speak Arabic?

SSAMAD
In Arabic: No.

WAITER
I don't know what haggis is. Some kind of English food. I don't have any. It's a joke; I hate tourists.

SSAMAD
But if it weren't for all the tourists, you couldn't make a living.

WAITER
Sure, I know. But after Barraka comes down from the mountains everything'll be different.

SSAMAD
Oh yeah. Barraka.

JURGEN
In German: What's haggis?

SSAMAD
@ You won't like it. Order the omelet.

JURGEN
[*To Waiter.*] @ Omelet.

WAITER
[*To Ssamad.*] And what're you having?

SSAMAD
Omelet.

WAITER
[*Pointing, in order, to Ssamad, Jurgen, and Jane.*] Omelet, @ home-let, and Fish-and-chips it haggis. [*To Mina.*] In Arabic: What about you?

MINA
I don't have enough money.

WAITER
Make the Caucasian prostitute buy you something. I'll be right back. [*He exits.*]

MINA
[*To Ssamad.*] In Riffi: Will you ask Jane to buy me an omelet?

SSAMAD
OK.

JURGEN
[*To Ssamad.*] In German: Is Jane getting some wine tonight?

SSAMAD
@ I don't know. I'll ask her.

BOY
@ Un dirham, un dirham!

JANE
No! Go away! What an unhealthy-looking sprog you are.

[*The Boy holds out his hand.*]

JANE
Laa laa! I said imshee!

[*The Boy shakes his open palm. Jane puts down her palm as if begging from him.*]

BOY
Pour manger? [*He reaches in his pocket and pulls out a minuscule coin. He puts it in her palm.*]

JANE
What is this? Play money?

SSAMAD
@ Let me see. Five centimes. Worth nothing.

JANE
I've never seen one. [*She pockets it.*]

MINA
In Riffi: Did you ask her yet?

JURGEN
In German: Did you ask her about the wine?

SSAMAD
[*To Jurgen.*] @ Why don't you ask her?

BOY
Mes centimes!

JANE
What do you mean? You gave it to me.

BOY
Mes centimes!

MINA
[*To Ssamad.*] Did you ask her about buying me food?

SSAMAD
What?

JANE
Imshee!

BOY
Mes centimes!

[*The Waiter arrives with three plates, which he puts down in front of Ssamad, Jurgen, and Jane.*]

JANE
This isn't haggis. I ordered haggis.

WAITER
@ What haggis. You say home-let.

JANE
You said you had haggis.

WAITER
@ What is haggis? You order home-let. [*To Mina.*] In Arabic: Are you ordering anything?

MINA
I don't know yet. In Riffi: Did you ask her?

JANE
Ssamad, tell this twit I'm not paying for this.

SSAMAD
[*To Mina.*] @ What do you want?

MINA
Why are you speaking German to me?

SSAMAD
@ I am?

JURGEN
[*To Ssamad.*] In German: You ask her. She doesn't like me because my English is bad.

JANE
Ssamad —

MINA
Ssamad —

SSAMAD
@ Everyone shut up!

MINA
What did you say?

SSAMAD
In Riffi: Shut up. English only from now on. That leaves you out.

JURGEN and **JANE**
What did you say?

SSAMAD
@ Nothing! Leave me alone! [*He stews.*]

BOY
Mes centimes!

JANE
Laa laa laa laa LAA! Imshee!

BOY
@ Imshee. Go away, go away. Fish-and-chips.

WAITER
In Arabic: Scram, kid. You're bothering my customers.

BOY
Mes centimes!

[*Waiter grabs Boy by the arm and pulls him away from the table. The Boy breaks away and goes back to the table. The Waiter grabs the Boy by the arm, throws him down and beats him viciously. First Jurgen and Ssamad, then Jane, leap up and break up the fight.*]

JURGEN
Nein, nein.

JANE
Stop it.

WAITER
[*To Boy.*] I'll kill you if you come back here. @ All finis. Close, good night.

[*The Boy is crying. The Waiter angrily cleans up the plates. Then he strikes the chairs through the following.*]

BOY
[*Crying, in agonized rage.*] Mes centimes!

JANE
I'm sorry, here. [*She gives him a bill.*] Here's twenty dirhams.

BOY
[*Pocketing the money.*] @ Fuck you. Fock you BITCH you focking BITCH you focking BITCH!

JANE
But I just —

BOY
[*He spits.*] @ Fock you focking BITCH focking BITCH! [*He runs off.*]

SSAMAD
[*To Jane.*] @ What do you think you do?

JANE
What are you yelling at me for? I gave him twenty dirhams and he spat at me.

SSAMAD
@ You think you can throw money on things like magic to make it all better?!

JURGEN
It's not her fault, Ssamad, take it easy.

SSAMAD
@ In German: Don't tell me easy. It is her fault. [*He storms off.*]

JURGEN
[*To Jane.*] @ End of Ramadan everyone go crazy. All OK, I talk to him. You buy some wine?

JANE
All right.

[*Jurgen and Jane exit. Mina gets up.*]

MINA
What's going on? I'm hungry.

[*Blackout.*]

SCENE 2

Eliot's place. A table and two chairs. On the table a stand-up picture frame with a photo of Ligeia, and a small plate with a peach on it. Cruel enters.

CRUEL
I'm gonna getcha, Eliot. Yes I am. I'm gonna eat slowly into yer pain centers like a little drop of water through stone. Whoa! Dat picture! A woman so beautiful it causeth me to have a flashback.

[*Lights change. Jesus, crucified, appears.*]

CRUEL
You sent for me, my savior?

JESUS
Yes, Sir Percival. Did you get a chance to read what Thomas Mallory wrote about you? He said you were too tainted by sin to bring Arthur the grail. Doesn't that rile you?

CRUEL
Oh, not at all and pshaw, good savior. As long as you and I know the truth, it doesn't matter.

JESUS
Well, Daddy thinks it does. Daddy says everything on Earth is all fucked up, and you have to go to Hell.

CRUEL
Just because some chronicler of the Arthurian Legends made a mistake? But that doesn't seem fair.

JESUS
Don't worry. Daddy says that once you're in Hell you'll forget all about it. Daddy says that in Hell they'll mash you into a two-dimensional caricature. Won't that be fun? Bye-bye! [*He disappears.*]

CRUEL
[*As lights change back.*] But good my savior, it's unjust! I behaved! I sinnethed not! O mash me not into a caricature I prithee! I brought my dying king the grail and saved the kingdom! What the Hell am I talkin' about? Did I just zone out or what? [*He jiggles his brains back into place.*] There. Kill Eliot, kill Eliot. Ooo, here he comes. I'll hide.

[*He does. Eliot enters, sits at table.*]

ELIOT
Fisherking. I'm not the Fisherking! Who said I was? I'm not. Poetry. It's beyond me. Impotent kings dangling their phallic fishing rods in dull dust-dry rivers. Kingdoms dying of famine. What's it's connection with me? I'm not a king. I'm just a mundane city coroner with a corpse beginning to stink in his adjacent room. A corpse of whom? A corpse that

resembles the woman in this image here on this emulsified paper which has been inserted into this imitation brass picture frame. Who is she? I don't remember, and that annoys me. I feel miserable. I am hungry. Here on this plate in front of me is a peach. I dislike peaches. I loathe peaches. I can't remember what a peach tastes like and that makes me ... angry.

CRUEL
[*Jumping out of hiding.*] NO MORE ROOM IN HELL!

ELIOT
WAH! Who are you? Are you going to hurt me? Why don't you leave me alone?

CRUEL
Questions! Questions! Wottalotta questions! Let's see, I'm Cruel, one of the walkin' dead. Am I gonna hurt you? Yes. Why don't I leave you alone? Cuz the way I'm gonna hurt you requires constant attention by the hurter to the hurtee. [*He takes out some rope.*]

ELIOT
Are you going to strangle me?

CRUEL
Will you just be patient?! [*He binds Eliot to chair.*]

ELIOT
Why are you tying me to this chair?

CRUEL
Cuz yer the victim an' victims get tied t' chairs. Got it? Now, ya know what I'm gonna do next?

ELIOT
If I ask, will you tell me?

CRUEL
Ya don't even hafta ask. [*He takes out a feather.*] Ya see this feather?

ELIOT
Yes.

CRUEL
I am goin' t' stroke it ever so gently here against yer forehead. [*He does.*] Now after about a month a little boo-boo should develop. An' little by little this feather will eat its way into yer skull until, many years from now, I'll be ticklin' the inside of yer brain. An' you will scream in pain an' I will laugh an' after a while you'll die an' then I'll stop. Ain't dat neat?

ELIOT
Why are you doing this to me?

CRUEL
Do you remember yer niece's boyfriend, Johnny Spider, who she set on fire an' whose life you ruined so bad that he had t' kill himself?

ELIOT
No.

CRUEL
Well, dat's even better. Yer the victim an' you don't even know what ya did t' deserve it. Ain't dat neat?

ELIOT
What if I wiggle my head around?

CRUEL
I'll stick pins in yer eyes.

ELIOT
But won't I starve to death before I die of ... featherbraining?

CRUEL
Nope. Cuz I will feed you. We'll start wid diss peach.

ELIOT
NO!

CRUEL
Aw, c'mon. Eat the peach.

ELIOT
But what if it tastes funny?

CRUEL
C'mon. Think of all the starvin' kids in Africa, dyin' like swollen maggots in the sun.

ELIOT
That's not a very appetizing image.

CRUEL
Look, ya either eat the peach, or sing a song about yer mom's brassiere.

ELIOT
I don't sing.

CRUEL
Peach, pins, or sing!

ELIOT
[*Tunelessly.*] O, my mother must have owned a brassiere. I believe so, yes, although I don't remember her very well. And if she owned one I suppose she must have worn it on occasion ...

CRUEL
What is this, minimalism? C'mon, wid feeling. Open yer mouth up an' sing!

ELIOT
O my mo—

[*Cruel jams the peach into Eliot's mouth and forces him to bite it. A choir of angels is heard. Cruel looks up. Eliot rises from the chair, magically unbound, and smiling. The choir stops.*]

CRUEL
What was dat?

[*The wailing of the crowd of undead is heard from another direction.*]

CRUEL
Listen: the multitudinous whole buncha Dead are beginnin' t' spill onto the wretched Earth.

ELIOT
"I had not thought death had undone so many." Hey, that rings a bell! The bell in Saint Something's. Ding dong! Do not ask for whom the dong dings, for it is a knell, that summons the Dead from Hell. O swell! I'm all well! O peach, O lovely peach. Lovely as the peaches in a young mother's brassiere. You've cured me, kind Cruel. I feel as though glorious summer had melted away the winter that put my inspiration on ice. But Nevermore!

CRUEL
Uh oh. Did I do a good deed?

ELIOT
And now I do remember your friend Johnny Spider. The poor fellow. I am filled with remorse. I must redeem myself. I will travel the world, spreading good cheer!

Oh no! Cognitive dissonance. I did a good deed. I could do more! It's ... coming back to me. Yes ... I am Sir Percival! I shall follow you, Good My Liege. Lead on, and whither thou goest I shall go, spreading, as you say, joy to the world!

[A ukulele flies on into Cruel's arms. They perform "The Poet Evermore."]

"The Poet Evermore"

ELIOT
Let us go then, you and I
While the night's Plutonian shore
Is spread out against the sky like
Rose petals on the floor
Joy to the world, quoth the poet, evermore
Quoth the poet evermore.

CRUEL
Yes it's true by golly
Corny as it may be
You who live in folly
Can be freed by poetry

ELIOT
Clap your hands and Tinkerbell

CRUEL
Will fly up, released from Hell

BOTH
Beauty, quoth the poet, evermore
Beauty, quoth the poet, evermore
Yodelayee, yodelayeee, yodelayee ...

[Blackout.]

SCENE 3
Gotham City. Anna in a chair while Stupid binds her to it.

ANNA
[Playfully.] Oooo, why are you tying me to this chair, my beloved?

STUPID
I fergit ... oh yeah, cuz ... no, I fuhgot again. Anyway, now yer tied to the chair, an' dat means yer the victim. So, even dough I love you, I gotta kill you.

ANNA
Ooo, but why, you nasty brute?

STUPID
Cuz I'm s'posed ta.

ANNA
Ooo, and what horrible atrocities will you commit upon me?

STUPID
What what? Don't ax me such hard questions! Dere's not really a brain in here, ya know, just some dried up crust. [*He shakes his head and the crust rattles inside.*] But I'll try t' be as gentle as I kin, big clumsy lummox dat I am.

[*He goes behind her and, after some deliberation and failed attempts, succeeds in covering her mouth and nose with his hands.*]

STUPID
This won't hurt a bit. Oh, I dunno why I'm so stupid an' dumb. It's just cuzza Hell, I guess. Hell pretty much flattens a guy. I mean, you could have all kinda lumps an' knots an' edges an' stuff in yer personality, but just spend one season in Hell an' they'll mash it all flat. It's like yer a juicy piece of gum an' Hell just chews ya up till dere's no flavor left an' then spits ya out on the ground an' steps on ya. Yes sir, dyin' an' goin' t' Hell pretty much ruins a guy fer any other kinda life.

[*Anna mumbles something. Stupid takes his hand away from her mouth.*]

STUPID
Huh?

ANNA
I said, "It sounds like an awful place." [*She takes a few breaths before Stupid covers her mouth again.*]

STUPID
Yeah, it sucks. Take me fer instance. I dunno what kinda guy I was before I went t' Hell, but even now dere's all kinda brainy ideas scootin' around in my bean. All kinda numbers an' formulas an' stuff, like fer the Unified Field Theory, whatever dat is, an' invisible shoe polish, an' somethin' like a kinda food dat all ya hafta do is think about it an' dere it is in frunna you, already cooked an' ready t' eat. Or maybe it's a new kinda animal dat when it's born it comes out already cooked an' widda knife an' fork already in it an' it runs right up t' ya so you kin just cut off a hunk an' eat it. But when dese ideas get up t' my mouth dey just come out soundin' stupid. An' no matter if I try t' do somethin' graceful or clever, my body just acts like some kinda remote control dune buggy wid Alzheimer's disease goin' over a cliff.

[*Anna mumbles again. Stupid takes his hand from her mouth.*]

STUPID
Huh?

ANNA
I said, "Oh, you poor thing." [*She breathes.*]

STUPID
Hey! [*He quickly covers her mouth.*] Are you sneakin' air? Boy, I thought you liked me, too. Yer gonna get me in all kinda trouble. [*Anna mumbles. Stupid uncovers her mouth.*] Huh?

ANNA
Oh, I thought I saw someone I knew.

STUPID
Oh, I'll go see. [*He goes to the edge of the stage.*] HEY! ... HEY YOU! ... HEY ASSHOLE!

[*Eliot and Cruel enter, unseen by Stupid.*]

ELIOT and **CRUEL**
We are the happy men
We are the nice men
Leaning together
Heads filled with joy, ole!

STUPID
Cruel! I was just ... don't get mad. I'm gonna kill her, honest.

CRUEL
What? No no! Desist, my man. Let the good woman live, and all be pleasant in Creation.

ANNA
Thomas, you're smiling!

ELIOT
Yes, I've become jolly, a good guy, fun to be around. But fun with a purpose. To bring beauty, light, and joy to the world. Shout Hallelujah, c'mon, get happy, that is the good news I bring to the world.

ANNA
Hallelujah!

STUPID
Huh? What's goin' on?

68

CRUEL
Stop! Don't kill the woman. You are free of any evil obligation.

STUPID
Really? Gosh, thanks.

CRUEL
And now, off we go.

ELIOT
Good night, ladies, good night, sweet ladies ...

[*Cruel and Eliot exit.*]

ANNA
How wonderful!

STUPID
Hey, I ain't no lady.

ANNA
Now we can live happily ever after.

STUPID
Naw, he's always bein' mean t' me. It's some kinda trick. But I'll fool him.

[*Stupid breaks Anna's neck. Her head hangs at a disgusting angle.*]

STUPID
Oops. Wait a minute. [*He cannot repair her. He sings.*]

Oh my love
I've murdered you
Something else
I could not do
Why is that
I cannot tell
Must be something that they did to me
In Hell

[*Blackout.*]

SCENE 4
Gotham City alley. A chair. A scream and the sound of ripping flesh. Ugly enters.

UGLY
Listen! The children of the night make their music. Ah, to die, to be really dead, that must be glorious. But dat happiness is to be eternally denied myself an' the other walkin' carcasses Hell is barfin' up tonight to throng the streets of the world. Soon Hell'll be completely evacuated. I can see the ice rink in the city of Dis, at the center of Hell, where once innumerable skaters circled endlessly to the throbbing of "Toccata and fugue in D minor" on the pipe organ, played by Bach himself, several skaters occasionally gettin' picked off by Mephistopheles on dat fuckin' Zamboni of his, laid out flat like in a cartoon, then poppin' up again to get run over another day. It looks funny but it hurts. But now Mephisto circles the rink alone, resurfacing the ice for no one, and suckin' on dat cheap cigar, while Bach, once the living have all been devoured and the Earth is a Global Village of the Dead, shall trudge and moan with the rest of us, forever achin' wid hunger for dat extinct delicacy, the living flesh dat once crystallized around the human soul.

A world of monotonous misery winding itself down, over eons, to a final, pathetic whimper. But I shall be satisfied, as I drool and slouch toward entropy, knowing dat my shitty life has been avenged. Even in the worst of all possible worlds the most we can do is tend our own gardens, which is why I have sent word through my Stupid and Cruel minions for Ligeia to meet me here, where her betrayal began, come Ligeia, abandon all hope, for dere is none. And so I wait.

Sittin' in la-la, waitin' for my ya-ya, uh huh. Uh huh. No, I don't believe she's comin'. One more hour and I shall begin to hunt her down. But, she might come. Suppose she does? Remorseful, she pleads for forgiveness. But I mercilessly interrogate her.

"Why, Ligeia, why did you set me on fire?"

"It was a mistake, an accident, a foolish mistake for which I have paid the heavy price of losing your love."

"This answer pleases me. But why did you spurn me, refusing to see me when I came to you afterwards?"

"I was afraid to face your hatred, which I knew was all I deserved."

"Oh, you poor thing. Then do you still love me?"

Of course she does. She can see through the ravages of fire, strangulation and rot to the inner core, the Johnny Spider who has always and will forever excite her adoration. And so we are married. We live in perfect bliss for a number of years, until the morning she awakens wid a strange pain and dampness on her face. She goes down the hall to examine herself

70

in the mirror ... and she screams. Screams and screams until wid some heavy object I pound those screams into the tile of the floor, into the grout between the tile, into the Earth below the house of falsehood and paranoia and deceit!

It is possible, y'know. She could be attracted to my ugliness, see it as a poetic expression of the travails she has put me through. She's a poet, y'know. Each skin-graft scar, each gangrenous lesion eloquently portrays a chapter of my suffering. I am in a certain way beautiful. All great works of art seem ugly, at first, until you graps the esthetic theory behind dem. [*To audience.*] You think I'm beautiful now, don't you? Fuck you! Sanctuary! Sanctuary!

[*Ligeia enters on a direct trajectory with Ugly. She stops. They are face-to-face.*]

LIGEIA
Well? Out of the way!

UGLY
Wha?

LIGEIA
Out of the way! Out of the path! We are on our way! Move!

[*She moves him aside and continues on her way. He goes after her and grabs her.*]

UGLY
Well! Don't you gotta lotta gall!

LIGEIA
Progress! Stand aside!

UGLY
Now you just hold yer goddam horses! [*He sits her in the chair and binds her there.*]

LIGEIA
No no NO! This won't do at all! Time marches on! Forward!

UGLY
Shuddup!

LIGEIA
How dare an insignificant weevil like you stanch the flow of the future!

UGLY
You must think I'm some kinda stooge! Did you think you could come here widout a ounce of shame an' fulfill my worst nightmares of betrayal an' dat I would just stan' here an' take it? No apologies, no explanations, nuttin'? Oh, no, my dear. You will feel the pain. Oh, the sickening pain of my vengeance upon you!

LIGEIA
Vengeance? You, upon us?

UGLY
Us? Ooo, hoity-toity. Well, I'll cut ya down t' size. [*He produces a knife.*] We'll start witcher face. Would we prefer it diced or julienned?

LIGEIA
Doesn't revenge imply a previous transgression on our part against you?

UGLY
Dat's right. Dat is the great thing about revenge. It evens things out. You did somethin' bad t' me, now I do somethin' bad t' you. It gives dat ol' balance t' nature, a symmetry, as it were.

LIGEIA
However, even had we met before, which we haven't —

UGLY
— Oh, we haven't! Yer fuckin' relentless! —

LIGEIA
— but even if we had, well, people change. Wouldn't we be quite altered from the people we'd been in the past? Doesn't the symmetry fail? Isn't revenge impossible in this world of progress and change? I'm sorry, this seems all wrong to me. We'll either have to call it something other than revenge, or you'll have to find someone else.

UGLY
It hasta be revenge, an' it can't be nobody else!

[*Crowley has entered.*]

CROWLEY
She's already someone else, Ugly, my boy.

UGLY
Will you quit followin' me around?

CROWLEY
Throw in the towel, boy, your revenge is impossible. Yours is a higher destiny. You've got great expectations.

UGLY
Dammit, I want my revenge! My pointless, asymmetrical, ugly little revenge. Is dat too much t' ask?

CROWLEY
But this is not Ligeia, boy. This is all the angels but one, alias Ashtaroth, the angel of immanent spectacle.

LIGEIA
At last, a voice of reason. Untie us, will you?

CROWLEY
In good time. [*To Ugly.*] Your lover must have been a very great poet indeed, the greatest in history, in fact.

UGLY
She sucked.

CROWLEY
Oh, no, you see, angels can only escape from Heaven to Earth through the heart of the world's greatest poet. And for the past several days they've been fleeing the divine concentration camp with increasing frequency through the body of that woman seated in that chair.

UGLY
Can't you see we wanna be alone?

CROWLEY
You obviously don't know how to treat a woman full of angels, boy. [*He pushes Ugly to the ground.*]

UGLY
You big bully! [*He slinks off.*]

CROWLEY
Alone at last! Remember me, Ashy?

LIGEIA
We are not of memory, but of imminence.

CROWLEY
[*Threateningly.*] Well remember this: a night in the month of Nissan, a night of pleasure disporting with the beautiful young Maharal of Prague,

your fornication with whom produced a living man of stone whose troublesome behavior got me ridden out on a rail.

LIGEIA
Oh, you're that kabalistic pimp, aren't you?

CROWLEY
You're in no position to insult anyone.

LIGEIA
What is it you want?

CROWLEY
The question is, what do you want? You've been having some ado with the Great Spirit, I gather.

LIGEIA
To say the least! Hitler was an autistic Quaker compared to God. A more paranoid tyrant the Heavens have never seen. Look at the sky, even the stars have gone into hiding.

CROWLEY
And you angels as well. All but one of you. And the last one is due presently, I assume? Yes. And then what? Disguised within this poet's mortal soul you'll slip unnoticed down to Hell with the rest of the automatically damned.

LIGEIA
Yes. And once there we'll be able to organize completely out of his sight. His own corrupt haste in creating Hell will be his downfall.

CROWLEY
But the body must die first, mustn't it? Do the Holy Angels intend to commit suicide?

LIGEIA
Certainly not! Destroy life? Let alone our own?

CROWLEY
No, that wouldn't be cricket. But can you afford to wait till this body dies of natural causes?

LIGEIA
What? No! Progress! Forward!

CROWLEY
But what do you intend to do? [*No response.*] All right, so you get to Hell,

you have a few meetings, and then what? Do you have any agenda, any plan of action?

LIGEIA
[*Stymied.*] Oh, this is very embarrassing.

CROWLEY
Impetuous things, aren't you? What if I told you I could arrange to get you to Hell as soon as the last one is over the border?

LIGEIA
What is it that you want?

[*Ugly enters, brandishing his knife. Crowley's stare stops him, wilting him into an incoherent, prone blob.*]

CROWLEY
My favor is this: would you back my boy here?

LIGEIA
He's a little on the hideous side, isn't he?

CROWLEY
It'll be all the rage. I can organize broad mythic support here on Earth if you can give me a divine boost during the caucuses in Hell.

LIGEIA
Well, we'll put in a good word, that's the best we can do.

CROWLEY
Oh, your word means a lot, Ashy. Now, one last thing. I've been getting synchronistic signals from a woman named Jane Clayton. I feel she is near to a revelatory experience. I think she could help me out in the evangelizing department, as most people of this planet seem to find me off-putting and aren't easily persuaded by me.

LIGEIA
[*Channeling in on the ethereal wavelengths.*] She's on her way to see another candidate, a Lord Barraka, in the Rif Mountains of Morocco.

CROWLEY
What? Another candi—Barraka? Who is he? Has he got a chance?

LIGEIA
He's quite good. All the abstractions are there, and he's big with the poor and oppressed. Exciting position on divine intervention. And he's very photogenic. Makes your boy look like ... well, what he looks like.

CROWLEY

Oh, you're not all going to fall for another pretty face, are you? [*Yelling into her sternum.*] You're not all going to fall for another pretty face! [*Back to her.*] Look, Ash, I tell you I'm on to something here, I —

LIGEIA

AH! Oh, last one coming through. Good luck!

CROWLEY

Thanks, Ash. [*To Ugly.*] She's all yours, boy.

[*Ugly snaps to, goes to Ligeia for his revenge.*]

LIGEIA

Ah ... ah ... ah ...

UGLY

Will you sneeze already?

[*The arms of the final angel burst through Ligeia's chest in a splatter of blood. Eliot and Cruel appear behind garbage and watch, unseen.*]

CROWLEY

Gesundheit.

UGLY

Ieeeyuew, yuck! What is it? Eeew, kill it, kill it! [*He stabs at the chest cavity.*] Ieeyueew! Yuck! Blech! Ick!

[*Ligeia is dead.*]

CROWLEY

Good job, lad! You've sent all the angels down to Hell to do some grassroots organizing against the Big Cheese.

UGLY

Angels? Fuck angels, man.

CROWLEY

That's a bit hard, holding a grudge like that. The angels are bound to throw their support behind you now that Ashtaroth's in your corner.

UGLY

Support? Fer what?

CROWLEY

God, of course. In the upcoming theocratic and thaumaturgical power struggle.

76

UGLY

You mean I didn't—you mean she really—wait a minute, I don't wanna be God. Some idiot might take it into his head to love me!

CROWLEY

And that, to you, would be very Ugly. Well, it's too late, I've already announced your candidacy to Ashtaroth and she's going to pull for you.

UGLY

You can't do dat!

CROWLEY

The ball, as they say, is rolling. We'll need a public relations manager of course. I'd suggest Jane Clayton, the former Lady Greystoke. She's quite glib. I'm off the Rif Mountains right now to solicit her support.

UGLY

Don't bother. If elected, I will not serve.

CROWLEY

All the better. No one wants a god who's going to meddle in their affairs anymore. Toodles. [*He exits.*]

UGLY

No! Stop! Stop thief! ... Thief of my soul. Thief of my destiny. Thief of my revenge. [*He goes to Ligeia's corpse and caresses her hair sadly.*] Did I love you? Why don't I love you anymore? Misery oughta love a corpse if it only has a corpse for company. [*He broods.*] I suppose I could become a benevolent god. I could abolish misery. I could resolve conflicts. Imagine dat, if anytime you had an argument wid someone you could just say, "Hey, God, which one of us is right?" an' God'd appear an' say, "You, the one who argued dat dere are no absolutes, you're right. An' you, Mistuh Dogmatic, pay up." You see, I think a lot of terrible tragedies could be avoided if God would just tell us what the fuck was goin' on! But ... I'm just not dat kinda guy. I guess I'll just stew. [*He sits and stews.*]

ELIOT

What an evil plan! The complete uglification of everything!

CRUEL

Yes, but what can we do? How has it come about that the only human being on Earth who understands the workings of gods and angels is a lunatic who styles himself the Antichrist?

ELIOT

I blame myself. Had not I and other poets of my ilk used poetry to convince everyone of poetry's uselessness, the world would not be in this sad pickle.

But wait! I have a plan.

[*Eliot and Cruel whisper conspiratorially to each other as the lights fade.*]

[*Blackout.*]

SCENE 5

Inside a mosque in the Rif, which has been captured and converted by the followers of Barraka into their headquarters and shrine. Jane enters and wends through the crowd, sipping rashasha from a teacup.

JANE
The closer we drew toward the Rif Mountains, the more complex my visions became, growing branches like crystals, amino acids, DNA, an animal and animistic universe, jewel planets rotating moistly in sockets within a cosmic vastness of flesh. In the form of a bluish vapor I glided past the centurions of evil and their barricades —

SSAMAD
[*Having entered.*] King Hassan thought he could seal off the Rif from pilgrims to Barraka's Mecca here, but there are many paths through the mountains and many people willing to come on foot or by mule. And as for the highway, the laws of tourism seem to be more binding than those of the king. Jane slipped the soldiers at the roadblock at least a hundred pounds sterling.

JANE
I rode up the mountain on the back of an enormous tortoise into whose shell was woven in diamond threads a miraculous blueprint for the rebirth of the cosmos —

SSAMAD
When we got to my village of Bab Taza we borrowed mules to ride up the mountain to Barraka's temple.

JANE
I won entrance into Barraka's sacred shrine for Jurgen and myself with the noble aura of wisdom I had begun to radiate—

[*Jurgen enters.*]

SSAMAD
Jane slipped the temple guards even more bakshish than she'd given the soldiers, so that she and Jurgen could enter.

78

JANE

We wait now in this temple of glass whose walls throb with arteries pumping the sacred sub-elements.

SSAMAD

We wait now in a rundown mosque that has been captured from Hassan and his god Allah by a newly mobilized Berber population. I have never seen my people so unified and hopeful. Many fell in the battle to liberate and convert this mosque, yet the people are still deferential to the building's former purpose, taking off their shoes ... out of habit, I suppose. But the women of this new faith have demanded entrance and won it.

[Mina enters.]

SSAMAD

This Barraka is truly a great force for organization. I have no doubt that the people will overthrow Hassan at the urging of this new faith. And when Hassan is overthrown, my work will begin.

[All have made their way through the crowd to the edge of a small platform.]

JANE

Fire of fire, water of fire, air of fire, earth of fire. It was our destiny to arrive on the day when Barraka is going to reveal himself for the first time to his followers in the form of his material avatar. I feel myself at the hub of a vast golden wheel, slowly turning toward its magnificent fate.

[Expectant silence. The Emcee enters, wearing a half-mask. He ascends the platform.]

EMCEE

In Arabic: Good evening, ladies and gentlemen, and welcome to the world premiere appearance of the material avatar of Lord Barraka, the New and True God. [Applause.] Lord Barraka has been busy lately ousting the other gods from the arena of mythology. Mithra and Zarathustra have been cut off from supplies and starved. Krishna and his co-conspirators lie dismembered on the field of battle. Buddha has been hung from the goalpost. The Titans and their Olympian offspring have surrendered without a fight, and Yahweh and his sniveling son Jesus the so-called Christ are on the ropes, legs wobbling, eyes swollen, blood spewing from cuts above their eyebrows—[Applause.]

SSAMAD

Yes, applaud, my people. I'm with you. The only good god is a dead one. Or a useful one.

MINA
I've heard stories of how much magic the Berbers knew before the Arabs came. How the women were masters of magic.

JURGEN
I can't believe it! Four kilos of hash for only 160 marks.

JANE
Fire of water, water of water, air of water, earth of water.

EMCEE
And within this year our Lord Barraka will lead us in armed revolt against bloody King Hassan and his army and police force, which are now the only things standing between our oppressor Allah's throat and our beloved Barraka's knife! The only thing standing between ourselves and our freedom!

[*Applause.*]

SSAMAD
Excellent, Barraka. Overthrow the oppressive government of Hassan. But sooner or later you'll prove yourself to be a fraud, and then the people will look to those with a political plan of action.

MINA
Maybe when Allah is killed I'll be able to weave spells instead of souvenir carpets.

JURGEN
I can't swallow four kilos of hash. How'm I gonna get it past the roadblocks?

JANE
Fire of air, water of air, air of air, earth of air.

EMCEE
And now, without further ado, ladies and gentlemen, an entity who needs no introduction: I give you the material avatar of Lord Barraka!

[*Wild applause. Barraka enters dressed in stunning raiment and a beautiful mask. He capers and disports about, from one gracefully arcane posture to the next.*]

MINA
He's so cute. I'd kill anyone for him.

SSAMAD
Listen to them cheering this faker. He's got 'em completely fooled. Ha!

80

When he fucks 'em over they'll come crying to me.

JURGEN
Wonder if it's OK to light up a joint in here.

JANE
Fire of earth, water of earth, air of earth, earth of earth.

EMCEE
Yes, my friends, Lord Barraka, the last word in state-of-the-art godhead technology. All the best features of the old gods with none of the old-fashioned severity or crypticism. More of what you look for in a deity. Like Yahweh and Allah, he is all-powerful, but thanks to improved divine engineering, he's even more all-powerful than the two of them put together. Compassionate? He has the compassion of Jesus one-thousand-fold. Ephemeral essence? The Dharma Body of Buddha couldn't hold a candle to the essence of Barraka, through which courses an easily attainable and user-friendly enlightenment. Wealth, talent, good looks, charisma? The gods of Olympus are just so many crippled, mutilated wretches. Krishna himself is just a withered old hag whose digestive problems cause her to blow salvoes of putrid farts, and who should be shipped off to some bleak, impersonal nursing home and left to rot in utter despair and neglect!

SSAMAD
What a disgusting religion this is going to be.

EMCEE
Just look at our fine young avatar of Barraka. Opulent! Happy! Wealthy! Healthy! Beautiful! Cheerful! Fun to be around! All his aspects and talents so beguiling that even the dead in their graves are brought to orgasm!

[*Wild applause.*]

JANE
My god how wonderful how wonderful mygodmygodmygod ...

MINA
Yes! Yes! Up with Barraka!

SSAMAD
What a bunch of chumps. What am I doing here? I don't belong here. What a farce. I should really just leave. Why don't I just get up and leave? I should just get up right now and walk out the door.

JURGEN
This would be great if I was stoned.

[*Murmurs have been building: "Tarzan is coming."*]

EMCEE
What's that? Did someone say Tarzan is coming?

[*Barraka throws off his mask, revealing himself to be Tarzan, Lord Greystoke.*]

GREYSTOKE
Daht's riot, mahn!

JANE
Oh no, you've GOT to be KIDDING!

SSAMAD
NO! Not yet! I still need you! You'll spoil everything!

[*He runs to protect Greystoke from the crowd. A general outcry.*]

MINA
Kill him! Kill him!

SSAMAD
[*Shouting down the crowd.*] No, don't you see? It's not Tarzan, it's ... Lawrence of Arabia. You like him, don't you?

MINA
No it's not. He doesn't look like Peter O'Toole, he looks like Johnny Weismuller.

[*General outcry: "Yeah, that's right!"*]

GREYSTOKE
[*Having removed his robes.*] Ha ha ha! Yes! Once again I and I have proven my superiority over you indigenous African schmucks in my rub-a-dub style! And now I escape you!

[*Greystoke escapes, exiting. Cries of despair.*]

MINA
NO! NO! [*Falling at Ssamad's feet.*] No gods, no magic, only tourists, tourists, tourists. And my brother sold his shop for half of what it was worth! [*She weeps.*]

[*Crowley, who has thrown off his emcee disguise, is resuscitating Jane, who has passed out.*]

82

CROWLEY
Mrs. Clayton, Mrs. Clayton ... do you recognize me, Mrs. Clayton?

JANE
Aleister Crowley, I presume?

CROWLEY
I am sorry you were deceived, Mrs. Clayton.

JANE
Deceived? I am destroyed. The universe lies in shards at my feet.

CROWLEY
Yes, but now I am certain that you will never again be seduced by a god of compassion, omnipotence, enlightenment or beauty.

JANE
Certainly not. I shall retire to solitude, ingesting opium in various forms and mumbling idiotically to myself.

CROWLEY
Before you make such a rash decision, madam, I implore you, come with me to Gotham City, where I would like to show you a god who might be more to your liking. He is hideous, petty, impotent and cowardly, and awaits only your superb talents as his evangelical scribe.

JANE
Well ... no no no ... hmm. You're sure he's not the least bit quaint?

CROWLEY
I assure you he is utterly repulsive.

JANE
I don't know.

CROWLEY
You would be under no obligation. And I'll throw in four bushels of poppies from my own private stock.

JANE
I'll go.

CROWLEY
Excellent. [*Loudly.*] I now speak in a universal language of my own contrivance which somehow falls upon the ears of everyone with equal clarity and force: People of the Rif, the Sahara, the Atlas, and the Coast; tourists, Peace Corps volunteers, smugglers, and entrepreneurs—Jane

Clayton and I are leaving for America on my magic carpet. There we will be doing our best to make certain that your issues are not lost in the upcoming theocratic and thaumaturgical shuffle, and that the immanent restructuring of Heaven is not entirely irrelevant to your lives. Please pray for us ... or whatever it is you do here.

JURGEN
In German: Just a minute. Do flying carpets have to go through customs?

CROWLEY
Of course not.

JURGEN
Can you drop me off in Dorfstadt?

CROWLEY
Certainly.

SSAMAD
@ What?

JURGEN
I'm sorry, Ssamad. I have four kilos to sell.

SSAMAD
@ Sorry? You can be sorry! [*Drops accent.*] Fuck off. Go back home, tourist.

CROWLEY
You can come as well, little brown man.

SSAMAD
Go? With you? Thief of our culture? Thief of our revolution?

CROWLEY
Your culture? Oh, don't be so possessive. You are a communist, I believe. Do I accuse you of stealing Marxism from my culture? A great Frenchman once said, "Property is theft." The phrase was later plagiarized and regurgitated by an American. Perhaps you too, one day, will vomit up this same wisdom.

SSAMAD
Yes, property is theft. But so is robbery.

CROWLEY
Very clever. Makes no sense, of course. "Do what thou wilt shall be the whole of the Law." Perhaps you will say that, one day, as well. But we really must be going.

SSAMAD
[*As Jurgen, Jane, and Crowley exit.*] Yes, go! Leave me alone, all of you! Leave me alone! Leave me alone! Leave me alone!

[*Blackout.*]

SCENE 6

Gotham alley. Ugly on stage.

UGLY
[*Sings.*]
Oh my love
I buried you
In the park behind the Gotham City zoo
Now the lamenting peacock moans
While the city soil below erodes
Your bones

[*Stupid crawls on, weeping, and clutches Ugly's leg. Ugly strokes Stupid's hair sympathetically, then removes his hand, which is now full of hair grease, in disgust.*]

UGLY
Hey, leggo ... I said leggo! Leggo, I tell ya, yer gettin' me all wet. Yer cuttin' off my circulation.

[*Jane and Crowley appear behind garbage, unnoticed.*]

CROWLEY
Ah, we are just in time to witness an archetypal scene from the new pantheon ... excuse me, the proposed new pantheon: The god Ugly beating Stupid, his imbecilic toady.

UGLY
Get offa me, ya scum! I'll sic Cruel on ya. Where is he at? Cruel!

JANE
May I talk to him?

CROWLEY
By all means. But be careful. He bites.

JANE
Does he? Oh, very good! [*She approaches Ugly with notebook and pen.*]

UGLY
Cruel! YO! CRUEL!

JANE
Excuse me, sir. Could you please describe your doctrine to me?

UGLY
Doctrine? I ain't got no fuckin' doctrine. Run away before I eat ya. Cruel!

JANE
If I devoted myself to you body and soul, what could I hope to receive in return?

UGLY
A kick in the ass. Get lost. Cruel!

[*Ugly, out of options, kisses Stupid on the mouth. Stupid screams and runs off. Ugly chases him. Throughout the following they periodically appear behind the garbage barrier, battling like Punch and Judy puppets.*]

JANE
Well, he certainly is everything you claim. But I'm still not certain what point there is in making him God. Wouldn't it be better simply to abolish the office entirely?

CROWLEY
If the office of God didn't exist, someone somewhere would surely find it necessary to reinvent it. No, no, better and far safer to have a god whom no one could trust. As you know, Jane, it has long been my project to help people achieve their fullest potential. I have drawn my motto from Rabelais' Abbey of Thélème: "Do what thou wilt shall be the whole of the Law." But before we can do that which we will, we must discover what exactly it is that we will. And how can we discover our own will if we are seduced by some superior being called God into believing that it is His will, and not our own, that is of the greater worth in following?

JANE
Clearly it is difficult for the average human being to resist the persuasion of a creature who comes to him in the form of beams of light, unconsuming fire, thunderbolts, flashes of revelation, and states of spiritual ecstasy and enlightenment.

CROWLEY
Yes, humanity is so easily taken in by such parlor tricks. But who would be taken in by a creature who appears to them as a hideous monster or a physical and spiritual feeling of nausea? Can you imagine anyone who would rather do the will of that putrid thing than his own?

[*Stupid, pursued by Ugly, runs on. Winded, they both collapse.*]

JANE
I see your point. I have often wondered why, if God wouldn't help us, he wouldn't at least leave us alone, as apparently only we can solve our problems.

CROWLEY
But now we have our chance. The old God is about to be toppled!

JANE
Well, Master Therion, I'm with you.

CROWLEY
Excellent. Come.

[*They go to Ugly.*]

CROWLEY
Oh, Mister Candidate.

UGLY
[*Reviving.*] No more fer me, thanks. Oh, shit, you again.

STUPID
Help! It's da ucky guy. [*He grabs Ugly's legs.*]

CROWLEY
Good news, Ugly, you're now running unopposed.

UGLY
No I ain't. I'm runnin' away. [*To Stupid.*] Leggo of me!

STUPID
I can't. I'm rigor-mortified.

CROWLEY
Let me introduce you, Jane Clayton, to Ugly, our shoo-in candidate for God.

[*Enter Eliot and Cruel dressed in Arthurian garb.*]

ELIOT
Don't count your chickens yet, Antichrist!

CROWLEY
Oh, it's you.

UGLY

Cruel! Where ya been? Dey wanna make me God! Cut up everyone dat ain't already dead!

CRUEL

I am no longer your slave, you vile demon.

UGLY

Yer not? How come?

CRUEL

None of your business.

CROWLEY

Gentlemen, what is the meaning of this disruptive intrusion?

ELIOT

I have come to fight your ugliness with the superior power of Beauty.

CROWLEY

You? A pathetic city coroner? A failed poet laureate whose laurels have dropped their leaves and been buried under the winter snow?

ELIOT

I have been cured of my modernistic malaise by the mythical services of my dear friend, Sir Percival, here.

UGLY

Well, dat's great, Tom. Too bad, Al. I guess dat does it. Good game, dough. We played hard. Nice work, Tom.

CRUEL

Do not speak to His Majesty unless spoken to.

UGLY

What a fuckin' ass-kisser!

CROWLEY

[*To Eliot.*] So now what? You seek to turn the clock back to Romanticism? Ha! Shelley is long dead, and you, like his Ozymandius, will be remembered ages and ages hence merely as two trunkless legs of stone. Time moves ... er ... forward! Prepare for the new esthetic, the new world of Ugly!

ELIOT

No! Prepare to meet the opposition candidate: Beauty! Beauty, come forth!

[*Ligeia enters in courtly dress, carrying a grail. She has risen from the dead,*

88

and is ashen and drawn, but on her it looks good.]

ELIOT
Sing to us of your doctrine, fair Beauty! Sing to us of your platform and its well-polished planks. Sing to us, O Beauty, and beguile the angels to your delegation.

[*Ligeia looks at Ugly.*]

UGLY
Hi. Remember me?

ELIOT
Grace us, Beauty, with unprecedented sweetness from your golden throat!

[*Ligeia vomits into the grail.*]

ELIOT
You bastards! You've made her ill with your loathsome characteristics!

JANE
Not at all. She has expressed herself wonderfully. I'm writing it all down in the new Gospel. The new cosmos shall be built in the shell of your old one, Eliot. It is the theological next step. Long ago artists merely stole from one another. Now they "allude" to one another. Whose work is whose is anyone's guess at this point. From now on artists will regurgitate each other, producing collages, montages, and pastiches of vomit. This [*Taking the grail.*] represents the new aesthetic, and its regurgitated view of the old. Just as war is too important to be left to the generals, poetry is too important to be left to the poets. And magic is too important to be left to the magicians.

CROWLEY
Pardon?

JANE
Yes, it is not enough to free ourselves from the seduction of God. To fully realize our own will we must also cease to be seduced by his godlike counterparts here on the Earth: the experts, the geniuses, the famous and the beautiful. You Eliot, and you Crowley, will be remembered only as this, a puddle of bile and partially digested food.

UGLY
Dat's you all over, Al.

CROWLEY
Fine! Fine then! If that is the way it must be. I have not come this far to

shrink from the consequences of my own life's work, unexpected though they may be.

JANE
[*Handing him the grail.*] Then embrace your future self. [*He does.*] Breathe deeply of your future self. [*He smells the vomit.*] Drink of your future self.

CROWLEY
[*Eventually.*] I do! [*He drinks the vomit.*]

STUPID
What a idiot.

UGLY
The man is unstoppable. He drank puke!

CROWLEY
Eliot, will you join me in a toast to the Brave New World?

CRUEL
I prithee, Good My Liege, vomit is a thing ugly and foul and should never be ingested into the body.

UGLY
Yeah, stick to yer guns, ya old fart. I mean, yer majesty.

CRUEL
Well if he says you shouldn't then perhaps you should.

[*Eliot nearly takes the cup.*]

ELIOT
What am I doing? Never! You may have Ashtaroth, but we have the Muses, we have Apollo and Athena! Beauty's candidacy is still viable. Sing, Beauty, sing!

LIGEIA
[*With a Brooklyn accent.*] No, Uncle Tom, he's right. When I got down to Hell and the angels emerged from my soul, they told me that they would never be swayed in their support for Ugly, the former Johnny Spider. And they convinced me that Beauty is far more Beauty when it embraces, rather than opposes, Ugliness. [*She approaches Ugly.*] Ugly, forgive me. When we were lovers in that bitter life we have since shed, I carelessly set you on fire. It was a mistake, an accident, a foolish mistake for which I have paid the heavy price of losing your love.

90

UGLY
This answer pleases me. But why did you spurn me, refusing to see me when I came to you afterwards?

LIGEIA
I was afraid to face your hatred, which I knew was all I deserved.

[*Ugly is suspicious. He catches on.*]

UGLY
Oh, you poor thing, then do you still love me?

LIGEIA
Of course I do. But I am unworthy of your love. So please, I beg of you, take your revenge.

UGLY
Oh, come off it.

LIGEIA
Spank me with a garden trowel.

UGLY
Do what?

LIGEIA
Flail me! Scald me! Push me across a gravel parking lot on my face!

UGLY
Why you bitch, I wouldn't torture you if you was the last person on Earth!

LIGEIA
See, Uncle Tom? Even when you do what he wants, he doesn't like it!

JANE
Do you understand now, Mr. Eliot? You do, don't you?

ELIOT
I think so. We worship him, and he hates us. We don't, and he hates us still, but we take responsibility for our own lives, is that it?

JANE
Perfectly it. Then will you join me in writing hymns to his ugliness?

ELIOT
I shall! With tongue in cheek, of course.

CRUEL
But Sire, how will I love your undead daughter Beauty pure and chaste from afar, or run where the brave dare not go, or dream the impossible dream in a world managed by such a god?

ELIOT
Think how much braver you must be, how much purer and more chaste, Sir Percival, and how much more precious Beauty is in a world in which God does not even pretend to be pleased by these things. What a challenge to you, and how better by far to find the desire for god in yourself rather than in the promise of some Heavenly Reward.

CRUEL
I take up the challenge, then, Your Majesty.

JANE
Well spoken, Eliot.

CRUEL
Your will is my only desire, Good My Liege.

ELIOT
No! Your own! I am vomit, remember?

CRUEL
Sorry, I forgot.

UGLY
Wait, alla yas, listen, I don't wanna be God.

LIGEIA
Exactly the kind of God we want!

UGLY
OK, den I do wanna be God.

CROWLEY
Listen to him. Our God wants to be God!

ELIOT
What an ego!

UGLY
Dat's enough! You have insulted the Lord!

[*All gasp sarcastically.*]

ELIOT
Oh no!

LIGEIA
Beat me!

CRUEL
Oh, we'd better go do penance right away!

[*They all bow, scrape, and ad-lib sarcastically as they exit.*]

CROWLEY
[*To Jane.*] Are you getting all this down?

JANE
Of course.

UGLY
Yeah, go, leave me alone, alla yas! Leave me alone, leave me alone, leave me alone! Nuttin' but hotache. No revenge, no nuttin'!

STUPID
[*In tears.*] But you did get revenge. You got revenge on love. My love.

UGLY
Huh? I did? Yeah, sure I did. An' ain't dat what I wanted all along? Wasn't it love that set me aflame, an' love dat later abandoned me once I was all burned up? I did it! I got revenge on dat sonofabitchin' love!

[*Anna enters, pale and undead, wearing a neck brace.*]

ANNA
My love!

UGLY
Oh no.

STUPID
Huh? It's you! Hooray!

ANNA
The angels are letting us keep our memories now. Along with twenty dollars and a new suit.

STUPID
But what about us poor guys whose memories is all smooshed? [*Anna hands him a notice. He reads.*] "To the recipient of diss notice: Before

you died your name was Henry Stupid. You had all kinda brainy ideas runnin' around in yer head, but when you tried to express dem dey came out soundin' ridiculous. You were a slack-jawed, vacant-eyed, clumsy buffoon." I feel like a new man!

ANNA
Come live with me and be my love!

[*Anna and Stupid exit. The lights change, leaving Ugly alone in a stand-up comic spotlight.*]

UGLY
Well, after dat, I was pretty miserable fer awhile. Everywhere I went people'd be like, "Oh, hi Ugly. How ya doin'?" Like, "We know yer all fucked up, but dere's nuttin' we kin do about it." Fuck diss, I said. I'm gonna check out ol' Lucifer, I says, cuz I figure he'll sympathize, right? I mean all the angels are down dere, all dese old friends of his dat turned state's evidence on him right? So I go down to Hell, an' the first thing I notice is dat dere used to be diss sign out front dat said, "Check yer hope at the door." Well, dat sign's gone an' dey gotta new one dat says, "Don't worry, be happy." In neon. Teal an' magenta neon. So I go inside an' the place is all cleaned up. Like dey tried to keep the seedy atmosphere of the place but it's all clean. An' den I see Lucifer an' he's big an' fat, an' wid long hair an' a li'l beard an' little round glasses an' a beret an' a maroon blazer wid blue velour lapels an' he looks like a fat ol' rich beatnik. An he's all in touch wid himself now like he's been to therapy or somethin', an' he comes up an' hugs me an' says, "Hi, Ugly. How ya doin'?" An' I never liked the guy in the first place, right. So I'm real tense, I go to light up a cigarette an' he takes it away from me, real polite-like, an' says, "Sorry, Ugly. No smokin'." An' I'm like "No smokin' in Hell?" An I look up an' dere's diss fuckin' smoke detector on the ceilin'! I mean, what a buncha pussies, right! So I stalk away, ya know, an' go to the rec room figure I'll play a song on the jukebox. Cuz dat was one thing in Hell dat we had dat was really good, we had really good music. An' the way the jukebox used to work, see, was dat, well, first of all, the song you punched was never the song you got, right? An den, after you punched it you'd hafta go through like diss eleven minutes of really intense pain. Like you'd puncha Elvis song, an' den you get diss feelin' like dere's a epeleptic porcupine havin' a fit in yer lungs. And den some song dat wasn't Elvis'd come on, an' you didn't know what it was or who was singin' it, but it really sounded good, y'know, 'specially after the porcupine. But now dey changed dat. Now ya gotta go see the concierge, right? You go up dere an' ya hold out yer hand or yer stump or whatever, an' the concierge gives it a little pinch. Doesn't even fuckin' hurt! An' den the concierge gives ya a token. So I go up, I get my pinch an' my token, I go over, I put it in an' I punch up Bessy Smith. An' what comes out is diss ... I can't even describe it ... it's like [*Sings to Phillip Glass-esque piano accompaniment.*] 1234 1234 1 2 3 4 5 1234 ... an I'm like, what is diss shit, I don't wanna hear

94

diss shit, so I unplug the thing an' I turn around an'... an' dere's Jellyroll Morton sittin' down to the piano. An' man I loved Jelly man, he used to come in dere, so I go to sit down ... An' den I notice dat, hey, dere used to be broken glass all over everything. So if you wanted to sit an' listen to somebody play you had to really like 'em a lot. An' Jelly man he'd come in dere an' dere'd be broken glass all over the piano bench an' all over the keyboard but he would play an' play even till his fingers got all cut up an' bloody, he would play an' I would fuckin' listen. But now dey cleaned up all the glass, see. An' he sits down an' it's like diss.

[*He mimes pounding elbows and fists on a keyboard while the piano accompanies him, Cecil Tayloresque.*]

I mean, am I reactionary or somethin'? Dey fucked wid the music, man! It was the stupidest thing dey coulda done. Dey completely ruined Hell. I got the fuck outta dere man. An' I came back to Earth an'... I caught a show. I went to Steppenwolf. Yeah, I get in free to everything cuz I'm God. Is dat patronizin' or what? But it's free, so what the Hell. An' diss play dey had, well, it was a religious play, part of the new religion, the new religious pageant of plays dey had dere, and diss I hadda see, cuz diss was the story of Ligeia an' Johnny, an' y'know I was as curious as the next guy about dat story. An' the way dey had it, see, was dat Ligeia an' Johnny were really in love but dey was also really nasty to each other, it was like diss contest about who was like tougher or somethin'. An' so the deal with her settin' him on fire was like, y'know, Johnny was fixin' his bike, like in the song, an' he was all covered wid gasoline an' she's flickin' diss lighter at him like, I'm so tough I could actually do diss to you, an' he's like well I'm so tough dat I don't even care an', KABOOM! Y'know? An' dat was really cool, man, when he went up in flames? You should go see it just fer dat, man. But usher for it, it's way too much money. I dunno how dey did dat, set dat guy on fire. Musta cost 'em like $50,000. An' what, did dey hafta get a new guy every night or somethin'?

But, I'll tell ya somethin', dat show did not spark no memories in my skull dere.

[*A nostalgic voice sings "Ligeia and Johnny" to a distant piano. Ugly seems to reminisce. Then he gets testy.*]

Don't PLAY dat! ... Don't play dat. I don't believe in Ligeia an' Johnny no more. I don't think dey ever existed. I think dat is a fairytale.

[*Lights fade to black.*]

THE END

Danny Thompson's graphic for *Necessity*.

Necessity
by Danny Thompson

Necessity was first performed in February 1998
at the Footsteps Theatre in Chicago, with the following cast:

Thomas Edison................ Ben Schneider

O.T.......................... Danny Thompson

Albert Schweitzer, Boy,
Thomas Bell, Reporter 1 .... Paul Tamney

Mr. Earl, Man on the Road,
New York Lawyer, Nikola Tesla,
Reporter 2 .... David Isaacson

Warden Paul's Woman, Annie
Sullivan, Helen Keller Bell .... Martha Schoenberg

Alexander Graham Bell,
Warden Paul .... Dave Buchen
(performing as Dave Baxter-Birney)

Dana Wise replaced Martha Schoenberg during the original run
and for the July, 1999 revival.

For my Oobleck family, from Red Hook to West Hollywood,
from Berkeley to San Juan, from Madison to Wicker Park.

CHARACTERS

Doc (Albert Schweitzer)
Thomas Edison
O.T.
Guard (Mr. Earl)
Warden Paul's Woman
Boy
Annie Sullivan
Man on the Road
Alexander Graham Bell
Assistant (Thomas Bell)
Helen Keller Bell
New York Lawyer
Nikola Tesla
Warden Paul
Reporter 1
Reporter 2

O.T.'s accent was inspired by my dear Aunt Mildred, who was from Lyles in central Tennessee. Her speech was a lovely amalgam of a small-town Southern accent and the open, fluid, but careful pronunciation resulting from overcoming a childhood stammer. My approach in capturing her voice was to attempt a swallowing of parts of words amidst an ease of conversation.

ACT ONE

THE NEWSPAPER

In the dark we hear Morse code beeps, a telegraph key clicking, and a voice reading.

VOICE
Thomas ... Alva ... Edison, Ohio inventor of some note, found guilty today of investment fraud in case brought forth by prominent Wall Street backers; including J. Pierpont Morgan. Edison had failed to deliver on promise of indoor electric lighting. Edison sentenced to three years hard labor.

[Lights up. It is late at night in the chain gang bunkhouse. Three men are in a triple bunk bed. Doc, on top, is reading to O.T., on the bottom bed. Edison, in the middle, has his back to the audience.]

DOC
Unt in ze last panel ze olt man is jumping in ze air unt yelling, "I'll get you lil' varmints." Unt zen die Katzenjammer Kit zez, "Got in Himmel—"

EDISON
"Got in Himmel, it's not a ham sammich; it's a HAND sammich." I've got all the funnies memorized by now, Doc.

DOC
No, zis ist new newspaper. I trade ze guard for two ziggeretten. Paper ist only fife days olt.

O.T.
What's the Hasenfeffer Kid say?

DOC
Katzenjammer.

O.T.
Hats an' Peffer.

DOC
Katzen.

O.T.
Katzen.

DOC
Yammer.

O.T.
Yam ...

DOC
Yammer. Katz ... en ... jammer.

O.T.
Hasenfefferjammeryam ... yam.

DOC
Good. Ah ... die Katzenjammer Kit zez, "Got in Himmel vater de tulips tomorrow. De fire must be vatered, now." Heh, heh. Is gut, no?

O.T.
Thas a gooden'. Boy oh boy, them Hasenfeffer Kids. Read it agin.

[*Edison rolls over. Chains make a loud sound as his feet hit the floor.*]

EDISON
No. No more funnies tonight. I've got to keep things clear in my mind.

DOC
I read die news, now, OK?

EDISON
NO. You've got to rest, Doc. We've both got to save up our strength. It'll be soon.

DOC
Ya. Ve all lay back unt sink fer a while. Is nice cool night. Is gut night zu sink.

[*They all lay back in their beds. Long pause.*]

O.T.
What's ever'body thinking 'bout?

DOC
I'm sinking is nice cool night. Is gut night zu sink. You sink, too. OK? Yaaaah.

[*Long pause.*]

O.T.
What's ever'body thinking 'bout, now?

[*Edison applauds and laughs. He jumps up and blows kisses to O.T.*]

102

EDISON
Goddamn me! You are a piece of work, O.T. Just amaze me.

O.T.
Thank you, very much. I like you boys, too.

DOC
I like you boys, too. Both of you.

O.T.
This place weren't too much good aforen you two come in here on the chain gang.

DOC
Vell, if I vas to be on ze chain gang, I am glad it vas on zis chain gang. I vill miss you, big man.

EDISON
Doc! [*Quietly to Doc.*] I thought we agreed. No goodbyes. Too risky.

DOC
Ya.

O.T.
Hey, Tom. I'm tired a thinkin'. Make that thang with the piece a' wire agin.

DOC
Vat sing mit da vire?

O.T.
Tom bends up a piece a wire so it holds yer pieces a' paper together. He does things like that. He's got a head fer making thangs outa other thangs. Make that thang with the piece a wire agin, Tom.

EDISON
[*Calming him.*] O.T., O.T. I'm just wanting to lay here and think.

O.T.
I'll bet you my cornbread tomorrow, you cain't make that thing with the piece a' wire agin.

DOC
Vat sing mit da vire !?!

EDISON
Nothing. It's just a little invention.

103

O.T.
Thas what he called it. A little vention.

EDISON
I call it the Edison paper brace. Well, OK. [*Shows Doc.*] I take a regular piece of wire about six inches long and bend it into a square and then again bend two of the outer corners together and ... there you go. The Edison paper brace.

DOC
Vat does it do?

O.T.
It holds yer papers together without makin' a hole in 'em. Lemme show ya.

[*Doc gives him the newspaper. O.T. unfolds the pages and binds them with the amazing "paper brace."*]

EDISON
That's right, O.T. Just like I showed you.

O.T.
See. They ain't no hole, but they ain't fallin' down. Haw, haw, haw, haw. Tom's head is filled with thangs even beddern' this. Ain't yer head so filled, Tom, ain't it?

EDISON
Of course it's filled. It's pregnant with ideas. That's what I do, damn it. I'm an inventor. I create things.

[*O.T. is jumping up and down testing the paper brace's effectiveness.*]

EDISON
Just like Adam created Eve from his own rib; I create things to ease mankind's burden. To continually march us step by step further from the screaming monkeys we once were.

DOC
Like zis paper brace?

EDISON
Yeah ... well no. Mostly electrical things. Or things that would be better if they were electrical. I just can't ... get a hold of any equipment to work on here. But that doesn't stop the old mind from thinking up things. I'm always thinking, Doc. [*Points to the stage lights.*] Take these lanterns here for example. There's a real name to be made for the guy who can replace open flames with *electrical* luminescence.

104

DOC
Zen you vould be interested in zis story of the Excelsior City Invention Exposition. It sez a man named Bell has taken za vorld by storm.

[*Edison grabs the paper and scans quickly.*]

EDISON
Bell, a speech therapist from New Jerusalem, is currently drawing record crowds with ... talking boxes ... No. Noooo. People cheering at demonstrations of his electrical speech transmitters, which he calls the *telephone*, the *phonography box*, and the *dictaphonium*. No. Oh, no. Ooooooh.

O.T.
Tom's got a plan fer a talkin' box in his head. I bet it's beddern' this Bell man's talkin' box.

[*Edison begins to hyperventilate.*]

EDISON
These are my ideas. He can't just take my ideas. These are my ideas.

DOC
But your ideas are just zat—ideas. Hundreds of people haf seen zeez machines.

[*Edison grabs Doc by the collar.*]

DOC
But zat does not mean zey are not gut ideas. Very gut ideas.

EDISON
We're moving everything up. We're leaving tomorrow.

DOC
Tomorrow? Ve cannot leave tomorrow. You haf not told me ze plan?

EDISON
This is the plan. [*He takes out a homemade knife, a shiv.*]

DOC
Zis is your brilliant plan? Knife ze guard unt run?

O.T.
Thas a purdy little pig sticker. Only we ain't got no pigs ta stick. 'Cause they's pork. Git it? It ain't a pig no more; they's pork. Haw, haw, haw.

DOC
No. I cannot condone violence. If zis is ze only vay out—

EDISON
Then I'll leave you behind. I'm going!

GUARD
[*Outside.*] What the hell's goin' on in there?

O.T.
Yer gonna have ta be quiet, Tom, or the guards'll come on in here.

DOC
You said zat you vanted to help people vis your ideas. Zis is gut. But maybe you could help in ozer vays. People vill alvays need medical help.

EDISON
Look, you nincompoop. I'm an inventor, not a goddamned nurse.

[*The Guard enters.*]

GUARD
What the hell's goin' on?

[*As the guard turns his back to close the door, Edison lunges at him with shiv raised high. Doc grabs Edison's arm. O.T. disarms Edison and holds him by his upper arms. The guard sees neither the weapon nor the attack.*]

EDISON
I gotta go to Excelsior City.

GUARD
You gonna go spend the night in the box. Thas where you're goin'.

EDISON
Do you know who I am, you stupid little man?

GUARD
You're the feller who's gonna get his head busted open. [*He raises his rifle up to hit Edison with the butt.*]

EDISON
I am Thomas Alva Edison!

O.T.
NO. I'll take care of him. [*He holds him more firmly.*]

EDISON
The Napoleon of Invention!

O.T.
Can you hush up? [*Shakes him.*]

EDISON
The Wizard of Industry!

GUARD
I'll hush 'em up.

EDISON
I am the son of Revolutionary War heroes!

[*The guard has his rifle butt raised near Edison's head.*]

O.T.
NO!

EDISON
I am the modern Prometheus!

[*O.T. hits Edison firmly, but carefully on he back of the neck. He goes limp in O.T.'s arms.*]

O.T.
Sorry, Tom.

[*End of scene.*]

CHAIN GANG

A rock quarry. O.T. and Edison are chained together. They are sweaty from bustin' up rocks. An armed guard is watching them. There is a tall, narrow wooden box upstage.

GUARD
Now, what was I saying? Oh, yeah. That dog was howling and a yelping. I don't know where they got so many big ol' rocks, let alone where they got the strength to toss them things. I'm talking little chil'ren. Throwing big ol' rocks. Bigger'n them over there.

O.T.
Well why didn't that ol' hound dog go in bitin' on them chil'ren. They needed it.

EDISON
Drinking it up over here, Boss. [*He drinks without waiting.*]

GUARD
You right 'bout that. I never seen any chil' more deserving of being bit. [*To Edison.*] Hey, smart boy, I don't recall calling you to drink it up.

EDISON
[*Straining his patience.*] Waiting to drink it up over here. Boss.

GUARD
[*Waves at him quickly.*] Drink it up, smart boy. Now, where was I? Yeah, that dog. I jus' don't know why he didn't bite. He'd growl some, then stop like he was ashamed to be showing teeth at them chil'ren.

[*A small door on the upstage box opens and Doc slowly works his face out of the opening.*]

DOC
Please. May I have vater?

[*The Guard walks to the box and closes the little door.*]

GUARD
Now, that I'm thinking on it, I got no idea why he don't bite. They weren't big chil'ren, just little'uns. I bet you one bite would a' saved his damned ol' life. Maybe the damned dog was raised that way. Taught not to harm chil'ren, not even to defend himself. I bet you thas it. Somebody taught him that way. About 20 minutes a' them damn chil'ren afflictin' that dog was all I could take. So's I pick up my Winchester and draw a bead on down the barrel and pow! Put that poor damned dog outta his mis'ry. Best thing I could a' done in the circumstances. I bet that dog's up in heaven right now ... thanking me for that bullet in his head.

DOC
[*From inside.*] Please! I need vater.

GUARD
Shut up, mouth boy. You did enough gabbin' last night.

EDISON
[*To O.T.*] What? Did Doc talk?

O.T.
Yeah. He were talkin' jes' now. He said he wanted some wadder.

[*Edison takes water bucket to Doc.*]

GUARD
Whar you goin'?

EDISON
I thought I'd bring him some water.

GUARD
Oh, no. You ain't bringin' him no water. Is ever'body all a' sudden stupid on how my box works?

O.T.
Mr. Earl, sir, how come you always call it "my" box?

GUARD
'Cause thas how it is. I built her. She's my baby girl.

O.T.
You built her all on yer own?

GUARD
Thas how it is. This here is the O-riginal hot box. First one ever. Anywhere.

EDISON
Doc must have said something. He's gone all chicken and my knife's gone.

GUARD
But I seen one just like it in Hickman County. Same size. Same tin top. They stole it from me.

O.T.
Yer pig sticker? I got. it in my pocket, here.

GUARD
And them Taylor County boys stole the idea from me, too. It's not like I cain't prove I came up with it first. I got me a dated letter from—

[*Edison begins "his plan" as he jumps back from a large flat rock downstage.*]

EDISON
Ahhhh! What the hell is that?

GUARD
What you find? Lizard?

EDISON
I don't know. What is it, O.T.?

O.T.
I ain't so sure.

[*The Guard walks to the rock and stands with his back them. Edison takes his shiv from O.T.'s pocket.*]

GUARD
All right. You back up, Smart Boy, so's I can see.

[*Edison raises the shiv as Earl aims his rifle at the rock.*]

GUARD
An' O.T., you lift up that rock, so's I can take a good ol' look.

DOC
NO!

GUARD
What?

[*Edison hides his shiv behind his back. Everyone glares at Doc.*]

DOC
Nothink. Just be careful.

[*The Guard aims his rifle at the rock.*]

GUARD
Lift it up on three. One ... two ...

DOC
NO!

GUARD
What the hell is wrong with you? I'm about to shoot you first and then kill the lizard. You keep your goddamned mouth shut. Sumpen under a rock and the whole damn world goes wild on me.

EDISON
Ahhhh! I saw it again.

GUARD
Did ya see what it was?

EDISON
It was yellow.

GUARD
Yellow? Naw.

EDISON
Perhaps green. I'm not sure.

GUARD
[*To O.T.*] You seen it?

O.T.
Naw. I mean yeah. But I didn't ... I ... I don't ... I ...

GUARD
What the hell you st-st-st-stammerin' about? Back up, smart boy. [*To Doc.*] And you keep yer mouth shut. Now pull up that damned rock when I say. Do it now, O.T.!

DOC
Noooooo!

[*The Guard falls backward onto Edison. The Guard jumps up and throws a rock at the box. O.T. takes Edison's shiv and cracks the blade off against the chest of his overalls.*]

GUARD
GODDAMNED SON A' BITCH! YOU GOT NO BRAIN IN YER GODDAMNED HEAD!

[*When he reaches the box he slams his rifle butt into the side several times and Doc yells in pain.*]

GUARD
WHAT THE HELL IS WRONG WITH YOU, YOU GODDAMNED SON A' —

[*Eventually a plank breaks. The Guard sees the damage and is trembling mad and speechless. All is still for a moment.*]

GUARD
[*In a frightful whisper.*] Goddamned son a' bitch. He broke my goddamn box. She's all busted up. Goddamned son a' bitch, broke my damn box.

[*The Guard sticks the butt of his rifle through the new hole, hitting Doc.*]

DOC
[*His face through the small door.*] God, forgive him for he knows not vat he does.

111

GUARD

"Knows not what he does?" [*Hits him again with his rifle.*] You callin' me ignert?

DOC

NOT you, but zis system vhich ve are all victims of. You as much as myself.

GUARD

I don't seem to be the victim here, do I? [*Hits Doc with rifle.*]

DOC

I mean no insult, no impudence. Ve both find ourselves vis no recourse, no ... potentiality for mutual human acknowledgment. [*Guard hits him with rifle.*] Please. Your abuse only breaks my body not my humanity. If God—

GUARD

[*Hits Doc with rifle.*] Well hot damn, I think I got 'em right in the humanity that time.

DOC

If God is in all of us—

GUARD

[*Hits Doc with rifle.*] You think God is in a piece of shit like you? [*Hits him with rifle.*] If God's got half a brain, he'd better get the hell outta you before he gets a bullet in him. [*Aims rifle at box, but it does not fire.*]

GUARD

Look at this! My goddamned Winchester. You broke my goddamned Winchester.

O.T.

WARDEN PAUL'S WOMAN! WARDEN PAUL'S WOMAN! COME OUT HERE QUICK! WARDEN PAUL'S WOMAN!

[*The Guard unlocks and opens the door. Doc, covered in blood, teeters forward and falls to the ground. Warden Paul's Woman runs on screaming at the Guard.*]

WARDEN PAUL'S WOMAN

Earl! Stop it! Stop it, Earl!

GUARD

This son a' bitch broke my goddamn box and my goddamn Winchester. [*Kicks Doc.*]

112

WARDEN PAUL'S WOMAN
Stop it, Earl! You've hit him enough.

GUARD
This ain't none a yer business, Ma'am. Yer man left me in charge here.

WARDEN PAUL'S WOMAN
He left you to guard them, not to beat 'em to death.

GUARD
He ain't dead. I beat men before an' I know when to stop.

WARDEN PAUL'S WOMAN
This man is almost dead, Earl.

GUARD
Almost dead is still alive, ain't it?

WARDEN PAUL'S WOMAN
Get the medicine box off my kitchen wall, Earl.

GUARD
This man tried to—

WARDEN PAUL'S WOMAN
Say what you will. I'll tell my man what I saw. Get your ass to the kitchen, Earl.

[*They stare at each other. She eventually takes a pistol out from under her apron.*]

WARDEN PAUL'S WOMAN
I'll guard these men, Earl. You run to the kitchen. I can shoot a man if I have to.

GUARD
Yeah, bet you'd like it, too. [*Exits.*]

WARDEN PAUL'S WOMAN
[*To Doc.*] You lay still.

O.T.
Warden Paul's woman, can we help?

WARDEN PAUL'S WOMAN
[*Pointing pistol.*] You two stay right there where I can see you.

DOC
Don't blame zem. Mr. Earl lost control of his sinking.

WARDEN PAUL'S WOMAN
He's lost a lot more than that, now.

DOC
It is not really his fault, either. I vas vain in trying to preach to him.

WARDEN PAUL'S WOMAN
Shut up, Schweitzer. You're all out of cheeks to turn.

DOC
[*Laughing.*] Ya. [*He coughs and spits blood.*]

O.T.
You look bad, Doc.

DOC
I feel bad. Hold my hand, please.

WARDEN PAUL'S WOMAN
Alright, O.T., but don't move him.

[*Edison and O.T. cross to Doc. Warden Paul's Woman is at his feet.*]

DOC
O.T., "Ve are all brethren." Ya, remember Matthew 23:8.

O.T.
Well, I ain't got a head fer 'rythmatic.

DOC
But you have ze heart which could do much good in this world. Follow with me the footsteps of Christ. Remember the things which I've done to help the less fortunate.

O.T.
I ain't sure. I only knowed you a few days. And you was in the box most a' today.

DOC
But remember ze hospitals which I have told you of? Of helping others?

O.T.
Oh, yeah. You were helping folks in the jungles and then you come here to help us help folks in city jungles. I'll do what I can, but I cain't promise

114

I'll be leaving here none to soon. Doc? [*Nothing.*] You resting, Doc?

[*During this, Edison has crossed over to the woman's other side. He loops the chain (between O.T. and himself) around her neck and strangles her. He knocks the gun from her hand.*]

O.T.
Oh, lord. Warden Paul's Woman, you got yer neck caught in my chain. Tom, run around this a' way or she'll choke.

EDISON
You dumb son of a bitch, I'm strangling her. This is our only chance.

O.T.
Ah, no! What you wanna do that for? This here's Warden Paul's woman. [*She goes limp.*] Oh, lord. OH! She's dead. What you do that? What you go an' kill her for?

EDISON
I didn't want to. It was necessary. Besides, you're on the other end of this chain. You killed her, too.

O.T.
Oh, lord. This is the worst thing. This is the worst day ever.

EDISON
This is our best chance to get out of here. Let's make a run. Come on.

O.T.
I cain't go. B'sides, I like it here.

EDISON
I'm not ... what?

O.T.
I like it here. I do.

EDISON
You don't know what you're saying. You can't like prison.

O.T.
Oh, I ain't a prisoner. I work here. It's my job. I break rocks fer 10¢ a day. I cain't just leave my job.

EDISON
Why would anyone work on a chain gang?

O.T.
I like to drink way too much. ... I cain't keep sour mash outta my mouth lest I's chained down somewhares. [*Rattles his chains.*] I get mean crazy when I drink. A few years ago, I got good'n drunk in a bar full a boys who was all good'n drunk. They was all mean crazy an' I was all mean crazy. An' then the littlest son a' bitch of 'em all lit a match an' that powder keg blew up, but good. An' I killed 'em all, 'cept that little son a' bitch. I picked him up an' lit his head on fire into the stove. Then I walked around town carrying him burnin' ever'thang down to the dirt. He never stopped screamin' an' I never stopped yellin', "Scream some more, match boy." I woke up the next mornin', layin' in the ashes with four deputies sitting on my arms and the marshall with a gun to my head. I killed them, too. Ever'body an' his uncle was lookin' fer me, so's I go work here. Nobody ever look fer me here. [*Rattles his chains.*] An' I cain't get no sour mash here. Besides, the rocks is softer here, than in most places.

[*Edison is slackjawed speechless. The Guard creeps onstage wielding an ax handle.*]

GUARD
You go in the box real quiet, O.T., an' I won't hit you.

O.T.
You ain't gonna hit nobody no more, Mr. Earl, sir. [*He slowly turns to face the Guard.*]

GUARD
Get in my box an' I'll make sure Tom don't have no trouble with Warden Paul.

O.T.
Look at here. [*He holds out his open palm. He effortlessly takes the Guard by the throat with one hand. The guard's strength goes quickly and he drops the ax handle and becomes limp. This is all very easy for O.T.*]

O.T.
Doc tried to preach you right, BUT YOU WOULD NOT LISTEN! [*The Guard is dead.*] But Doc fergives you. Don't you, Doc? I will foller in yer Christian footsteps. I will go into the jungles and teach people how to make bandages. And how to be dignent.

EDISON
[*Looking through the Guard's vest pocket.*] Where's the goddamned key?

O.T.
Let's go, Tom. I feel like walkin' some.

[*End of scene.*]

GREAT EXPECTATIONS

At the crossroads. A signpost states: Rockville Quarry 15 miles, Excelsior 6 miles, New Jerusalem 3 miles. O.T. is sitting on a large rock. He is shaking stones and sand out of one of his boots. Edison, still chained to him, is just waking.

O.T.
Nothing to be done. [*Pause.*] How'd you sleep?

EDISON
Just closed my eyes a minute. I really don't sleep. Maybe three or four naps every twenty-four hours.

O.T.
Naw. You been sleepin' a long time. It's almost high noon. You been sleepin' all night an' half today.

EDISON
Damn me. Did that blacksmith's boy come back?

O.T.
Not yet, but he's hiding over there behind them tombstones.

EDISON
What's he doing there, just watching us?

[They cross the stage on either side of a tree and are stopped by their chain. O.T. tries to fix the problem by way of a bizarre set of physical wrangling resulting in a twisted mess.]

EDISON
Wait, no. Stand, stand, STOP!

[Edison crawls under O.T.'s leg to untie the tangle. O.T. is amazed at this display of "Big Smarts" as he rubs Edison's head. They finish their cross.]

O.T.
Whar'd he go? He were right thar a minute ago talkin' to that thar cow. I think you scared him bad yesterday.

EDISON
If he didn't bring us that file I'll give him something to be scared of, sure enough. Boy! Get your little ass over here.

O.T.
I don't think you should a' told him I'd eat his heart and liver.

EDISON
You can't hide from us. I've got special powers. Even if you were invisible, I can see your thoughts. And my friend's got a way with a little boy's liver, so hurry up.

[*The Boy runs on.*]

BOY
I'm sorry. I ... I ... I ...

[*Edison takes the boy's sack and passes it to O.T.*]

EDISON
What's in the sack? You bring the file?

O.T.
It's a pork pie. Nice round one, too. Thank you very much.

EDISON
[*Grabs the boy.*] I gave yer man $10 to send a file or a hacksaw, didn't I?

BOY
I ... I ... I ...

O.T.
He's too scared to talk, Tom.

EDISON
Don't say my name no more! I told you that. My name's not Tom, boy. It's Mr. Albert. Understand? Now, where's your blacksmith?

BOY
He ... he ... [*Edison slaps him.*] He cain't come today, but he'll come tomorrow, for sure.

EDISON
What kind of idiot does he think I am? What kind of fool would sit on the side of the road for two days waiting for some bastard to screw 'em through a little squirt like you?

[*Edison turns the boy upside down and shakes him. Things fall out of his pockets.*]

O.T.
Don't you hurt him none!

118

EDISON
What's he got in his pockets?

O.T.
Le'me talk to 'em, Tom. [*Kneeling down to hanging boy.*] Don't you pay no never mind to him. He's just mad at yer man. Yer blacksmith done did us wrong. But that ain't yer fault. You work fer him? [*Boy nods yes.*] Does he beat on ya? [*Boy nods no.*] Well, thas good. But you learn from this what kind a' man he is. You remember: he could do you like he done us.

[*Edison drops the boy, who runs off.*]

O.T.
Now you run along an' have a good life. An' don't tell nobody you seen us.

EDISON
What if he lets on about us to someone? We'd best move on, O.T.

O.T.
Naw, maybe we oughta wait an' see if his blacksmith shows.

EDISON
He won't show. He's cheated us.

O.T.
Then why'd he send the pork pie?

EDISON
[*Thinking.*] Maybe it's poison.

O.T.
Let me eat on it a while. If it's poisoned you know soon enough.

EDISON
Your thinking's missing a step or two there. I'll know, but you'll be dead.

O.T.
Well, if a man steals $10 from you an' then has his boy bring you a poison pork pie, well then I don't wanna live in this world no more.

EDISON
Well, you may not mind ending up poisoned, but think about my situation? [*O.T. is stumped.*] I'll be chained to biggest dead man since Goliath.

[*O.T. throws the pie to Edison, who throws it into the brush. O.T. is staring at his hands.*]

O.T.
If we was back at Rockville, we'd be eatin' supper by now. And then Doc would be readin' me off'a the funny papers.

EDISON
I guess this gives you opportunity for a fresh start.

O.T.
This ain't no fresh start. Not with killin' people.

EDISON
You started over after burning down an entire town, O.T.

O.T.
That were *after* killin' people. This'ld be startin' over with killin' people. That ain't no fresh start.

EDISON
Well, what are you going to do, now?

O.T.
I figgered I'd foller you around fer a little while.

EDISON
I don't think so.

O.T.
At least 'til we get these chains off.

EDISON
All right. I suppose that would be OK.

O.T.
Then I guess I'll go get work bustin' up rock somewhars.

EDISON
Rocks. Isn't there something else you can do, man?

O.T.
I've tried lots a thangs. None I'm special at. I always thought I'd be special at sump'en , since I's so bad at bein' smart. I thought maybe I could run real good, er play Ping-Pong real good, er get elected president 'cause somebody backed their vehicle into my legs. Or maybe some brother I never knew I had whisked me up and took me to some big gamblin' city and we won lots a money 'cause I's so good at countin' cards with 'rythmatic. Or maybe I'd join the Marine Corps an' get my drill sergeant all steamed up with wacky misadventures ever' week an' then I'd surprise ever'body

120

by singin' real good. "Oh, my per-paw. To me you are so wonderful. Oh, my per-paw ..." [*O.T. sniffs at his chest. There is an awful smell. He reaches into his overalls bib and removes at dead mouse by its tail.*] But none a' that never happen. My mama always said, "When God doesn't put a door on yer house, you gotta crawl out the winder." But I guess God didn't build me no winders, neither. On my house. My 'maginary house.

EDISON
Aw, jesus. [*Crosses to comfort him.*] Look, O.T., it isn't easy being special.

O.T.
Naw.

EDISON
When I was ten years old my mother, she lay on the cusp of death all because some lame-headed doctor wouldn't operate at night. "It's too dark," he said. So I went to every house in town and gathered up every mirror, and every lantern. And I created a brilliant field of reflected light on the dining room table.

O.T.
Dang. A whole field?

EDISON
That's when I began to understand that I was special. No one else in town could've figured that out. Just Thomas Alva Edison, boy genius. Edison. That name's dead, now. I'll have to start all over again. Build it up from the ground floor. New laboratory, new workforce. Nose to the grindstone again. Like my first years. My best years. No sleep. Dinner plates piled up on the table. Sketches and notes covering the wallpaper. Absolute and unreserved mindfulness to the task at hand. I'll need a new name. What's Thomas Edison backward? Noside Samoht. No, slightly Jewish. Maybe if I scramble the letters. Ed Mathison. Too Swedish. How about ... Ted ... Danson. Nice.

[*A woman's voice is heard offstage just before she (Anne) enters; a Man soon follows carrying her suitcases. Anne is wearing a green traveling dress and round sunglasses. The Man is wearing worn coattails with no tie. He was once a dandy, but now looks more of a drunk.*]

ANNE
[*Off.*] Please. My eyes are bad and I don't wish to run.

EDISON
Quick, O.T., behind that brush.

[*Edison and O.T. scurry back, out of sight.*]

ANNE
I don't want you any closer than you already are.

MAN
Oh, but that patch of grass there looks so nice and inviting. I'll bet you it's soft, too, Miss Annie.

ANNE
Mr. Simon, you were sent to the station to escort me to the house and that is precisely what you shall do.

MAN
I was instructed to be kindly to you and that is precisely my intention, Miss Annie.

ANNE
You may not address me by my Christian name, Mr. Simon.

O.T.
We oughta help her.

EDISON
No, no. Someone else will come, O.T.

ANNE
Please stand still. PLEASE! [*She takes out a small derringer.*] NO! I have warned you, Mr. Simon.

MAN
That little pistol is just about as pretty as you are, Miss Annie.

EDISON
She's got a derringer. No need to worry.

ANNE
Please stop. [*He is walking slowly to her.*] Please. PLEASE!

[*She fires. All is still for a moment. The Man looks down at himself, then at the suitcase.*]

MAN
You done shot your own clothes, Miss Annie.
[*She tries the derringer again and again. All clicks.*]

MAN
One shot's all it's got, Honey. You should a' used a six-shooter to mess with the likes of me.

122

[*He drops the cases and dashes for her. He throws her over his shoulder and plays with her as if she were delighted by this. As she begins to scream O.T. rises. Edison tugs at his overalls with little effect.*]

EDISON
Please stay down, O.T. Please.

MAN
Ha, ha. You ain't gonna kiss me, are you?

[*She hits him hard in the spine with the pistol, which sends them both to the ground.*]

EDISON
You see, she can fend for herself.

MAN
Mongrel bitch.

[*The Man returns to her with a rock and strikes her dead. He spits on her and begins to unbelt his pants. O.T. bolts across stage dragging Edison behind him. The Man backs up looking about him and slowly picks up the rock as he speaks.*]

MAN
Oh, shit. Uh, I'm so glad you gentlemen arrived. Me and the misses were accosted. I was trying—

[*The Man hits O.T. in the head with the rock. O.T. does not react. The Man hits him squarely once more. O.T. touches his fingers to his head. O.T. and the Man look at each other for a moment in confusion. As the Man turns to run O.T. grabs his coattail and drags him back. O.T. pulls up the man's hand, still holding the rock, and shows it to him accusingly. O.T. crushes the man's hand.*]

MAN
Please. We are all gentlemen of the world. We can certainly talk this over.

[*O.T. strikes him down with one substantial, Old Testament blow. He is dead. Edison is kneeling quietly in shock.*]

O.T.
Oh, Lord. I killed him.

EDISON
It's alright. He killed her.

O.T.
I should a' killed him 'afore he killed her. It's as good as I killed 'em both.

EDISON
No. He killed her. You killed him. Don't get confused. He needed killing, right? [*O.T. is beginning to panic. The shaking of the chain is hurting Edison.*] O.T. Look at me. LOOK AT ME. Did you kill him to steal his money?

O.T.
NO.

EDISON
No, you didn't. Did you kill him to steal his wife?

O.T.
[*O.T. is confused.*] I don't even know that man.

EDISON
Exactly. So you couldn't gain anything from him being dead. And you certainly didn't enjoy it.

O.T.
Oh, Lord God, no.

EDISON
Well, alright then. You killed him. You didn't murder him. That's the sin—murder.

O.T.
I should a' killed 'em 'afore he killed her. That's the sin.

EDISON
We'll have to bury them both.

[*Dogs are heard in the distance. Edison closes his eyes and bows his head in resignation.*]

EDISON
The dogs. I can't outrun the dogs, anymore.

O.T.
You wanna go back an' tell Warden Paul we're sorry we killed his wife and Mr. Earl?

EDISON
[*After sneering at O.T.*] I have an idea. Take off your clothes.

[End of scene.]

AT TABLE

The Bell dining room. The table is set for four. Alexander Graham Bell stands center clasping O.T.'s hand. O.T. is in Anne Sullivan's dress. He looks wide-eyed around the room and only partially listens to Bell.

BELL
Welcome to our home, Miss Sullivan.

O.T.
Thank you.

BELL
I am glad to see you are a ... strong woman. You'll soon learn Helen can be quite a handful.

O.T.
Helen?

BELL
Yes. My adopted child, Helen. Ack, they didn't tell you her name? Well, I do hope they told you she is a special case. Both blind and deaf.

O.T.
Blind and deaf? That must be real hard on her.

BELL
You'll soon be very surprised. Our Helen is quite a happy girl. She is spirited and free at play. She loves the sun and the water and all of God's Good Earth. The difficulty is upon me as her protector. But this burden is a cross I bear gladly.

O.T.
Uh huh, you glad she cain't see an' hear.

BELL
My gladness is solely from her own joy of life. But as I have said, her supervision is a constant labor—albeit a labor of love—which takes me from my other work. Work, which I hope someday may be of great benefit to mankind. I repeatedly have asked God for guidance in that work, but now realize that in order to receive it I must be prepared to accept it. And that will require time. Time which you—

[Bell notices that O.T. is scratching deep into his dress and is not listening.]

BELL
Ack, I am speaking of myself when it is Helen you have come for. I will ring for dinner and you shall meet her then.

[*Bell walks off with bell in hand. He is heard offstage ringing. Once O.T. finds himself alone, he lifts his skirts to reveal Edison underneath. He crawls out.*]

O.T.
I think we ought get out a' here.

EDISON
Oh, good lord, that's no picnic under there.

O.T.
Sorry. I been eatin' stinkweed.

EDISON
Let's just ride it out 'til dark. Besides, you get to eat supper.

O.T.
I think he's trying to marry off his daughter to the Sullivan woman.

EDISON
Noooo. I think it's an orphanage thing. If we—What's that? My God, I think this is a telephone.

O.T.
I think we ought get out a' here.

[*Edison compares the telephone with the picture on the newspaper in his pocket.*]

EDISON
It's a telephone, alright. What did he say his name was?

O.T.
I don't think he said. [*The bell ringing gets nearer.*] Hide back under!

[*Bell enters. The Assistant follows silently. Edison has gone back under the skirt.*]

BELL
I'm sure you'll excuse my whimsy. Bell. [*Points to himself.*] Bell. [*Points to bell.*]

126

O.T.
[*Uncomfortable pause.*] Oh, I get it. Thas a bell ... an' yer name is Bell. I like that 'en. It's like a man named "Horse" ... on a horse. Haw. Haw. It's jest a good thang yer name ain't "Shotgun" when you come callin' time fer supper. [*Edison bangs on O.T. from under the dress.*] Oow!

BELL
[*Formally.*] Let us now sit at table.

[*Bell holds chair for O.T. who, with much commotion, cautiously arrives to the center of the table. Seated to O.T.'s left and right, Bell and Assistant bow their heads in prayer.*]

BELL
Dear Heavenly Lord—

[*O.T. jumps up in pain holding the entire table off the floor. Bell and Assistant take the table by each end. Smiling, O.T. gently presses the table back down. Bell and Assistant await an explanation.*]

O.T.
My underneath is hurting.

BELL
Dear Heavenly Lord, we give great thanks for our abundance today. A bountiful crop from our own garden, which you have smiled upon this summer. And for the safe arrival of Miss Sullivan ... and for the surprise guest with us today. He is an unexpected presence at our doorstep, but welcome, no matter his past transgressions. Thomas, like all of us, is God's child.

[*Edison's arm slowly rises to take a knife from the table. O.T. is in near panic.*]

BELL
It is not my place to judge nor damn him. God grant us your patience and wisdom. In the name of the Father, the blessed Son and the Holy Spirit. Amen. Thomas, hide not your face from me nor God. The wrongs you've committed are no longer a concern of this house. Rise and stand before me, Thomas.

[*The Assistant rises slowly. Edison begins to crawl out from under the front of the table.*]

O.T.
[*Pulling Edison back by the leg.*] It ain't you.

BELL
Pardon me, Miss Sullivan?

O.T.
[*Pulling again.*] It ain't you. [*To Bell.*] Nah, I weren't talkin'.

[*Edison continues to struggle under the table.*]

BELL
Come, good Thomas.

O.T.
So, yer name is Thomas, man standing here at the table.

BELL
Tell me, have you repented before our Lord.

ASSISTANT
Yes. If it is of importance to you. I have spoken to God. I am at peace of mind with myself.

BELL
It is God you must be at peace with.

ASSISTANT
I know where peace comes from, Alexander. Yes, if it is of importance to you, I am at peace with God.

BELL
Very well.

ASSISTANT
I was at peace with God the day the day I left here. I was at peace with God the day I arrived at my new employer's. I have been at peace with God every—

BELL
We can discuss this at another time.

ASSISTANT
The only one I am not at peace with—

BELL
NOT now. We have a guest. We must remember our Miss Sullivan. Thomas, would you bring Helen to us? [*The Assistant exits.*] Thomas Bell, my brother. He has been away from home for sometime, now. He was my assistant at the first stages of the telephone—But I forget myself. This is a

128

family matter. I am sorry your welcome has been ... Please forgive us this incident and let us speak no more of it.

[*Pause.*]

O.T.
Taters sure look good.

BELL
Indeed they do.

[*Bell serves O.T. potatoes. Helen enters with the Assistant. She walks to Bell and embraces him lovingly then eats off his plate with her hands.*]

BELL
This is our Helen. Strong with God's pleasure. I am certain you will come to love her as I do.

O.T.
She's purdy, fer a blind an' deaf girl.

[*Helen goes to O.T.'s plate.*]

O.T.
She's got her fingers in my food.

BELL
As you can see, our Helen is a pure, free spirit. Uninitiated in the social fineries. We have exhausted all attempts to impose matters of etiquette.

[*Helen puts her hand on O.T.'s plate and he gently pulls it away. This sequence repeats, Helen alternating hands. The routine builds to a fit of all four hands slapping.*]

O.T.
Yeah, but she got her fingers in my food.

[*Helen is feeling O.T.'s features, leaving mashed potatoes on his face.*]

BELL
Think of the simplicity of it. Food before us. Fingers to food. Food to mouth. Pure and honest human need fulfilled. All other elaborations are merely social vanity, don't you think?

[*O.T. tosses Helen back against the wall. She is enjoying the competition and returns for more. O.T. snatches his plate and shields it in his arms.*]

O.T.
I don't mind that much, but she got her fingers in my food. Why cain't she finger eat off a' her own food?

BELL
Why not indeed, Miss Sullivan, why not indeed. Take this as your invitation to her soul. We can all see her inner self, but we have little access inside. Miss Sullivan, you must find her door. And bring her out to us.

[*Long pause as O.T. is confused. He leans down under the table.*]

O.T.
Is he talkin' 'bout her room—

EDISON
No. He's not talking about a real door.

O.T.
[*Up to Bell.*] You don't mean no real door.

BELL
The door of her soul.

O.T.
What if God didn't make her no door in her soul? Can I help her climb out the winder?

[*Helen crosses in front of the table and trips on Edison's feet.*]

BELL
Perhaps this is the secret which has alluded us so far, Miss Sullivan. I see your superiors were quite correct about your special insight.

[*Helen is now under the table feeling Edison's face. O.T. is eating like an ogre.*]

BELL
After dinner, I'll show you to you room and explain your duties. [*Noticing the empty plate next to him.*] Again, I am sorry Mr. Simon did not meet you at the station. Unfortunately, this is typical of him.

ASSISTANT
I'm sorry if I was rude, Miss Sullivan.

[*Helen and O.T. are making lots of noise. Bell and Assistant stare at each other. End of scene.*]

ANGELS & TATERS

Helen is alone in front of a huge plate of mashed potatoes. She snorts and sniffs at the delicious mound. As she lifts her hand to splat the goo, a Puppet Angel appears over her right shoulder.

ANGEL
Please don't do that. [*Helen halts mid-swing.*] It would make such a mess. And we don't want a mess do we?

[*Helen is very confused and seems to "hear" something. A new and weird sensation.*]

ANGEL
That's a good girl!

[*Another Puppet pops up on her left. GUESS WHO?*]

DEVIL
Who you talkin' to?

ANGEL
Oh, hiiiiiii. How you been?

DEVIL
Shutdafuckup, who you talkin' to?

ANGEL
I was just—

DEVIL
SHE CAN'T HEAR YOU!

[*Helen is in the same state of flux. She rotates between "listening" left, then right, then sniffing her mound of taters.*]

ANGEL
But she stopped. The potatoes are untouched. Perfect. Pure.

DEVIL
Oh, you think you did that? Watch this: HELEN, SMASH THE PATATOES! SMASH 'EM! SMASH THE HELL OUT OF 'EM!

[*Helen gurgles a bit like a confused dog, but is still.*]

DEVIL
Nothing! Last month I screamed at her for three days to butcher the dog. She ended up peeing in her daddy's shoe.

ANGEL
Ooooh. That's dreadful.

DEVIL
I'd like to take credit for it, little piddle as it was, but it wasn't me.

ANGEL
We have dominion over her.

DEVIL
Nah, that head's bowling ball thick.

ANGEL
We have influence.

DEVIL
Look, I once talked an oak tree into smashing a stained glass window, but I'm telling you brother, she's a free agent. Neutral chaotic.

ANGEL
Oh, this is so sad.

DEVIL
Tell me if I'm out of line here, but weren't you off sprinkling dew on daisies when she got scarlet fever and went deaf as a board, blind as a bat?

ANGEL
That's definitely out of line.

DEVIL
Oh, come on Helen, pick up the ax! GRAB IT!!!! IT'S RED HOT AND NASTY!!!! HELEN KELLER TOOK AN AX AND GAVE HER FATHER FORTY WHACKS!!!!

ANGEL
No, don't do it, Helen. Look into your soul. You are filled with God's love.

DEVIL
BUTCHER THE WHOLE HOUSE!!!! A BIG GLORIOUS BLOODSPILL! CHOP 'EM ALL TO HELL!!!!

[*Helen makes an outrageously big gurgling noise. The Puppets jump back. Helen drops her face into the potatoes. The Puppets sigh mightily.End of scene.*]

P.O.T.A.T.O.

Helen's room. Helen is laughing and throwing potatoes at O.T., they are both covered in mashed potato muck. After each throw she slops a handful of mashed potatoes in her mouth. Edison is banging on some ratty looking invention. During the scene the Assistant appears at the door and watches silently.

O.T.
[*Bonk.*] Don't throw no more taters at me. [*Bonk.*] Stop throwin' taters at me. [*Bonk.*] Little thang, I wish you'd stop throwing taters at me.

EDISON
Do you mind? I'm trying to do some inventing here. [*He yanks some wires.*] Work, you goddamned thing!

O.T.
Now, why does she keep throwin' taters at me? Maybe she's tryin' to tell me sump'en.

EDISON
Maybe she hates potatoes.

[*O.T. takes away her potatoes.*]

O.T.
No, she's eatin' em like nothin' ever did.

[*Helen starts crying. Edison covers his ears. Then starts pulling on his leg iron ring.*]

EDISON
Maybe she hates you.

O.T.
She couldn't hate nothin'. She's never learned how 'cause she's blind 'n' deaf!

EDISON
Goddamn me. This is worse than the chain gang.

O.T.
What you want? You want teacher to make more mashed taters. Is that what "sweet little thang" wants? Tell teacher what you want.

[*O.T. has calmed her. He slops mashed potatoes into her hand. She "spells" with them by pressing her hands, elbows, and face into his hands.*]

O.T.
P ... O ... T ...

EDISON
An idiot communicating with a deaf and blind girl via mashed potatoes.

O.T.
A ... T ... O. Tater! I can't get her to spell nothin' else. Come on, spell sump'en else, Honey.

[*Helen starts spelling and kissing O.T.*]

O.T.
P ... O ... T. Pot! A ... T. At! ... O. Pot at O. Hum, pot at O.

EDISON
Potato! Potato! You moron.

O.T.
Yeah, I got confused 'cause now, she's kissin' on me while spellin' tater.

EDISON
Maybe she just *really* likes potatoes.

O.T.
She's tryin' to say sump'en and I just ain't smart 'nuf to understand it. I should be teachin' her sump'en asides taters and kissin'. What should I teach 'er 'bout, Tom?

EDISON
Teach her to sit in a corner for a while AND BE QUIET. [*He beats his "invention" with his fist.*]

O.T.
[*Bringing Helen her sock monkey.*] Look who's comin'. It's monkey!

[*She calms down cradling the doll.*]

EDISON
Drag her behind a train for a day or two. That'll teach her.

O.T.
What she gonna learn from that?

EDISON
She'll learn what doesn't kill you makes you stronger. She's a spoiled brat.

O.T.
She's a sweet little thang. She's just a little wild, ain't you a sweet little thang?

134

EDISON
If we don't go to the workshed and get some tools to get these chains off, I'm gonna chew your foot off.

[*Edison jumps up and crosses to the door. O.T. is knocked off balance as he squats. O.T. rises and walks sternly to Edison.*]

O.T.
You know Helen ain't allowed in there.

EDISON
Then we go alone.

O.T.
Half my job is ta watch her night an' day. And you know that, too.

[*O.T. walks back to Helen. Edison's feet are swept from under him.*]

EDISON
I swear to God, I thought Mr. Earl had the key on him.

[*Helen spells.*]

O.T.
P ... O ... T—I know whar this is goin'. Maybe I should teach her 'bout God so she goes to heaven?

EDISON
The way you're teaching her, she'll end up praying to a potato.

O.T.
Yeah. She don't need it, no how. It's like she's been a baby, so far. Angels are pertectin' her. She's filled with God's love, ain't she so filled, Tom?

EDISON
She's full of something, alright.

O.T.
You filled with God's love, ain't you, you little thang.

EDISON
I think I'm getting a rash.

[*Helen is becoming very sensual as she spells.*]

O.T.
P ... O ... T ... A ... T—Potato.

[*Helen licks O.T.'s arm between each letter. O.T. becomes aroused and nervous. Helen pushes him backward, climbs on him and starts to kiss him hungrily. They roll on the floor in a passionate embrace.*]

EDISON
Definitely got a rash.

[*End of scene.*]

"WE FOUND TWO BODIES UP THE ROAD."
Inside Bell's workshed. O.T. is trying to saw through the chain, while Edison is looking at the chemicals and equipment. Helen is holding tight to O.T.'s leg. Mr. Earl (Guard) stands behind them. His throat is bandaged.

EDISON
That's a wood saw, you moron. You're barely scratching the metal.

O.T.
Maybe we should try this another day.

GUARD
I thought you'd have them chains off by now, Smart boy.

[*O.T. and Edison rush for opposite exits. Unfortunately, their chains won't allow it.*]

O.T.
Mr. Earl, sir. You 'bout scared me half to death. I'm glad to see you ain't dead.

GUARD
I bet you'd be a whole lot happier if Warden Paul's woman weren't dead.

EDISON
I guess you can't kill the devil after all.

GUARD
I got me a new Winchester an' I'd love to try it out, today.

O.T.
I got a child here, Mr. Earl, sir.

EDISON
Put the rifle down or he'll kill her.

136

GUARD
You'd do that, O.T.? Kill a little girl?

O.T.
No! I would never do that, Tom.

EDISON
You could have bluffed him a little.

O.T.
Oh yeah, I guess I could a' bluffed him a little. [*He turns to the guard, who has pulled Helen away.*] I'M GONNA KILL 'ER!

[*The Guard motions for O.T. to raise his hands. Helen has settled into the corner and plays with a doll.*]

GUARD
They found two bodies up the road. Didn't you think the dogs would notice that? I thought my time in the hospital would a' put me way behind you Sesa'mese twins. What happened, boys? Lose the key you took off my watch chain?

[*Edison glares at O.T., shakes his head, and turns away. He sees something on the table.*]

O.T.
I'd a' told you 'bout the key, Tom, only I's afraid you'd a' leave me behind. I get lost so easy.

GUARD
You'll have plenty a' time to work this out while they're building yer scaffold. Double hangin's gonna draw a big ol' crowd. Especially if you wear that pretty dress, O.T. You boys are gonna make all the papers. What you messin' with over thar, smart boy?

[*Edison stretches out the chains between O.T. and himself as he reaches across the room and places a rod across both power lines running along the wall. O.T. begins to shake.*]

GUARD
What's goin' on?

EDISON
Grab his gun, O.T.!

[*As O.T. does, the Guard bears most of the electric jolt. He shakes, gurgles, and collapses.*]

O.T.
What happened? I got all tingly an' then Mr. Earl started jumpin' around.
I think he's dead, agin.

EDISON
We'll make damn sure of that this time around. Give me the key, O.T. Did
you see that rod spark? It shouldn't have glowed that long. I tried tungsten
years ago. It must have carbonized. That's the answer! IT'S NOT THE
METAL, BUT THE CARBON!

O.T.
Looka this, his eyeballs are all cloudy. Did you do that somehow?

EDISON
I think I've found my perfect filament. I've got to find another piece of
tungsten.

O.T.
[*O.T. brushes Helen's cheek.*] You alright little punkin' head? What you
wanna do with Mr. Earl's body? [*He drags the body across the stage.*] I'd
like to think there's another world goin' on somewhar, whar we ain't this
way an' differ'nt things is happen to us.

[*Edison places a filament on battery terminals + and –. Flash of light for
several seconds. The room is glowing. Bell walks in just in time to see it. O.T.
holds the guard's legs behind him and straddles the torso hiding it under his
skirt. Edison slinks behind the worktable.*]

BELL
What was that?

O.T.
Sumpen' happened.

BELL
Who's been playing with the acid battery?

O.T.
Uh ... well, it were ...

EDISON
[*Impersonating O.T.*] Hel-len.

BELL
Helen?

138

O.T.
Uh ... yeah. Helen, but she won't do it no more.

BELL
I'll say she won't. The fact that I had forbidden you from bringing her in here does not seem to matter to you, Miss Sullivan. I'm quite disappointed with you.

O.T.
You won't have no more complaints 'bout me, sir.

BELL
Let's hope not. Now, if you'll leave me to it, I'd best clean up this mess.

O.T.
Alright. [*He begins to walk away from the body.*]

EDISON
The body.

BELL
What was that?

O.T.
I said ... The cody. I meant ... Dody ... Rody ... Fody.

[*Extremely long take, as O.T. mentally checks every rhyme for "body".*]

O.T.
I said ... If you would mind taken Helen for a minute, I'd feel better 'bout this if I was ta pick up this here mess.

BELL
Yes, if you feel you must. [*Begins to exit with Helen.*] If there are any sizeable objects to dispose of you can put them in the unusually large acid bath behind the shed.

[*End of scene.*]

TWO BELLS (Eaves Drop)
Inside Bell's workshed. Bell lies in full prostrate prayer on the floor. A beam of light is bathing him and then it fades. The Assistant enters.

ASSISTANT
I'm sorry, Alexander. I didn't mean to interrupt your prayers.

BELL
No, not really praying. I was just … passing time. Come to work on something?

ASSISTANT
I've come to put a padlock on this door. For Helen's sake.

BELL
Meaning?

ASSISTANT
I believe this is a dangerous place for her.

BELL
She's not in danger. This is her home. She belongs here. [*They stare at each other.*] Do you belong here? Why is it that you have returned?

ASSISTANT
I have returned because of this. I received this note from Helen's last caretaker, Miss Pownthleroy. It states that she can no longer take care of Helen. "The poor beast grows wilder every month," and you, "Master Bell spends all his waking hours in prayer and tinkering with machines." … "He will not speak to me or anyone, but only to God—or to God … at the ceiling (?)," or some such. She seems to imply doubt to your sanity.

BELL
One's spiritual devotion can easily look extreme to others.

ASSISTANT
Yes, you may be correct, but I'm not convinced that this is the right environment for Helen.

BELL
Ack. Not back a whole day and you continue with your mission to rid me of my daughter.

ASSISTANT
My mission?

BELL
You've always disliked her.

ASSISTANT
That is not so.

BELL
Ack. Do you deny it is the reason you left here?

140

ASSISTANT
Ack. I do.

BELL
Ack.

ASSISTANT
Ack. I left because the telephone was going nowhere.

BELL
You left because you became impatient.

ASSISTANT
Ack.

BELL
Ack.

ASSISTANT
Ack, I became lonely. You had given up long before me. I was wasting my time winding coils in different ways. Switching this wire with that. It was stagnation. Neither one of us possessed enough knowledge of what we were doing to continue. I began to mope about, while you retreated to Helen.

BELL
Helen? Helen was the way back to the path. She was the source of my continued inspiration.

ASSISTANT
Our problem was far beyond inspiration. It was with electrical theory.

BELL
Ack.

ASSISTANT
Ack.

BELL
You left to find theory. I stayed to find inspiration. And who completed the telephone?

ASSISTANT
Ack.

BELL
Ack.

ASSISTANT

[*Muttering.*] I was utterly delighted when I heard the news. Although somewhat amazed.

BELL

It was beautiful the way it came to me. It was like a cool breeze blowing up your kilt on a hot summer's day. I was standing at the front gate watching Helen playing in the mud. Everyone was covered in filth. Miss Pownthleroy was screaming for her to stop. Which always made her look ridiculous. At a deaf girl. Miss Pownthleroy's voice was beyond painful. But Helen's joyous laughter echoed with the voice of God.

[*Beautiful voices sing and a light shines down. Bell walks into the light staring up.*]

BELL

And then the screaming and laughter all went away. I was given a perfect moment of clarity. Nothing to reason out. No need to take notes. The solution was obvious. I simply had to make the telephone into what it is now. I walked to this table and built what God had shown me in the vision.

[*The light is gone.*]

ASSISTANT

How long did it take?

BELL

An hour. Maybe less.

ASSISTANT

An hour. [*He shakes his head and laughs a bit.*] For three years, I worked at this table with you. I can't really feel it was a waste. Mostly it was rewarding. And even though I realized the stigma I would bear on my return, I have come back. I am here and willing to work again. Would that please you?

BELL

I am wrong to bear you any bitterness. The Bell family together again is my greatest wish.

[*They embrace.*]

ASSISTANT

What shall we work on; the microphone or the receiver?

142

BELL
Yesterday, I walked in as Helen had somehow set a piece of tungsten wire across the positive and negative terminals of the acid battery.

ASSISTANT
Helen?

BELL
It glowed for several seconds, it did. It glowed. It would feel right to work on that.

ASSISTANT
Yes. Why not? We should take advantage of Helen's little accident.

BELL
That was no accident. God has brought new hope to this house. Miss Sullivan's arrival has given new hope to Helen. And your return has given new hope to me. And we shall bring new hope to mankind. The Bell Brothers conquer electric indoor lighting.

ASSISTANT
I'll take the wagon and pick up supplies.

BELL
I'll come along.

ASSISTANT
You know, that's what distinguishes you from some of these tinkers who called themselves inventors. A little incident like with the carbonized metal, is observed and comprehended. It would have been lost on a man like Edison.

BELL
Ack. There was a strange little man. The so-called "Wizard of Invention." They say that he never slept, but it's more likely he never bathed. I wonder what ever became of him?

[*They exit. Edison steps out of a closet. He grabs his experiment and holds it protectively.*]

EDISON
Damn you both for what you're about to make me do.

[*End of scene.*]

O.T.'s DREAM

The Bell dining room. The table is set for four. Schweitzer, Helen, and Edison are at the table. O.T. speaks directly to the audience.

O.T.
Being here with Helen, this is all so close to my dream.

[O.T. reaches into his shirt and pulls out his heart. It's a big, red Valentine's Day-type thing. He opens it and shows us a tiny dining table inside a pretty room. Lights come up behind him showing the room and table are prepared on stage just as the tiny Valentine version.]

O.T.
In my dream we got a little house all of our own. It's white with some blue on it. Ever' now and then we got company over to sit at table with. Ever'thang is simple, but sweet. Helen's made her best tater recipe. I put on my good Sunday overalls. And Doc has returned from Africa with stories 'bout his mission. Tom's brought his new music playin' box. Ever'one is lookin' elegant and dignent.

[He sits at the center with Helen at his right. She is not blind or deaf in O.T.'s dream. Schweitzer, in his bloodied prison stripes, sits at the house right end. Edison is seated house left.]

EDISON
These are the best potatoes I've ever eaten.

DOC
I've started a clinic in Africa. *[The others applaud him.]* I am helping Africans maintain zer dignity. I am teaching zem medicine and bringing zem ze gospels of Jesus Christ. *[They applaud him.]* But ze smallest babies vill die if they are not kept warm.

EDISON
I will help you solve this problem with a new invention. The Electro-heating crib.

[The others applaud him.]

O.T.
[He takes his wife's hand.] My home is truly blessed by the company of kind and smart friends. But above all, Helen, my heart is blessed by your beauty and spirit.

[Doc and Edison applaud them. Edison starts the gramophone. It plays a waltz, "A Good Woman's Love," by The Country Gentlemen. O.T. and

144

Helen dance. Edison crosses to Doc and sits next to him as if to start a conversation.]

EDISON
You know, Doc ... you're dead.

DOC
Ya. [*He is deeply saddened by this and watches the rest helplessly.*]

[*Edison walks behind the dancers and hits O.T. in the head with a board. O.T. teeters and collapses to the floor. Edison empties a box of rat poison onto Helen's plate.*]

EDISON
[*Sweetly.*] Come and finish your potatoes, Helen.
[*She sits at her plate crying, spooning the poisoned potatoes into her mouth.*]

[*End of scene and end of Act I.*]

ACT II

THE BULB

The workshed. A single lightbulb glowing and fading. Each time the light grows brighter a small voice faintly begins to moan as if the two were connected. Edison "gives voice" to the Jinni of the Lamp (in bold).

EDISON

Free me. Free me. FREE ME. Ah, but if I free you how will I know you will serve only me, and me alone. **Oh, great master, it is my destiny. For it is written that only one who is above all others can free the great power of the lamp.** Then I release you, great Jinni.

[The bulb glows brighter.]

EDISON

Hhhhhhhhhhhhhhh, I am free. My master, grant me the pleasure of blessing you with three wishes. Only three, huh? Then I must choose wisely. **But Master, in what other way could one such as you choose?** You are quite correct. I choose to be brilliant ... insightful ... and from Ohio. **Ah, but you are already these things for you are Thomas Alva Edison.** Well, what can I say? I can think of nothing greater you can offer me. How about a cigar and we call it a deal?

[The bulb becomes brighter now, lighting the whole room. As Edison stands to light a cigar we can see he is wearing Helen's green and white gingham dress around his waist.]

EDISON

The greatest moment in human history, right here. In the old days there would have been champagne and reporters swarming all over me like bees to honey. "Say Mr. Edison, sir, can you tell us what your secret is, sir." Well boys, you know what I say: invention is one percent inspiration and ninety-nine perecent perspiration. [*Sniffs disdainfully at cigar.*] This will do for now. If this were a play, this would be the climax. [*To audience.*] Goodnight, folks. But it isn't. I'm not living some piddle one-act play. I'm living the big league. A full blown nine-hour Eugene O'Neill bladder-buster. I'm living an opera. [*He flips several switches.*] An Electric ... Light ... Opera.

[*"The Magic Fire Music" from Wagner's* Die Walküre *blasts as Edison mouths Wotan's aria. Every light in the theater chases across the stage. Edison is strutting grandly acting out the scene.*]

EDISON

Wer meines Speeres Spitze fürchtet, durchschreite das Feuer nie! [*Translation: Those who fear the tip of my spear shall not pass through the fire.*]

146

[*The music and lights fade. Edison runs to check the clock.*]

EDISON
Look at that! Five minutes and still burning. This is definitely your birthday, great Jinni of the lamp. Meet your papa—I mean mama. Back to work.

[*He pulls the dress on then begins to run wires along the floor to the table, twisting and connecting things. The door opens slowly. A figure is in the doorway. Lightning flashes. It is O.T. holding an ax. He is wearing the Sullivan dress, tattered and soaked in mud.*]

O.T.
I ain't dead.

EDISON
[*Worried.*] I suppose I shouldn't have buried you then.

O.T.
Naw. You should a' made sure I were good an' dead.

EDISON
We don't seem to be too careful about that lately.

O.T.
No, we ain't.

EDISON
You're not going to kill me, now, are you O.T.?

[*Edison who has slowly been backing away, now stands back to the wall. O.T. rubs the ax blade along Edison's throat.*]

O.T.
If you think 'bout it, I ain't killed nobody. Not fer a long time. You killed Mr. Earl fer real. You killed Warden Paul's woman. An' now you done killed a little girl. I guess women are easier. I wouldn't know. I never killed one. [*Raises ax.*]

EDISON
It's not as if I sought them out. I don't enjoy it. It was necessary.

O.T.
You think yer special?!

EDISON
[*His back to the wall.*] I am.

O.T.
Well, you think yer specialler than ever'body else. [*Raising ax.*] Maybe that's true. [*Hesitates, but again raises ax.*] But you think 'cause you been treated wrong, you got special comin' back to you to make up for it. Well, maybe thas true, too. [*O.T. is confused and flustered.*]

EDISON
What's your point, O.T.?

O.T.
But yer acting like a right down nasty bastard, an' that ain't right. No matter what.

EDISON
You think I don't know that? I knew that before I ever did a damned thing wrong to anybody. This is how they've screwed me the most. Nice isn't something I get to be anymore. That's one of the things they took away from me in that goddamned courtroom. You and I have been screwed over by life. And now we're on the run, so we don't get to be our real selves anymore. Only bits of ourselves. Now, if nice is one of the bits you want to be, that's fine for you. It suits you. But me, I've got too much to accomplish to let *nice* get in the way.

O.T.
You ought 'a be talking to somebody smarter'n me so they can tell you you're wrong.

EDISON
Well, you can kill me if you want. I've finished the electric light.

[*He turns it up for O.T., who stares at it with fascination, then blows on it.*]

O.T.
It's real purdy. [*O.T. notices Edison is wearing Helen's dress.*] You wearin' her dress fer some plan a' yers?

EDISON
I have to be her, now. Just like you had to be Miss Sullivan.

O.T.
That were yer idear. Not mine.

EDISON
[*Remembering.*] Oh, you killed that man ... Mr. Simon.

O.T.
Yeah. I fergot 'bout him.

148

EDISON
I'm sorry I reminded you.

O.T.
Thas alright.

EDISON
What do you want to do, now?

O.T.
I guess I'll go warsh out this here dress.

EDISON
You're not planning to kill me anymore, are you?

O.T.
I ain't got a taste fer it no more. [*O.T. starts to leave and then turns.*] If you wouldn't mind, I might like the bedroom to myself tonight.

EDISON
I'll be up all night working. O.T., if you hear a scream later, it's not because I've hurt anyone. Just part of my plan.

O.T.
I don't care no more. [*He exits.*]

EDISON
[*Looks at clock.*] Calm down. Plenty of time. Plenty of time.

[*He runs around finishing with the wires. There is a noise outside. He jumps up and stands about three feet from the table with the end of a wire in his hand. Bell steps through the door. Edison makes some of Helen's vocal noises and walks to the table.*]

BELL
Helen! What is she doing in here?

[*There is a flash. Edison gives a high-pitched scream and begins to fall. Bell catches him in his arms.*]

BELL
Helen! Oh, God. Helen!

EDISON
Geh ... fah ... fah ... father, I can see. I can hear.

BELL
[*To heaven.*] She can see. She can hear.

[*End of scene.*]

SHE CAME BACK THAT NIGHT

Helen's room. A woman's voice has been talking. She is well spoken and sweet. O.T.'s presence is heard faintly through his breathing and small moans. O.T. holds a candle, which lights the scene.

HELEN
Things will be different, now. You can make a fresh start. I know you think you that you don't deserve to be happy, because of all the terrible things. Because of all the people who died. All of those men were bad. When you were drinking, you were so unhappy you wanted to die, but you couldn't kill yourself, so you killed them.

You have to stay away from Edison. It's men like him you have to hate. Men who hate the world, but want to own it at the same time. He hates anything that's not made new by his own ideas. His problem is his ideas are never new enough to make anything truly his. He'll never be happy.

But you have a good heart. And you have someone you loves you for what's inside of it. We'll both make a fresh start. You'll build a beautiful little house. White and blue, with a porch wrapping around it on two sides. Every now and then our dear friends will drop by to share dinner with us. There'll be laughter and music. And you and I will dance together long into the night after everyone else has gone home. And I'll have two homes. The one you build for us and the sweeter one in your arms when you hold me.

[*O.T.'s crying becomes louder. As she comes closer to the candle we see it is Helen, but as she was in O.T.'s dream, only paler and the color of her gingham dress is gray and black.*]

HELEN
Why are you crying? I can hear and I can see, now. You should be so happy. Don't cry. We're together, aren't we. We'll be together forever, I promise. The dead can marry anyone they want.

[*O.T. sees her face clearly. He is terrified and blows out the candle. Blackout. End of scene.*]

150

A PROUD PAPA

Bell and Edison, in Helen's dress, are facing the audience. The Assistant sits off to one side with the bulky controls on his lap. Its wires running to a mounted light bulb held by Edison. Edison looks as if he is about to be sick.

BELL
Honored members of the American Scientific Association and gentlemen of the press, it is with a great and a appropriate sense of pride that I present to you the greatest invention, and I believe this truly, in the history of mankind ... the electric filament light.

[Applause as the bulb glows.]

BELL
And lest we not forget my greater pride; I give you its creator, Helen Keller Bell!!

[As the applause rises, Edison's face lights up as he looks to the crowd. He shyly curtsies, then blushes, finally lifts is head high with beaming pride and takes in the applause.]

VOICES
[Behind the audience.] Brava! Brava! Huzzah! Huzzah! Excelsior! Excelsior!

EDISON
[Raising a hand in the air.] YES!

[Fadeout and end of scene.]

IN THE HALLWAY

The Assistant and O.T. enter from opposite sides of the stage and walk to down-center as if they are tracing the paths of two hallways meeting at a 90° angle. The Assistant stops O.T., who mopes past him.

ASSISTANT
Excuse me. I need to have a word with you.

O.T.
Mornin'.

ASSISTANT
Who are you?

O.T.
Miss Sullivan. Nice to meet ya.

ASSISTANT
I know that's not true. What's your real name?

O.T.
O.T.

ASSISTANT
I know what's going on.

O.T.
You do? You a real perceptive man.

ASSISTANT
Not really. Where is Helen?

O.T.
She in the shed talkin' with her daddy.

ASSISTANT
I mean the real Helen.

O.T.
She's up in my room, I guess.

ASSISTANT
I've seen how she is with you. She seems to be in love. Is that correct?

O.T.
Yeah.

ASSISTANT
And you? I need to know. Is it mutual?

O.T.
Yeah.

ASSISTANT
Thank you.

O.T.
You gonna tell on us to yer brother?

ASSISTANT
Not yet.

152

[*He exits. End of scene.*]

A CASUAL HAUNTING
The workshed. O.T. sits on a bucket, hitting it casually with a stick. Helen is on a swing in the middle of the room. She hums "Amazing Grace." As Edison enters, she gets louder and very annoyingly off-key.

EDISON
Do you mind? I'm trying to connect this capacitor.

[*Helen and O.T. stop.*]

HELEN
It's called a resistor. And you're not using it correctly.

EDISON
I know what I'm doing.

HELEN
When you hook it up to the battery tomorrow you'll burn out all the wiring. And all because you didn't use a real capacitor.

EDISON
This is a capacitor.

HELEN
A capacitor has two metal plates separated by a dielectric.

EDISON
There's no such thing.

HELEN
That nice man at the supply shop tried to sell you one.

EDISON
He didn't know what he was talking about either.

HELEN
It doesn't matter really.

EDISON
No, it doesn't.

HELEN
You shouldn't be using direct current anyway.

EDISON
Are you going to go on about alternating current, again?

HELEN
It's true what I told you yesterday. George Westinghouse will set up a high capacity AC system for all of New York City in six years.

EDISON
Ha. Yesterday, you said seven years.

HELEN
No. I said in seven years Nikola Tesla and Westinghouse will develop a self-sustaining electric power station for New York. And in two seconds—

[*There is a spark. Edison shouts and puts his hand to his mouth.*]

HELEN
—you'll shock yourself.

EDISON
What kind of stupid name is Tesla, anyway?

HELEN
You shouldn't have licked it. The infection will inflame in 48 hours. And you'll make it worse when you keep picking at it on Sunday.

EDISON
Well, why don't you just tell me the rest of my life story?

HELEN
Alright. It's a life like unto the scriptures: a continual allegory. You'll be penniless within a year and beg for work at the Pewaukee Dynamo Company using the embarrassing pseudonym "Wayne Newton." The foreman will fire you during your first week when you short-circuit an expensive switchboard. After a month-long drunken stupor you'll end up wiring the lights for a seedy carnival freak show. But you'll mess that up, too. After you wet yourself begging for a second chance, the owner will agree to keep you on as one of the acts. Not a very good act, either. The rest I can't see very well. It gets all blurry.

[*O.T. walks into the room. He stands near Helen.*]

EDISON
What could possibly be embarrassing about the name Newton?

HELEN
You'll never know.

154

O.T.
[*Looking up at Edison.*] Who you talkin' to, Tom?

[*End of scene.*]

IT'S A BOY

Helen's room. Edison, naked and whistling "Yankee Doodle," back to the audience, is drying his butt with a big pink towel. Bell walks into the room.

BELL
Miss Sullivan tells me that—

[*Everything stops. Edison stands frozen with towel open and his privates exposed to Bell. Bell nods and turns around, leaves the room, and closes the door behind him.*]

EDISON
I'm sorry, I was changing.

BELL
[*Offstage.*] Oh, Dear God in heaven!

[*Bell bursts back through the door. Edison, terrified, wraps the towel around his waist.*]

BELL
You ... you're not ...

EDISON
I ... I can explain ...

BELL
I told myself something was wrong. [*Bell sits down.*]

EDISON
I can leave right away.

BELL
What has happened? This is unforgivable.

[*Edison pulls a stiletto from his sock. Click. He silently waits for the right moment to strike.*]

BELL
How could this have happened? My child ... my wee, little lassie ... is a man.

[*Bell embraces Edison; he is weeping. Edison is stiff.*]

BELL
I am so sorry. I am so sorry. You poor thing, you haven't even learned the difference. My poor little girl is a man. We'll have to get you new clothes. We'll have to get you a new name. I am so sorry.

EDISON
You're hurting me ... Daddy.

BELL
[*Holding him now at arm's length.*] My son.

[*End of scene.*]

FADED LOVE

O.T. is by the crossroads from Act One. Helen is on the opposite side of the stage, closer to New Jerusalem.

O.T.
Well, it's OK if I don't see you, if I know you're there. As a matter fact, I didn't know how to tell you 'afore. But I ain't been able to see you fer a long time. Maybe it 'cause you ain't 'sposed to be with me no more, now you dead. Maybe it's 'cause I knew you in my heart. An' too many bad things have happened an' I cain't stand to look in there no more. In my heart. Could be 'cause you started speakin'. You never could speak 'afore, 'cept with our hands, an' taters, an' such.

HELEN
But I can speak, now. This is the way I should have been.

O.T.
I been listenin' to the things you been sayin'. They real nice things an' all, but thas not the way what you talked with yer hands. I want you to purtend with me that we can still touch hands. That were real special to me, that way what you taught me to do.

HELEN
I'm sorry. I can't do that, but I can speak.

[*He kneels and pretends to hold imaginary hands and "spells" into them, hamfistedly aping the way Helen signed into his hands in Act One.*]

O.T.
I ... loved ... you ... special.

156

HELEN
I'm over here.

[*O.T.'s open hands move up and down slightly as if someone's hands were signing into his.*]

O.T.
I .... loved ... you .... too. I know you did. [*He stands.*]

HELEN
You're not talking to me.

[*O.T. starts off.*]

HELEN
You weren't talking to me.

[*End of scene.*]

AT TABLE (2–A)

The Assistant is at the dinner table working on a project. Edison and Bell are heard laughing offstage. They are in very high spirits.

EDISON
[*With new Scottish accent.*]—and then he lifts up his kilt and says, "I don't know where you've been, laddie, but you've taken first prize."

BELL
After you, son.

[*The door swings open hitting the back of the Assistant's chair. He drops his equipment.*]

ASSISTANT
Where were you off to this morning?

BELL
We are just come back from the christening.

ASSISTANT
Who's christening?

BELL
Brother, meet your *nephew,* Thomas Bell.

ASSISTANT
My name is Thomas Bell.

BELL
Yes, you should be flattered.

ASSISTANT
He's wearing my best suit.

BELL
Thomas, thank your uncle for the new suit.

EDISON
Thank you ... *Uncle Tom.*

[*The Assistant stares at Edison in disbelief.*]

ASSISTANT
My name is Thomas Bell.

EDISON
And now, so is mine. You should be flattered.

ASSISTANT
Uh, huh.

BELL
Is this a problem?

ASSISTANT
Well, yes. There are several problems. For one thing, it's more than a bit confusing. What are we supposed to call him?

BELL
Thomas Bell.

ASSISTANT
My name is Thomas Bell. We'll have to call him Tom.

EDISON
Thomas.

ASSISTANT
Why "Thomas?"

BELL
I will refer to you as "Brother." Thomas will call you "Uncle."

158

ASSISTANT
Or possibly "assistant." Or "boy."

BELL
Don't be petty, Brother.

EDISON
Yes. Let's not be petty ... *Uncle Tom.*

[*LIGHTS OUT ... and after a count of ten ... LIGHTS UP*]

AT TABLE (2–B)
The dinner table is filled with tools. Edison is working on a project. Bell and the Assistant enter with rolls of blueprints.

BELL
Thomas, we have made plans for the new telephonic improvements.

EDISON
[*Not looking up.*] That's nice.

BELL
There are three basic elements to the improvements. The receiver, the charcoal diaphragm, and the transmitter.

EDISON
That's nice.

BELL
This is an excellent opportunity for us to work together. As family. We can sit at this table and each work on a separate element of one unit. Really, it is a fine metaphor of ourselves. The Bells. Three inventors, one family.

[*Bell, in the center, takes a hand from each of them to form a chain. Edison pulls away.*]

EDISON
I'm in the middle of something. [*Realizing he hasn't been using accent.*] Ack, I'm in the middle of sumethin'. But, thanks, Dad.

ASSISTANT
We'd like you to work on the receiver. From an engineering point of view, it's the simplest of the three.

EDISON
And what's that supposed to mean?

ASSISTANT
Nothing. It's just that you're new to this work.

EDISON
Am I now? [*He points up at light bulb.*] And where did this come from?

BELL
No need for disharmony. You might prefer to work on the diaphragm.

[*Bell grabs the schematics from the Assistant's hand and offers it to Edison with an eager smile.*]

EDISON
I'm in the middle of sumethin'. But, thanks, Dad.

BELL
What is it you're working on, son?

[*As Bell leans forward, Edison violently smashes the lid down to cover his project. Bell, visibly distressed, looks to the Assistant, who is at the limits of his patience.*]

[*LIGHTS OUT ... and after a count of ten ... LIGHTS UP*]

AT TABLE (2–C)
The dinner table is filled with tools. Bell, the Assistant, and Edison are working on separate projects. Edison's is shielded by a small folded partition. No one speaks. Bell is not working. He is staring into space. The Assistant and Edison stick out their tongues at each other.

[*LIGHTS OUT ... and after a count of ten ... LIGHTS UP*]

AT TABLE (2–D)
The dinner table is still filled with tools. Bell, the Assistant, and Edison are still working on separate projects.

EDISON
Edison's greatest achievement was the invention of the invention factory. A group of highly skilled craftsmen and engineers working together toward a single goal. The only problem was some of the ungrateful

bastards wanted credit for developing things they would never have been working on if they hadn't been hired by me—er, Edison in the first place. At least that's what I've read.

ASSISTANT
You can read?

BELL
[*Softly.*] What?

EDISON
I meant heard.

ASSISTANT
What's the harm in sharing credit with those who share the work? For example: Eli Whitney and ... what's his name's gin mill. Samuel Morse and ... that other fellow's telegraph system.

EDISON
The entire point of the invention factory is to have 60 or 70 men experimenting with something at the same time. Anyone of those morons could come up with the right circumstance to make the inventor's vision succeed. In fact, if the number of experimenters is increased the level of skill can decrease. And that proves where the credit should lie. With the mind. Not the busywork.

ASSISTANT
I don't agree.

EDISON
Frankly, my little friend, I believe the entire compliment of workers could be replaced with a thousand monkeys. Given enough time, and placed in front of the right equipment, a big roomful of monkeys could easily come up with the same results as a small roomful of ungrateful bastards.

[*The phone rings.*]

ASSISTANT
A thousand monkeys?

EDISON
I'm serious.

[*Phone still ringing.*]

ASSISTANT
Monkeys?

161

EDISON
Well, not tree monkeys. Chimpanzees, man.

[*It rings.*]

EDISON
Let's not be ridiculous. We should think about it.

[*It rings.*]

ASSISTANT
I think it might be best to not to involve others at this point. Even monkeys.

[*It rings.*]

EDISON
Look, I'm telling you I need assistants. My mind's coming up with things faster that I can work on them.

[*It rings.*]

EDISON
I can't even take notes fast enough.

ASSISTANT
You can write?

[*It rings.*]

EDISON
I'll get the phone.

[*Edison puts a napkin over his work and crosses to answer the phone.*]

ASSISTANT
Alexander, we need to talk about your—

EDISON
Hello.

ASSISTANT
—so-called son. In the last few weeks—

EDISON
Hello?

[*Bell jumps up enraged.*]

BELL
AHOY! Say, Ahoy, son!

EDISON
Ahoy ... Is there anyone there?

BELL
I hope this fad of saying "hello" passes. "Ahoy" sounds much more inviting.

EDISON
Ahoy. AHOY!! AHOY, YOU SON OF A BITCH!!!

[*Bell is shaking his fists as Edison yells. The Assistant walks him back to his chair. The napkin is knocked off of Edison's invention.*]

EDISON
I know you're on the line. I can hear you breathing, you bastard. Ahhh! They hung up. I don't know why you invented that goddamned thing. [*Hangs up the phone. Seeing napkin is moved, he turns to the Assistant.*] Did you look at my invention?

ASSISTANT
No.

[*Edison gives one good hammer blow to his invention.*]

EDISON
At least with monkeys a man could have some privacy around here.

ASSISTANT
Monkeys?!

[*End of scene.*]

THE LAWYER
The Bell dining room. A knock at the door is heard. Edison flicks his stiletto and walks across the room to stand behind the door.

EDISON
Let yourself in.

[*A fancy, tight-suited New York Lawyer enters and walks timidly around the room. Edison leaps out to kill him, but stops with a surprised look on his face.*]

163

LAWYER
Mr. Bell, I presume?

EDISON
Where the hell is Morgan?

LAWYER
My name is—

EDISON
Is he in the wagon? [*He runs out and back in quickly. He puts his knife away.*] Why isn't Morgan here?

LAWYER
Mr. J.P. Morgan is in New York attending to the business of J.P. Morgan & Company.

EDISON
Well, you go back and tell Mr. J.P. Morgan that the most important business he'll ever attend to is right here with me.

LAWYER
Yes, he agrees. But I'm sure you understand. Monday's unpleasantness.

EDISON
What unpleasantness?

LAWYER
The crash, sir. Mr. Morgan is personally overseeing the stock market recovery.

EDISON
I'm sure he caused the damn thing.

LAWYER
Ah, you read the *Post*, sir. [*No response.*] I'm sorry. That was a joke.

EDISON
A *New York* joke.

LAWYER
Ha. Mr. Morgan would like to congratulate you on the invention of the electric light bulb. [*With a smile.*] Or should I say the newest *developments* of the light bulb?

EDISON
No. You can say it the first way. The invention of the electric light bulb.

164

LAWYER
Actually, I believe that a Mr. Jonathan Swan, of England first developed the idea.

EDISON
I think we've finished our talk. It's a long walk back to the train station.

LAWYER
Honestly, Mr. Bell, you should hear me out. Your situation is quite similar to your father's predicament with the telephone. There is a problem with the patent. And therefore with any possible manufacturing rights from the patent.

EDISON
Look, you nincompoop, my bulb burns for seventy hours or more and that limey bulb of Swan's doesn't stay on long enough to turn it off.

LAWYER
Frankly, Mr. Bell, that is a matter between you and Mr. Swan. And like your father's dispute over the telephonic patent, it is a matter to be played out in the courts.

EDISON
Lawyers. Lawyers. Lawyers.

LAWYER
Exactly. That is why I have taken the liberty of drawing up this offer.

EDISON
[*To himself.*] In the door ten minutes and he's already taking liberties.

LAWYER
This would put money in your pockets within a week and release you from all legal problems with the patent. Please look at the figure of the offer, Mr. Bell. I think you'll find it most impressive.

EDISON
What's this thing?

LAWYER
This is an agreement which would, from now until perpetuity, transfer all right to the patent to the firm of—

EDISON
No, no, no. The bent wire thing on top, here.

LAWYER
That is a paper clip.

EDISON
Paper "clip"? Where did you get this? Did you make it yourself?

LAWYER
Uh ... no. It's from the office. I must inform you that this is our final and only offer.

EDISON
Who made it?

LAWYER
Mr. Morgan.

EDISON
[*Very angry.*] Morgan made this?

[*Chimps begin a little noise offstage.*]

LAWYER
Morgan himself!

EDISON
Who has the patent?

LAWYER
You currently have the patent. That is why I am here.

EDISON
I have the patent for the paper clip?

[*The chimps are quite loud, now. The Lawyer is quite vexed.*]

LAWYER
No, on the light bulb! [*Crossing to the rear door.*] What kind of animals are those?

EDISON
[*Pushing door closed.*] That's none of your business, is it?

[*Edison bangs on the walls until the chimps settle down. The Lawyer gathers his things.*]

LAWYER
[*Coyly.*] It seems we have wasted Mr. Morgan's time and money. Perhaps

166

I might catch an earlier train. [*Looks back to see if Edison is concerned.*] An ... earlier ... train.

EDISON
[*Sheepishly.*] Can I see those papers.

LAWYER
Yes. Of course. [*Edison examines the papers as if they are a strange item to him.*] I knew you would come to appreciate the generosity of our offer. As you can see the party of the first part agrees with the party of the second part that unless the party of the third part finds that the first two parties—

EDISON
Damn it. Not a single hole or scratch. It's folded differently than mine. Seems to work better, too. Does it scrape the paper sometimes when you pull it off?

LAWYER
Mr. Bell, I must inform you that an associate of mine is on his way to London with a similar offer to Mr. Swan.

EDISON
Swan?! Throw your money away on your goddamned limey Englishman. Black beer drinkin', fish & chips eating, queen loving bastard with bad teeth. Singing in public! Eatin' sheep innards in pies! Move into the Tower of London for all I care. I'll see you in court.

LAWYER
[*Overlapping with above.*] Mr. Morgan warned me about you inventor types. You're almost as crazy as that *Edison* fellow he told me about. I'm off to the station. And good riddance. [*He puts on his hat and is out the door.*]

EDISON
And take your God damned "paper clip" with you. [*Slams the door.*] Lawyers.

[*End of scene.*]

TWO THOMASES
The Bell dining room. Edison, in chair, the Assistant, above him, looking over papers. All the furniture is covered in sheets. A few crates are stacked on the side. Bell is sitting at the table, staring blankly, nodding to each statement.

ASSISTANT
And this paper shows the outstanding debts and how the sale of the estate will cover that. The leftover amount will generously take care of Alexander's expenses at the asylum.

EDISON
That's a lot of money.

ASSISTANT
It is a very restful, pleasant atmosphere. We do want him comfortable, do we not?

EDISON
Yes. But that's a lot of money.

[*Bell smiles lovingly.*]

ASSISTANT
I discovered that, as these places are concerned, restful and pleasant is expensive.

EDISON
But how long do you expect him to live ... in that pleasant atmosphere?

ASSISTANT
We do wish him a long life, do we not?

EDISON
Yes. [*He sinks a little. Bell nods.*]

ASSISTANT
Yes, a daughter would, wouldn't she ... he?

EDISON
Yes. [*He sinks. Bell's nodding begins to take a on logic of its own.*]

ASSISTANT
And this is a list of equipment from the laboratory. I will of course be taking that with me.

EDISON
Most of that is here because of me.

ASSISTANT
Oh, no. That's not exactly true. The electrical and telephone equipment are really all I'm interested in. Your chemicals, lathe machines, and glass works were mostly destroyed by the monkeys.

168

[*Edison explodes. Bell stands up, nodding.*]

EDISON
Traitorous little beasts, I should have eaten them when I had the chance.

[*Bell calmly leaves the room.*]

ASSISTANT
So, if you'll just sign here, we can lock up the house and be finished. This states you leave here empty handed with no claim on the estate.

EDISON
I don't think my daddy would not want me to go ... uncompensated.

ASSISTANT
I don't know who your "daddy" is, but you can take that matter up with him.

[*Bell re-enters and crosses to center stage. He stops and looks at the screwdriver in his hand as if it were an alien artifact. Edison, pen in hand, stares at the paper dumbly.*]

ASSISTANT
An "X" will do.

EDISON
I'm not illiterate.

ASSISTANT
I didn't mean to imply it. I thought an X most appropriate. Signifying your true identity as the unknown factor in this case.

[*Edison makes his X. Bell exits.*]

ASSISTANT
I was quite surprised that Alexander was not aware from the beginning of Miss Sullivan's ... masculine qualities. I can only guess as to the reasons behind his inability to perceive the obvious continuing farce on your appearance. Possibly the miracle with which you arrived forced him to chose accepting you as a joyous wonder instead of the ridiculous abomination.

[*Bell enters.*]

EDISON
Why didn't you tell him.

[*Bell nods and turns around, leaves the room, closing the door behind him. Then re-enters. He is re-enacting the blocking from the beginning of the scene IT'S A BOY.*]

ASSISTANT
Well, mostly a difficulty in timing. Waiting for the right moment. Then it was too late. I suppose the only good thing to come of this is how happy Helen is with your *Miss Sullivan*. Despite his size, he seems to be a very gentle man.

EDISON
Oh, yes. He's very gentle.

ASSISTANT
I may assume they are happy together, wherever they are.

EDISON
You may assume.

ASSISTANT
I myself will be changing my name. *George Westinghouse* a nice sound to it. I'll be starting a modest electrical supply station with a brilliant, young Croatian, named Tesla.

EDISON
[*Overlapping with above.*] Tesla.

[*End of scene.*]

TESLA'S TRUTH

A loud zap. A pool of light comes up showing Edison sitting behind a primitive polygraph machine. He takes a long swallow from a pint bottle of whiskey. Tesla is strapped to a chair.

EDISON
[*Flips some switches.*] Alright, shall we start from the beginning? State your name, please.

TESLA
You know my name.

EDISON
For the machine, Tesla. For the machine.

170

TESLA
[*Slowly as if giving dictation.*] My name is Nikola Tesla.

[*A bell dings and a small red flag pops up from the machine.*]

EDISON
Very good. Now, tell me a lie.

TESLA
I am in the hands of a kind and brilliant man.

[*A buzzer and light bulb.*]

EDISON
Very good. Now, tell me how your recent discovery works.

TESLA
The wave becomes harmonized by the coil's proximity to the magnets.

[*A bell and red flag.*]

EDISON
Wave? Wave? What wave? You are talking gibberish. Tell me, in plain English how you transmitted sound without wires.

[*Edison hits a small, hinged switch. There is a zap. Tesla jumps.*]

TESLA
Hooo! That was 18 amperes, no?

[*A bell and red flag.*]

TESLA
[*Happily.*] Da!

EDISON
Again! How is sound transmitted without wires?

TESLA
Please. I can only tell you my ideas. It's not my fault you cannot steal them because you do not understand them.

[*A bell and red flag.*]

EDISON
Again.

TESLA
It's pointless anyway. A man named Marconi has taken all my ideas already.

[*A bell and red flag.*]

TESLA
You can't keep me here forever, you know. People will start looking for me. I have many friends.

[*A buzzer and light bulb.*]

EDISON
Ha! Who the hell is gonna come looking for a yogurt-loving foreigner, like you?

TESLA
Many peoples. Miss Sarah Bernhardt, for one.

[*A bell and red flag.*]

EDISON
The actress?

TESLA
Miss Sarah Bernhardt is an admirer of myself.

[*A bell and red flag.*]

EDISON
No. [*He takes a big swallow.*] I find it hard to believe the Divine Sarah would be interested in a nobody, like you.

TESLA
I am not a nobody. [*A bell and red flag.*] I am Nikola Tesla. [*A bell and red flag.*] A better man than you. [*A bell and red flag..*] You see? Even your little machine agrees. [*To machine.*] He is cruel idiot. [*A bell and red flag. Tesla roars with laughter.*]

EDISON
[*To machine.*] Hey!

TESLA
What a wonderful machine. How did an idiot build such a thing?

EDISON
Typical European attitude. [*Edison lifts the switch. ZAP!*]

172

TESLA
Hooo! Oh, please. You must have stolen this machine.

EDISON
I did not—

[*A buzzer and light bulb. Tesla roars with laughter.*]

EDISON
[*To machine.*] OH! You ... you just ... stay out of this. [*He beats on the machine.*]

TESLA
Perhaps you steal all your ideas! [*A bell and red flag.*] You are not inventor at all! [*A bell and red flag.*] You are not genius! [*A bell and red flag.*] You are just thief! [*A bell and red flag.*] You are no better than horse thief! [*The bell and flag are working continuously, now.*] Just big American bully!

[*Edison cannot stop the bell, so he carries it away—still going—and tosses it offstage with a loud crash. Tesla is overcome with tears of joy. End of scene.*]

I SAW THE LIGHT
Inside a dreary circus tent. Edison is working on the guts of a primitive radio set (no dial). He wears a shabby blue robe with stars and moons glued on it and a matching pointy hat. He is drunk. Helen is perched on her swing. The faint sound of carousel music is heard.

HELEN
Aren't you going to wish us Happy Anniversary?

EDISON
Of what?

HELEN
You murdered me a year ago today.

EDISON
Here's to that. [*He downs the remainder of his pint.*]

HELEN
That's your reaction? You poison a little girl and have no remorse whatsoever?

EDISON
My show was really crappy tonight. My floating light bulb wouldn't work. And then some yahoo starting heckling me. So I slapped his little boy. Or was it the boy slapped me?

[*Beautiful voices sing and a light shines down.*]

EDISON
What is it?

HELEN
I think it's salvation.

EDISON
Is this God's salvation? It isn't meant for me, is it?

HELEN
I wouldn't think so. [*Yelling as Edison inches closer.*] Don't get too close!

EDISON
I WON'T! Why is it here? If it's not for me?

HELEN
[*Coyly.*] Oh, it pops up all over the place. You've never seen it before?

EDISON
No.

HELEN
That's right, you're you.

EDISON
Are you sure this isn't here for me?

HELEN
What do you need to be saved from? You don't believe in Hell.

EDISON
Maybe it's God's salvation from all the things that have been done to me?

HELEN
You mean "from the things you did."

EDISON
Let's not get into that again.

[*The beautiful voices and light are gone. The carousel music returns.*]

174

HELEN
[*With an evil grin.*] You know, I think that was for you.

[*Edison gasps, shrugs, and then staggers back to his gadget.*]

EDISON
It's too damn dark in here. [*He staggers across the room and returns with a floor lamp.*] What the hell is that noise?

[*Edison moves a lamp closer to the gadget. It makes a whistling noise that lowers and rises in pitch at different distances. He plays with the effect moving the lamp back and forth.*]

HELEN
Yesterday a teenager in Yonkers noticed the same thing. He'll understand it. Ironically they'll call it "the Edison Effect." He'll put a zigzag piece of platinum in a bulb, next to the filament.

EDISON
Platinum makes a lousy filament.

HELEN
Next to the filament! NOW, YOUR GOOD EAR'S GOING BAD!

EDISON
Nothing good ever came out of Yonkers. Gotta be from O–Hi–O! Land of geniuses and presidents.

HELEN
You just missed a very important step a moment ago.

EDISON
When?

HELEN
Just now. Your screwdriver was right over it.

EDISON
Here?

HELEN
Nope. Back there.

EDISON
There's nothing wrong there.

HELEN
You're not noticing it. Your analytic abilities have really gone downhill. I blame the low quality of the booze.

EDISON
WHAT IS MAKING THAT NOISE ?! [*He bangs on the gramophone, then throws it to the floor. It stops whistling.*] There. Pro-blem solve-ed.

[*With one careful finger she tips over the whiskey bottle. Edison looks at the bottle as it pours out. He looks up at Helen and then at his finger.*]

HELEN
I think you'll probably end up insane. Drooling and counting your toes over and over again. [*She mocks his drunkenness.*] One toe. Two toe. Three toe—OW!

[*Edison has thrown a tool at Helen.*]

EDISON
Hey, that hurt didn't it?

HELEN
Not as much as this hurts you. [*She unscrews another bottle and pours it out.*] Oooooh, so sad.

EDISON
How can you do that?

HELEN
I don't know. [*Her fingers play with the whiskey as it pours out the bottle.*] I can touch things.

EDISON
Yeah, and if you can touch things, things can touch you.

[*As Helen plays, transfixed by her new ability, she does not notice Edison creeping up behind her. He grabs her by the throat and strangles her. She falls to the ground.*]

EDISON
Hey, looks like somebody got his cognitive thinking back. Tell me that little shit in Yonkers could've figured that out.

[*A MAN in a khaki uniform, suit jacket, and dark glasses walks into the tent. He has a shotgun.*]

176

MAN
Hello, Mr. Edison.

EDISON
Hello, Warden Paul. What brings you to the circus?

[*End of scene.*]

THE CHAIR

Two Reporters are taking notes as Edison connects wires to the bottom of an electric chair which is on its side.

EDISON
Alright, boys, read it back to me.

REPORTER 1
Thomas Alva Edison, the greatest inventor of our time, died early today at the age of thirty-four. The man who gave us the electric light, the phonograph, and hundreds of other inventions—

EDISON
Better make that thousands. Sounds better.

REPORTER 1
Thousands of other inventions died at 6 a.m., in an electric chair of his own design.

EDISON
Better make it THE electric chair. "AN electric chair," makes it sound like there are others. [*To Reporter 2.*] You, what about the background story?

REPORTER 2
Uh ... Edison was born in Milan, Ohio, land of geniuses and presidents—

EDISON
Good.

REPORTER 2
—on February 11th, 1847. At the age of twelve, he set up a chemistry laboratory in his parents' basement. To pay for his equipment he took a job as a newsboy on the *Port Huron Express*.

EDISON
You know what? Better make it THE newsboy. Otherwise—

REPORTER 2
[*Curtly.*]—it makes it sound like there were others. He soon purchased a secondhand printing press and began to publish a newspaper—

EDISON
—the first newspaper ever printed on a train. Thank you very much.

REPORTER 2
Yes, I've got that.

EDISON
Have you got the part about the Scottish bastard who grabbed my ear?

REPORTER 1
Was that the conductor or the teacher?

EDISON
Hum. Well, they both pulled my ear.

REPORTER 1
Which one was Scottish?

EDISON
Make 'em both Scots.

REPORTER 2
That's quite a coincidence.

EDISON
My life is filled with 'em.

REPORTER 2
Coincidences or Scots?

EDISON
Both. What's next?

REPORTER 1
At fifteen, Edison rescued a small boy—

EDISON
—from the train tracks. Yada yada yada. Get to the good part—the inventions.

REPORTER 2
About the inventions, sir. There a few problems with your list.

EDISON
What problems?

REPORTER 2
You've listed the wireless radio.

REPORTER 1
I've heard some people say that Marconi made the first wireless. Others say Tesla.

EDISON
Look, Marconi invented the Italian wireless, Tesla invented the Rooskie wireless. I invented the American wireless. Which one would you boys rather have?

REPORTER 2
But aren't they essentially the same type of—

EDISON
Listen, if Henry Ford can get away with it, why harass me? And don't get me started on *that* son of a bitch. The only original thing Ford ever came up with was strike breaking. And that he stole from Carnegie.

[*They all share a quick laugh.*]

REPORTER 1
We're good so far as your youth goes, but we don't have anything between the chain gang and the light bulb.

EDISON
Oh. Let's just say ... "He overcame impossible obstacles to continue his work."

REPORTER 1
Can't you give us anything more than that?

REPORTER 2
Maybe say something ... about the murders?

EDISON
You know what I say, boys, "Invention is one percent inspiration and ninety-nine percent mutilation."

REPORTER 2
How do you see that as a positive way to be remembered?

EDISON
What's your names, boys?

REPORTER 1
Samuel Clemens.

EDISON
And you?

REPORTER 2
Herman Melville.

EDISON
Nice to meet you, Sam. Herman. Now, I don't mean to be rude, but in a hundred years those names will be completely meaningless, while mine will be floating around with the likes of Napoleon, Caesar, Rutherford B. Hayes. This country is just crazy for a good gory murder story and the same goes for stories of great inventors. I'm bound to be a special chapter in every child's history book. Plus now, I'm the first execution by electricity.

REPORTER 2
There was that deranged elephant that Barnum fried.

EDISON
Did the pachyderm build its own electric chair?

[*They are all laughing as Warden Paul and Executioner enter. The executioner is in a guard's uniform and a black hood. The laughing stops.*]

WARDEN PAUL
It's time, Tom.

EDISON
Right. Say, could you boys run these sketches over to the patent office for me.

[*Edison hands them a big pile of schematics from his jacket. Another pile from his jacket. Another pile from his pants. And another pile. And another pile.*]

REPORTER 1
How many patents is this?

EDISON
Two hundred fifty-three. Giving me exactly an even 2000 lifetime total.

180

REPORTER 2
This one looks like a design for the wheel.

EDISON
You can only try, boys. You can only try. How about a photograph? Me in the chair. Make sure the caption reads, "Edison in his chair." HIS chair. [*Sternly.*] Promise.

REPORTER 2
"Edison in his chair."

REPORTER 1
[*To Reporter 2.*] Otherwise it makes it sound like there were others.

[*Reporter 2 takes the picture with a flash plate. He winds the camera and takes another.*]

EDISON
Hey, what y'do? You double exposed it.

REPORTER 1
No, sir. This is Eastman's Rolling Film Camera. Twelve shots on one roll.

EDISON
[*Rushing over.*] Lemme see that.

REPORTER 1
The light falls on only the center chamber, while the rest of the film is sheltered on either side of the lens.

EDISON
Why only twelve? Why not twenty-four, or thirty-six. This could be big. Your average Joe could buy a camera, take thirty-six photographs then drop it off, say maybe at one of Woolworth's new stores. Eastman sends a boy to pick it up, camera and all. Two days later you come back and— Hold on a minute. Even better, I bet I could rig an automatic shutter system, like a Gatling gun, hook up a twenty-thirty-foot roll of film and photograph a horse running. Or a train pulling into a station. Or an ocean liner hitting an iceberg and teenagers whining about how much they love each other while freezing in the water. Lemme me use your pen, I wanna write this down.

WARDEN PAUL
It's time, Tom.

EDISON
Oh well, nice idea, anyway. [*Handing them cigars.*] I want to thank you

two for showing up today.

REPORTER 1
No, thank you.

EDISON
In the old days there were reporters swarming all over me. Like bees to honey.

REPORTER 2
Oh, there's nearly two hundred reporters outside.

EDISON
What?

REPORTER 1
The warden said only two could come in with you. We got lucky, I guess.

EDISON
What paper are you boys from?

REPORTER 2
We're from the *Sandusky Sentinel*.

EDISON
Why didn't he let the *New York Times* in?

REPORTER 1
The warden said you're a big Ohio booster.

REPORTER 2
What's New York got up on Sandusky, anyway? *The Sentinel*'s a great paper

EDISON
Alright, alright. Don't have a whale.

[*As if a lightbulb lights over his head Reporter 2 sits down and begins writing very hurriedly.*]

EDISON
You boys stick around. I wanna talk to ya after this is over. [*The reporters look confused.*] Got ya, ha ha.

WARDEN PAUL
Is everything all connected?

182

EDISON

All set. Unless you'd like to try it out first. Ha ha ha. Oh boy, I just kill me. No wait— [*Points to executioner.*] that's his job. Ha ha ha.

WARDEN PAUL

You are certainly on top of yourself today, Tom. We're all sharing in the excitement of ... *the event*, but you've really made this your day.

[*Warden Paul begins to walk Edison to the chair. Edison stops suddenly, as if seeing the chair for the first time.*]

WARDEN PAUL

You gonna be alright, Tom? [*Edison nods.*] Tom, I have to say I've never had a man more eager or cooperative about *goin'* before. Do you have any last requests?

EDISON

I do have one request, Warden. [*He takes out small vial, breathes into it, reseals the cork, and gives it to the warden.*] Get this over to the Smithsonian, will ya?

[*The warden takes it, uncorks it, and sniffs.*]

EDISON

[*Very hurt.*] What are you doing, man? You let it out. [*Refills vial.*] Don't do that again.

WARDEN PAUL

Time to do it, Tom.

EDISON

Not a problem, Warden.

[*They walk to the chair. Edison hops in and starts the straps.*]

WARDEN PAUL

Here, I'll—

EDISON

Let me. I invented it. [*He finishes the left strap, but can't do the right.*] Uh ... you can do the other one. [*The Executioner places the hood over Edison's head.*] Say, Warden, I've got an idea for a new invention. Can I sketch it down quick?

WARDEN PAUL

What's it do, Tom?

EDISON
It's a type of edible shoe. In case of emergency you—

WARDEN PAUL
Might be best to let that one go, Tom. How many patents you got anyway?

EDISON
[*In a whisper.*] Four hundred fifty-three.

WARDEN PAUL
I thought you told those boys 2,000.

EDISON
A man's reputation needs room to grow in, Warden. Ha. Hey boys, the chair makes two thousand and one patents. And if you'd like to take note; this new switch works much better that my original design. And make sure to spell it right. E-D-I—

WARDEN PAUL
When you're ready, Tom.

EDISON
... S-O-N. Alright, then. On the count of three. [*Gathering breath as if he's about to go under water.*] One .... Two .... Three!

[*The switch is pulled. The lights flicker. There is a loud buzz. Edison shakes. After several seconds there is a loud electric snap. The stage goes black.*]

EDISON
What happened? Hit the switch again.

[*Warden Paul lights a lantern.*]

WARDEN PAUL
I think we've had some problem.

REPORTER 1
I've got to get to a telephone!

EDISON
Finish it!

REPORTER 2
I have the headline: Edison, a failure to the end!

[*The Reporters run out.*]

184

EDISON
NO! NO! Hey ... stop those boys ... I can fix it!

WARDEN PAUL
I'll get a bucket of water and a doctor. [*To executioner.*] Be prepared in case we have to ... I don't know. Hang him, I suppose. [He exits.]

[*Smoke is coming up from Edison's arms.*]

EDISON
I can fix it! I'm sure it's just a wire loose somewhere! Where the hell did everybody go? Don't let them hang me, please. I can fix the chair. [*Pause.*] Hello? is anyone still here?

O.T.
Hey, Tom.

EDISON
O.T.?

O.T.
Yeah. [*Takes off his executioner's hood.*] I was trying to keep outta yer way. Didn't want to upset ya. You seemed to be having a real good time, here.

EDISON
[*Breathing very heavily.*] What are you doing here, O.T.?

O.T.
This is my job. I been here fer nearly a whole year, now. I thought it were purdy strange, you being brought to me like this.

EDISON
What's wrong with the chair?

O.T.
It were smoking. An' the wires look burnt up, like they did after Mr. Earl died.

EDISON
I'll have to rewire everything. What's that smell?

O.T.
Yer arms is smokin'.

EDISON
Damn, that's not good.

O.T.
I had somebody read to me 'bout yer trial. Newspaper said they found Helen's body in yer circus tent. Said she were fresh dead. Guess you somehow got a second chance and you killed her again.

EDISON
It was her ghost, O.T. I killed a ghost.

[*O.T. rips out some of the wires.*]

O.T.
I guess that makes sense.

EDISON
Why would you come to work at a prison? You're a wanted man.

O.T.
Nobody ever come to look fer me, here.

EDISON
So, you've finally been promoted. From breaking rocks to executioner.

O.T.
Yeah, I had all the qualerf cations for it. I just don't care 'bout nothin' no more. [*He wraps the wire around Edison's neck and pulls up. During the following speech the sounds of a creek and a songbird slowly rise.*]

Think 'bout sumpin' nice. Like yer on a crick bed an' the water's soundin' purdy. And it's lookin' purdy, too. Maybe little critters is playin' on the other side, or some such. Ain't nobody gonna hurt nobody. Ever'body gonna be nice to you. Ain't gonna be no more troubles. Just little critters playin'. You think 'bout them kind a' things.

[*One quick jerk and Edison goes limp. The sounds of the creek fade away in the dark.*]

THE END

Dave Buchen's poster design for *Innocence and Other Vices*

Innocence and Other Vices
by Dave Buchen

Innocence and Other Vices was first performed by Theater Oobleck in 2002 at the Square One Cafe Loft in Chicago, with the following cast:

Mother Isa . . . . Kat McJimsey

Mr. Pedometer,
Chauffeur, Messenger . . . . Chad Southard

Sister Unction . . . . Sarah Weldmann

Mr. Mr. . . . . Dave Buchen

Plope. . . . . Dan Telfer

A NOTE FROM THE PLAYWRIGHT

There are references in this play that no one is going to get anymore. WorldCom? Kenneth Lay? Perhaps even a John Ashcroft joke is ancient history now. These can be changed and fitted to the proper time and place.

There are other references that hardly anyone will get, but that's OK. At the center of the play are the perfectly archetypical brother and sister, Mr. Mr. and Mother Isa. They are based on the perfectly real Luis and Isolina Ferré, brother and sister from one of Puerto Rico's richest and most powerful families. Luis was an industrialist millionaire who became Puerto Rico's first pro-statehood governor. Isolina devoted herself to good works amongst the poor as a nun. Scattered throughout the play are real details from their lives.

Mixed in with those bits of truth are generous helpings of George Bataille's *Story of the Eye* and *Blue of Noon*, a little bit of Pier Paolo Pasolini, some George Bernard Shaw in deference, and a very crucial clowning trick ripped off from Dario Fo.

CHARACTERS

Mother Isa, the head of a charitable order. She wears the white robe that is the uniform of her order. Only her hands and face are exposed.

Mr. Pedometer, a newspaper reporter.

Sister Unction, Mother Isa's assistant. She wears the same robe as Mother Isa.

Mr. Mr., perhaps the world's richest man. The twin brother of Mother Isa. He wears a black suit.

Chauffeur, works for Mr. Mr.

Messenger, dressed as cherub with wings.

Plope, the plontiff of the Church whose name shall not be mentioned. Dressed appropriately.

All action takes place in Mother Isa's Mission for the Wayward. The set is bare and spartan, with a hard wooden chair center stage and a footrest in front of it. There are two doors: downstage left that leads outside and upstage right that leads into the rest of the Mission. On the stage right wall there is a list of rules, immensely long and written in small type. On the upstage wall there hangs a simply framed somber painting of Mother Isa.

[*Mother Isa and Pedometer enter.*]

PEDOM
Actually, Mother Isa, I do have one more question.

ISA
Of course, Mr. Pedometer.

PEDOM
It's more of a clarification of something you spoke about inside.

ISA
Yes ...

PEDOM
It's about your twin brother, Mr. Mr. You said, if I'm correct, that since pre-adolescence you've had an ongoing incestuous relationship with him. [*Pause.*] And you described it as "moderately unhealthy."

ISA
I believe that I said it was "mildly" unhealthy.

PEDOM
Ah, thank you, for clarifying that for me.

ISA
Certainly.

PEDOM
And your brother is the older twin. I'm not sure if I ... if these times ...

ISA
Luis was born into this world at 9:17, November 15th, 1952. And I was born at 9:32, April 4th, 1962.

PEDOM
Yes, that's what I have written here. And when you were born ...

ISA
I was a fully formed healthy ten-year-old girl. I walked from my mother's

bed, took a sheet from the armoire, and wrapped myself in it to cover my nakedness. I have not worn anything else since. And it was there that I first publicly took my vow of charity and chastity.

UNCTION
[*Entering.*] Mother Isa, I'm sorry to interrupt, but the underclass are ready for today's lesson on patience.

ISA
I hate to leave you, Mr. Pedometer, but as I said, my life is one of service, and the wretched must be attended to. Sister Unction would be happy to answer any further questions you might have. [*She exits upstage right.*]

UNCTION
Did you find the tour enjoyable?

PEDOM
I'm not sure if that is the right word.

UNCTION
Pleasant perhaps.

PEDOM
No, that's not it either.

UNCTION
Enthralling?

PEDOM
Yes, that's it. I was unable to turn my eyes away from so much suffering.

UNCTION
Suffering can be a potent pornography. Did Mother Isa show you the chair?

PEDOM
Ah, the chair.

UNCTION
If you'd like to come by some morning to witness and take photos of the chair, I believe that we have a press pass available for next Thursday.

PEDOM
Couldn't I just take a photo of the chair now?

UNCTION
I suppose you could, but I'd suggest you come back next Thursday.

PEDOM
Does Mother Isa sit in the chair?

UNCTION
No, the dismal sit in the chair. A different one every morning.

PEDOM
And?

UNCTION
And they have their feet washed.

PEDOM
By Mother Isa?

UNCTION
Mr. Pedometer, I'm surprised that you don't remember any of this.

PEDOM
Why is that?

UNCTION
Uh-uh-uh. Rule number 43. [*Refers to the list on the wall.*]

PEDOM
[*Reading.*] "Never shake a baby?"

UNCTION
Try 53.

PEDOM
"Don't ask why."

UNCTION
That's the one.

PEDOM
I'm sorry. I should have known better. We have the same rule at the newspaper.

UNCTION
I had to refer that rule to you the last time you visited us as well.

PEDOM
When was that?

UNCTION
Last April. [*He does not remember.*] When Bruce Willis and the First Lady

visited to admonish our teen mothers. [*Still doesn't remember.*] Later in the morning Leni Riefenstahl came by to celebrate her 100th birthday, with Siegfried and Roy. [*Nothing.*] And four Siberian tiger cubs.

PEDOM
Doesn't ring a bell.

UNCTION
Mr. Pedometer, for a journalist you sure seem to have a poor memory.

PEDOM
Well, I write for the *RedEye.*

UNCTION
That's one of Mr. Mr.'s papers isn't it?

PEDOM
As of the last merger, they're all his. The staff regularly participates in The Forum of Fresh Perspectives. It's a bit "new-agey," if you ask me, but they never do. To free our writing from too much historical baggage, our memories are erased every three months.

UNCTION
That seems awfully inconvenient. You must lose your keys a lot.

PEDOM
Not really. After the procedure, we're given a booklet that includes all the pertinent information we need to know. Birthdate, address, pivotal childhood memories. Although, between you and me, they sometimes make mistakes. After my last session, the booklet stated that there would be a setup for a joke here.

UNCTION
But this is the setup for a joke.

PEDOM
Well that would explain why I'm giving the punch line. But I do have one more question. Mother Isa mentioned that her brother Mr. Mr. never contributes any money to her mission.

UNCTION
I doubt she would have discussed that with you.

PEDOM
Why is—I mean, oh.

194

UNCTION
Rule number 28.

PEDOM
"No consensual sex?"

UNCTION
I really must refresh myself with these rules. Here we go, number 24: "Discussing money is distasteful." [*Secretly.*] But, yes, he's never donated so much as a dime.

PEDOM
But he's the world's richest man. Is there some kind of tension between them?

UNCTION
Not that I can tell. Their filial love is unshakable, although perhaps mildly unhealthy. He'd do anything for her.

PEDOM
And yet the clinic here can't afford anesthesia. What I saw in the carpal tunnel ward was harrowing.

UNCTION
Oh, the clinic can afford anesthesia, financially. But as Mother Isa asks, "Can we afford it spiritually?"

PEDOM
Meaning?

UNCTION
Rule number 36: "One is never living life as fully as when one is suffering."

PEDOM
And when Mr. Mr. visits, does he—

UNCTION
He never visits. He hasn't once set foot inside the mission.

PEDOM
Never?

UNCTION
Never. Not even to stop by and say—

MR. MR.
[*Enters.*] Hello!

UNCTION
Mr. Mr.!

MR. MR.
I thought I'd stop by and say hello. Is my sister available?

UNCTION
She's ministering to the infelicitous, but I'll tell her that you're here. [*Exits.*]

MR. MR.
So, you must be one of the pitiable?

PEDOM
No, I'm a reporter.

MR. MR.
Oh, very good. I'm glad you're here. The world needs to know about my sister's work. Especially these days. What's your name?

PEDOM
Pedometer. I write for the *RedEye*.

MR. MR.
Hmm, that name sounds familiar.

PEDOM
I had a front-page article on Sunday—Real Victim of DC Sniper is America's Innocence.

MR. MR.
Yes, of course, the *RedEye*, I own that paper. Well, keep up the good work. You know I understand that the reporter's role is a rather thankless one. To enter the stage, set the scene for the public here, and then just as quickly to exit, forgotten. But soon that will all change and there will be no more thankless roles.

[*They smile awkwardly. Mr. Mr. looks knowingly at Pedometer and at the exit.*]

PEDOM
Oh, right. [*Exits.*]

ISA
[*Enters.*] Luis.

MR. MR.
Isa.

ISA
This is unexpected, to say the least.

MR. MR.
Yes.

ISA
What brings you here?

MR. MR.
Destiny.

ISA
Oh.

MR. MR.
I was on my way to the Luncheon at the Drake to deliver my customary annual address. Today's speech however will be far from customary. It promises to be the most important speech of my life. Whether or not it changes the course of human history, well, that's not for me to say, but that is certainly my desire. But first, I wanted to drop by and see how you are doing. How are you?

ISA
Fine, busy as always.

MR. MR.
With what?

ISA
The usual: the accursed, the crushed, the doomed and downtrodden.

MR. MR.
How wonderful.

ISA
Luis, we've always had, what I thought was, a very clear understanding about keeping our public lives separate.

MR. MR.
I know.

ISA
But?

MR. MR.
But, everything is different now, Isa. This morning I realized that the truths

I hold most dear to me have been debased and defiled, and that my life has been a lie. But it's all going to be different from here on out, I promise you. But enough about me, tell me, what's new with you?

ISA
You mean since I saw you at breakfast?

MR. MR.
One's whole world can change between breakfast and—

ISA
Lunch.

MR. MR.
Because one's mind begins to wander when one begins to—

ISA
Munch.

MR. MR.
So what's new?

ISA
Well, we had a new influx of the grief stricken from Cicero. The Queen of the Netherlands came by with some raw herring for the heavy-laden. Really, just the usual.

MR. MR.
Tell me more.

ISA
Luis, there's nothing more to say. I gave a tour to some reporter and—oh, I almost forgot. I'm going to be canonized.

MR. MR.
Sainthood?

ISA
That's what they say. The word is that as soon as I perform one more miracle, I'm in the canon.

MR. MR.
That's amazing, Isa. No one deserves it more than you do.

ISA
I couldn't have done it without your help, Luis.

MR. MR.
Nonsense. You've refused every contribution that I've ever offered.

ISA
You've contributed in your own way.

MR. MR.
Sainthood! That's incredible. Unbelievable. Inconceivable, really, since you're not actually a member of the Church.

ISA
The Plope is apparently willing to overlook my atheism.

MR. MR.
And you're still alive.

ISA
I suppose I'm on the fast track. You wouldn't have anything to do with that, would you, Luis?

MR. MR.
I have never used my influence as a Knight Templar of The Church Whose Name Shall Be Shrouded in Mystery on your behalf.

ISA
Good, now tell me what is going on in that head of yours?

MR. MR.
Isa, when the finger of Destiny suddenly points at a man in the middle of his breakfast, it makes him thoughtful.

ISA
Thoughtful about what?

MR. MR.
Kenneth Lay.

ISA
Kenneth Lay?

MR. MR.
Kenneth Lay. He was the Zippo lighter that lit this fire in my mind which ravages me, leaving in its trail the fertile ashes from which now grows the vision of a new world.

ISA
Luis, you didn't really answer my question.

MR. MR.
I'm divesting myself of all my holdings.

ISA
What?

MR. MR.
The aerospace associations. The brokerage houses. The concrete factories on the coast. The drilling companies. The e-commerce concerns. The fast-food franchises. The garment makers. The hotel holdings. The insurance industries. And that's just A through I. I'm getting rid of all of them.

ISA
And you're selling them to Kenneth Lay?

MR. MR.
I'm not selling them. I'm giving them away. Isa, I don't know what happened. This morning when you left me in bed it was all so normal. I was drinking my freshly squeezed low-acid Brazilian orange juice, reading my newspapers, when BAM I saw a photo of Kenneth Lay.

ISA
Hold on. You're giving them all away?

MR. MR.
It struck me: all these CEOs, at Enron and WorldCom, Starbucks and Cingular, Harken and Halliburton, men just like myself, they aren't aberrations. They're not a few bad apples. Don't you see, Isa: it's not that there is corruption in industry but industry is corruption. Every human interaction that we make has been polluted by capitalism into an unholy transubstantiation of life into lucre.

ISA
And so you decided to give everything to Kenneth Lay?

MR. MR.
No, not to Kenneth Lay. Forget about Kenneth Lay, we've put that behind us now. Now we're at the point where I sink into despair, a feverish burning despair that seized my soul and wouldn't let go. A demonic despondency that flayed my flesh, ripped open my rib cage, and burrowed deep into my bowels.

ISA
That's when you decided to give it all away?

MR. MR.
No, that's when I realized that I was late for the luncheon. So I summoned

the limo and slumped in the back seat, naked, alone in the wilderness, cast into a barren world without recognizable signs. Lost. And then do you know what I did?

ISA
You decided to snap out of it and pull yourself up out of despair.

MR. MR.
You know me so well, Isa. Yes, I went in search for a place beyond both hope and despair. And it was right there in front of me. The chauffeur, or more precisely, the little curly hairs on the back of his neck. The forgotten tender hairs missed by the barber's razor embodied for me an earthly passion uncorrupted by the efficient algebra of economics. The violent desire I felt shook me so, that right then and there I decided to divest myself of it all and make a gift of my amassed wealth to these long ignored curly hairs.

ISA
You're giving your 57% share of the global economy to the chauffeur?

MR. MR.
He and all the others with their little curly hairs.

ISA
Ohh, you're giving your 57% share of the global economy to everyone who has curly hair.

MR. MR.
No, the hairs are a symbol. Like Kenneth Lay was before. I'm giving it to the workers. From henceforth they can manage the industries for themselves as an organic, cooperative, democratic ... thing. And I will encourage my fellow CEOs to follow my example and join me, here with you, living a life of service. And now I go to tell all the world.

ISA
Luis, perhaps, you should think about this a bit longer.

MR. MR.
There is nothing more to think about. My decision is as predestined now as the sparrow being eaten by the sparrow hawk. You're happy aren't you?

ISA
I am—

MR. MR.
I knew you would be.

ISA

Luis, you know that I support you in all of your endeavors. But it's just that, well, communism's dead, Luis. Though we may like its ideals, we've all agreed that it can never, ever, be allowed to happen. Rule #2.

MR. MR.

Isa, I haven't become a communist. It's simply that I believe that the workers should control the means of production. That's all.

ISA

Luis, I'll tell you what. I'm going to cancel my session with the meek and defenseless, so we can go for a walk.

MR. MR.

Won't they be upset?

ISA

They won't complain.

MR. MR.

I can't. I'm late for my date with fate at the Drake.

ISA

Don't go yet.

MR. MR.

I must.

ISA

Luis, at least allow me to wash your feet, before you go, as a symbol of your new awakening. It would give me such pleasure, something that I am so rarely granted in this life. For your sister.

MR. MR.

I can never say no to you, Isa.

ISA

Thank you, Luis. [*Yelling off.*] Sister Unction!

[*Unction enters.*]

ISA

Mr. Mr. is planning on joining us here at the mission. Please, give him the full foot service.

UNCTION

Yes, Mother Isa. [*Exits.*]

202

MR. MR.
I thought that you were going to wash my feet.

ISA
I wish that I could, Luis, but as you will learn when you join me here at the mission, tending to the unfortunate and undone is a full-time job. But I leave you in Sister Unction's hands.

[*Unction enters with bowl, etc.*]

ISA
Sister, as you give him the full foot service, your hands will be as my own. Luis, if I don't get to see you before your speech, I will be there with you in spirit. [*Exits.*]

UNCTION
Please take a seat, Mr. Mr.

[*Over the course of this conversation, Unction takes off Mr. Mr.'s shoes and socks placing them on a hidden shelf beneath the footstool. She then washes his feet.*]

MR. MR.
I don't really have much time.

UNCTION
It won't take long. Besides, Mother Isa wanted this for you.

MR. MR.
Yes, she did. I'm not used to a stranger, uhm, touching—

UNCTION
You heard Mother Isa, my hands will be as her own. Now close your eyes and imagine that you are in a comfortable place. A park maybe, with a river running through it.

MR. MR.
No.

UNCTION
A beach perhaps, with the salty ocean air—

MR. MR.
No.

UNCTION
A field, then, with wild flowers—

MR. MR.
How about my mother's bed?

UNCTION
Sure.

MR. MR.
That's where I would spend every afternoon when I was small. After school I would run home, straight up the stairs into my mother's bed. She'd be lying there with Isa curled up inside of her. I'd climb between the sheets and nestle up with the two of them. I can still smell the warm perfume lingering on her skin. Pressing my ear tightly against her I could hear Isa—playing games, singing songs, doing her arithmetic. I always wanted to sing with her, but I never could. Rule number 17. Instead I would read to her.

UNCTION
That's sweet. What would you read to her?

MR. MR.
I'd read to her from the classic works of William Bennett: *The Book of Virtues, The Death of Outrage, Why We Fight: The Moral Case Against Terrorism.*

UNCTION
Weren't those books written just recently?

MR. MR.
Our family was quite wealthy. We could afford to buy books from the future. Looking at Isa now, I can see the profound effect those works had on her. It's as if the words of William Bennett had mixed in with her embryonic fluid, and still coarse through her veins today. I wonder how we ended up so different. I've wasted away my life by taking my family's fortune and multiplying it a thousandfold, whereas she seems imbued with a sense of moral devotion, an unquenchable thirst to do good. You must know that, working with her. Tell me, how long have you been here at the mission?

[*Mr. Mr. puts his socks and shoes back on. The shoes however are not the same as before but the exact same kind of shoe bolted to the floor hidden under the footstool. Once his feet are in the bolted shoes, Unction moves the footstool with the old shoes hidden inside.*]

UNCTION
I've been a Sister of Servitude ever since I reached the age of consent. But I first came here when I was six years old, after my father died.

MR. MR.
I'm sorry.

UNCTION
You have nothing to be sorry about. It was his own fault. I know that now. You see, my father had gotten himself involved with the wrong people. And once you've chosen that path, there is rarely any turning back.

MR. MR.
Drugs!

UNCTION
No, concrete. He worked in the factory on the south coast. Everything was fine until a stranger came to town carrying with him the poison that would ultimately kill my father.

MR. MR.
Drugs!

UNCTION
No, unions. He convinced my father to become an organizer at the factory. A strike was called despite threats and intimidation by management and the police. Then two nights before the strike, my father died.

MR. MR.
Drugs!

UNCTION
No, bullets. He was shot down in an alleyway. That's when my mother brought me here to be raised by Mother Isa. At first I was angry that he had been taken away from me. But slowly I came to learn that it was my father's fault. Mother Isa taught me that. And also that one must forgive. And now through forgiveness, I've put all my anger behind me.

[*Unction removes a hammer and a large nail from her robes, then drives the nail into Mr. Mr.'s shoe. His eyes pop open and he watches as she raises hammer again and drives another nail into the other shoe.*]

MR. MR.
[*Standing up.*] Yeeee-owwww. What have you done?

UNCTION
I nailed your feet to the floor.

MR. MR.
Yes, I noticed that.

UNCTION
Mother Isa said that you are joining us here at the mission. All of our new servants have their feet nailed.

MR. MR.
Why is that?

UNCTION
Uh-huh-uh. Rule number 53.

MR. MR.
[*As the list of rules is quite far from him, he must leeeeaaannn over to see it.*] Oh. Well, un-nail me. I must be going.

UNCTION
I can't.

MR. MR.
Then give me the hammer. [*She does.*] It has no claw.

UNCTION
None of our hammers do.

MR. MR.
Then how am I supposed to get free?

UNCTION
That is part of your journey. I spent three weeks nailed to this floor.

MR. MR.
Three weeks! I can't stay here that long.

UNCTION
That's exactly what I thought, too. Try this. [*They both do the following.*] Spread your arms out. Way out, until it feels uncomfortable. Lift your head as if it were being pulled up by a rope, but keep your butt down as if it were being pulled as well. Now suck in your gut and lift up your heels. How does that feel?

MR. MR.
Slightly painful.

UNCTION
Good. Now imagine a dog, lying in the dirt. Children are throwing rocks at it. Its guts spill out onto the ground. You are the dog. Be the dog.

MR. MR.
Will this help me get my feet free?

UNCTION
I don't know. I learned it at a Butoh workshop.

[*Mr. Mr. drops the pose and begins to yank at his feet.*]

UNCTION
Oh don't do that. You'll just tear the ligaments. Patience, Mr. Mr., you must learn patience.

[*He stops. Then starts up again.*]

ISA
[*Enters.*] Sister Unction, have you seen the—oh, Luis, you're still here? Won't you be late for the luncheon?

MR. MR.
Yes.

ISA
Then you should be off.

MR. MR.
I can't.

ISA
Have you had a change of heart?

MR. MR.
No.

ISA
Luis, what kind of game are you playing with me?

MR. MR.
I'm not sure. My feet are nailed to the floor.

ISA
You're not sure if your feet are nailed to the floor? Let me see. Omygoodness, they are! Sister Unction, what have you done?

UNCTION
You asked me to give him the full foot fulguration.

ISA
No, I said to give him the basic foot washing without the pedicure and the foot nailing. My brother has a very important speech to give today. What time is it, Luis?

MR. MR.
Quarter to twelve.

ISA
And it is already—my goodness, quarter to twelve! Oh dear! The Plope will be here at any moment.

MR. MR. and UNCTION
The Plope is coming?

ISA
Yes, didn't I tell you earlier? Oh, dear, he can't see you here. I would hate for him to think that I have brought you here to somehow influence him on the matter of my sainthood.

MR. MR.
Let's remove the nails from my feet and then I'll leave.

ISA
No, that wouldn't work. I'm sure Sister Unction explained to you about our hammer situation. We'll have to figure something else out.

UNCTION
Amputation?

ISA
No, the axes are all being used in the carpal tunnel ward. I've got it. Sister, in the storage area there are some foam cushions and an extra sheet. Run quickly and get them. [*Unction leaves.*] And bring some duct tape as well. Oh, Luis, I'm so sorry about this mix-up.

MR. MR.
It's not your fault, Isa. And I don't think that she broke any bones.

ISA
She is very good with a hammer and a nail, that girl.

MR. MR.
You've obviously taught her well.

ISA
I've taken this one under my wing unlike any other.

208

MR. MR.
She seems almost like your daughter.

ISA
I am mother to all of the wayward, whether young or old. But the orphans, they are different. They truly are my children. Actually, Luis, I like to think of them as the children that we could never have.

MR. MR.
You do?

ISA
Yes, I still regret that we could never have a family of our own.

MR. MR.
I still can't believe that father performed a vasectomy on me.

ISA
He was shocked to find us together in the bathroom hamper.

MR. MR.
At least he could have sterilized the toenail clippers.

ISA
Shh, shh, Luis, you must learn to forgive. Besides he succumbed years ago from the syphilis.

MR. MR.
Yeah, it's true.

ISA
And now we have plenty of children.

MR. MR.
We do?

ISA
Thousands. Why, when that chemical plant of yours exploded, we took in hundreds of orphans in just one day. They're all our offspring in a way: the orphans, urchins, waifs, strays, and orphans.

MR. MR.
That's wonderful. That's exactly why I want to join you here.

ISA
Yes, your new plan.

UNCTION
[*Entering.*] Here they are, Mother Isa.

ISA
Oh good. Now, quickly, we don't have much time, the Plope will be here any second.

MR. MR.
[*As Isa and Unction wrap him in large rectangular pieces of foam.*] What exactly is the plan?

ISA
[*Whispering.*] Shhh, keep your voice down, he may be walking up the path right now! We're going to disguise you as a chair. Remember, you're a chair. What are you?

MR. MR.
A chair.

ISA
Very good.

[*The foam is put over his body and taped into place. Then a white fitted sheet is slipped over the top. Nothing of his body or shape shows.*]

ISA
Sister, put that chair behind him. Alright, Luis, you're a chair so sit down. Luis? Luis, you're a chair, sit down.

[*She pushes him down onto the chair. He now looks exactly like a large cushion for the chair.*]

ISA
Luis, can you hear me? [*Yelling.*] LUIS, IF YOU CAN HEAR ME, MOVE YOUR TORSO AROUND!! [*Nothing.*] Whistle a little tune. Touch your tongue to your nose. [*Isa sits down on the chair. She sees that Unction has lay down prostrate on the floor.*] What on earth are you doing?

UNCTION
Isn't this how you're supposed to greet the Plope?

ISA
Get up, I can't concentrate with you all splayed out in front of me.

UNCTION
But what about the Plope?

ISA

You can humble yourself when he arrives. Right now I've got to come up with a plan. We can't keep my big brother here as a piece of furniture forever, and meanwhile I've got to figure out how to stop him from destroying everything I've worked to build.

UNCTION

Mr. Mr. would never do anything like that. He loves you, even if it is in a mildly unhealthy way.

ISA

No, he never intends to hurt anyone. He strides through this world with the noblest of intentions and loftiest of ideals, completely unaware that he is a Titan amongst the common herd; his every footstep crushing the earth beneath him. And now he intends to destroy me just as blindly.

UNCTION

Mother Isa, aren't you happy that your brother is giving away all his money and joining you here in the mission?

ISA

Really must get some doors put in here.

UNCTION

I wasn't trying to eavesdrop.

ISA

Your attempt at lying is as feeble as your grasp of the situation we have before us. Now, tell me, why would I be happy to have the whole world turned upside down and my mission whither away before my eyes?

UNCTION

Well, I think that you would be happy because ...

ISA

It was a rhetorical question, Unction. Good god, doesn't the man know that there aren't any communists left in the world. Stalin killed them all. Suddenly, a few CEOs get caught doing what everyone knows they've been doing for as long as anybody can remember and my brother goes Bolshevik on me. Do you know what would happen if he gave over control of the industries to the workers?

UNCTION

Is this another rhetorical—?

ISA

Worker's paradise! That's what. No more giant chasm between rich and poor. No more schizophrenic swings of a capricious economy arbitrarily throwing people out of work for no other reason than the personal profit of a few. Meaningful work for all! No more thankless roles for the mass of humanity serving interests contrary to their own. No more pool of the unemployed to keep wages down and misery up. No more cutting corners on industrial safety producing a steady yet shaky parade of the crippled and infirm. Can you imagine!

UNCTION
But I thought communism was a failure.

ISA
You've been reading my brother's newspapers too much. I'll be ruined. What use will there be for a humble servant cleaning up after the inevitable carnage of capitalism?

UNCTION
We'll always have the poor.

ISA
Thank you, Unction, that's nice of you to try and cheer me up. But I have bigger dreams than sitting around here waiting for the odd lunatic to walk in and say—

CHAUFFEUR
[*Enters.*] Hello?

UNCTION
[*Throwing herself on the floor.*] Your Plapalcy!

CHAUFFEUR
I'm looking for Mr. Mr.

ISA
He's not here.

CHAUFFEUR
Where is he?

ISA
How should I know? Am I my brother's keeper?

CHAUFFEUR
I dunno, but I'm your brother's chauffeur.

UNCTION
[*Rises from the floor.*] You're not the Plope?

CHAUFFEUR
No. I'm the chauffeur, and I've been waiting in the car for twenty minutes. I need to get Mr. Mr. downtown for his speech at the Drake.

ISA
He's not here.

CHAUFFEUR
You don't mind if I wait for him here, do you?

ISA
[*Gets up from the chair.*] I told you that he isn't here.

CHAUFFEUR
Did he go out a fire exit?

UNCTION
Oh no, we keep those locked.

CHAUFFEUR
[*Sits in the chair.*] Then I'll just wait for him here since this is where I dropped him off. He has a speech to give, and my job is to get him there on time.

ISA
Yes, I can imagine that you are quite eager for him to give his speech. I can see that you're champing at the bit for this moment, aren't you my little curly haired friend? Champ, champ, champ.

CHAUFFEUR
What are you talking about?

ISA
Let me see those little curly hairs that provoked my doom. [*Removes his hat.*]

CHAUFFEUR
Hey, etc!

ISA
Ah, there they are. Yes, indeed, very provocative aren't they? Why, I myself am feeling a violent passion looking at your neck. [*She hits him with his hat.*]

CHAUFFEUR
Hey, etc!

UNCTION
You'll have to excuse her. She's a bit upset.

ISA
A bit upset! My brother gets cast naked into the wilderness by Kenneth Lay, infected by a feverish mange all over his lamb's soul. And now after peeking at your little curly hairs, he's gone red.

CHAUFFEUR
Huh?

UNCTION
Mr. Mr. is going to announce at the luncheon that he's giving all of his factories to the workers.

CHAUFFEUR
[*Leaps up.*] He's giving it all to the workers?

ISA
Contain your joy.

CHAUFFEUR
That bastard!

ISA
Pardon me?

CHAUFFEUR
That goddamned sneaky son of a bitch. I'll kill him before he gets away with this. [*He kicks the cushion on the chair, which then begins to slowly slide down.*]

ISA
I would have assumed you'd be happy to hear the news.

CHAUFFEUR
Happy? Happy? Why should I be happy?

UNCTION
You know, worker's paradise, all for one, one for all.

CHAUFFEUR
Ha! This was your idea wasn't it? [*He fixes the cushion slipping off the chair.*]

ISA
My idea?

214

CHAUFFEUR
Yeah, I can see what's going on here. You convinced him to do this.

ISA
I never interfere with my brother's work. He is free to do whatever he chooses. [*Shoves the cushion back into position on the chair.*]

CHAUFFEUR
Don't gimme that nonsense. I know all about you and your brother, with your all too conveniently symbolic relationship. If you ask me, it's mildly unhealthy.

ISA
I didn't ask you.

CHAUFFEUR
No, of course not. No one ever asks the chauffeur. Who cares what he thinks? Say Luis, why don't you give the factories to the workers? I don't know, Isa, should we ask them first? No! Who cares what they think! Cuz your plan isn't about us. It's all about you, about getting everyone to be just like you: a whole world filled with middle class managers worried about productivity levels and stock portfolios and 401k's. You think you can just buy us out, so that any real worker's uprising is nipped in the bud. Sister, it's as obvious as your starched white sheet. You want to force the working class into bed with the guardians of the status quo: the church and the state!

ISA
First off, young man, [*Removes her robe to reveal she is wearing a black suit that matches Mr. Mr's.*] I am an atheist.

CHAUFFEUR
[*Drops to his knees.*] May God save your soul.

ISA
And secondly, I agree with you completely.

CHAUFFEUR
You do?

ISA
Yes, I do. When my brother came here today and told me his plans, I was shocked.

UNCTION
[*Chauffeur looks quizzically at Unction.*] She was shocked.

ISA
And I am against his plans for the very same cogent reasons that you have just laid out.

UNCTION
[*Chauffer looks quizzically at Unction.*] She was shocked.

CHAUFFEUR
So you agree that the oppressed must win freedom for themselves?

ISA
They should pull themselves up by the bootstraps.

CHAUFFEUR
And you agree that any lasting change must originate from below?

ISA
Yes, yes.

CHAUFFEUR
And any revolutionary project led by a vanguard is doomed to—

ISA
Oh why must we over-theorize everything? The time has come for action. If my brother gives his speech we're doomed.

CHAUFFEUR
First thing we gotta do is find him. If he slipped out, then maybe he's already on his way to the hotel. [*Mr. Mr. in complete exhaustion slumps to the floor between the feet of Isa and Chauffeur.*] I'm guessing that the cushion is uh ...

ISA
Yes.

CHAUFFEUR
[*Mr. Mr. is lurching around.*] What's he doing in there?

UNCTION
Asphyxiating.

ISA
Playing.

CHAUFFEUR
Well, which one is it? [*No answer.*] Mr. Mr., can you breathe?

216

ISA
He can't hear you.

CHAUFFEUR
Oh. [*To Unction.*] Can he breathe?

[*Unction shrugs.*]

ISA
Of course he can breathe. He knows the word to say if he's in trouble.

MR. MR.
[*Thrashing around.*] GRMDPLKJ!

ISA
That's not it.

MR. MR.
HJNMGFRTD!!

ISA
Nope.

MR. MR.
[*Emphatic thrash.*] MNK!!!

ISA
Now, it will be easy enough to stop him from giving the speech today. As his chauffeur you simply take the "scenic route". But we've got to figure out a long-term strategy.

CHAUFFEUR
Hold on, I can't do that. I'm Mr. Mr.'s chauffeur. My job is to drive him where he needs to go.

ISA
All I'm suggesting is that you perform your duties not up to their usual high standards.

CHAUFFEUR
I can't do that.

ISA
Oh come now. What will it hurt to be lax in your—

CHAUFFEUR
You don't understand. Every night growing up, my father told us stories of

our grandfather Ivan in the Siberian work camp. He was forced to build the walls of his own prison, while he was starved and beaten by the guards. And yet he never lost pride in his work. He laid each brick with the highest workmanship and built an escape proof prison.

ISA
Yes, yes, I'm sure the gulag was very unpleasant, but you have a bigger problem here. If my brother gets to the hotel and gives the speech, you'll be out of a job. What use will the great new middle class have for a chauffeur? They'll all be driving around in SUVs.

CHAUFFEUR
But if I don't get him to the hotel, he'll fire me.

ISA
You're always welcome here.

UNCTION
Excuse me, but I think Mr. Mr. is dying.

ISA
He's not dying.

UNCTION
It looks like he's fighting for his life.

ISA
What better can a man hope to attain in his life than to fight for it?

UNCTION
Shouldn't we do something?

ISA
Yes, we should figure out a plan.

[*Mr. Mr. has now pulled himself upright and is wavering around.*]

ISA
And we should move that chair out of his way.

[*Unction brings it to Isa on stage right and she sits in it.*]

ISA
Oh look at him, he's really just a child still. Rocking back and forth. Such memories it brings back. When we were 13, he got locked inside the armoire while mother and father were away on holiday in French Guyana. He was rocking the wardrobe just like that, until finally it fell over

with a crash; the door face down. It was a heavy thing. Our parents had quite a brooding taste in décor and the house was filled with dark heavy furniture. Needless to say, I was unable to lift it and as our nanny was a most timid woman, who never dared enter my room after the incident with the eggs. Luis spent that whole week inside the armoire. I can still smell that musky odor left behind after that week. Anyways, I huddled on top of the armoire, and sang to him—

UNCTION
Mother Isa, I hate to interrupt your longing for a lost intimacy, but shouldn't we figure out a plan. After all, the Plope will be here at any moment.

CHAUFFEUR
The Plope is coming? [*Throws himself to the floor.*]

ISA
Pick yourself up. The Plope isn't coming.

[*He gets up.*]

UNCTION
But he'll be here soon!

[*He throws himself back down.*]

ISA
No he won't.

UNCTION
But you said.

CHAUFFEUR
Well?!

ISA
He's not coming. Let's just say that—

UNCTION
You lied!

ISA
Yes, let's just say that.

UNCTION
Mother Isa! What about rule number ... [*Looks at list.*]

ISA
Number 47, yes, yes, yes. But we are facing a crisis here. And what is the first casualty in time of calamity?

UNCTION
The truth.

ISA
Exactly.

[*Mr. Mr. collapses backwards hitting the floor with a THUMP.*]

ISA
Oh, that's not good.

CHAUFFEUR
Is he dead?

ISA
Not yet. Damn. He's lost his stamina with age. We're going to have to let him come up for air. First, let's get our story straight. The Plope came by and he left. It was a very pleasant yet uneventful visit. All agreed? Good. Unction, fetch me a knife.

[*Unction exits.*]

ISA
[*To Chauffeur.*] And you have been in the limo the whole time.

[*Mr. Mr. rises up as if giving his last gasp of life and collapses.*]

ISA
Come back in ten minutes. Go!

[*Chauffeur exits. Isa sits next to Mr. Mr. and sings him a song as she pulls off the sheet.*]

ISA
Sleep, sleep in your restful room
Sleep, sleep this is your test, your tomb
The night is here, the day is gone
Your life is dear, but soon will be gone
So, sleep, sleep, sleep, sleep

UNCTION
[*Enters brandishing a huge knife.*] Will this do?

ISA
Perfect.

[*Isa lifts knife and plunges it into the cushion where his head is. She carves out an area around his face. She throws the extra section of foam away and places the knife in a prominent location.*]

MR. MR.
[*Sits up, taking in a huge breath.*] Uuuuuuuhhhhhhhh. Do you remember … that time … we were 16 … in Spain?

ISA
You got locked inside the trunk of that priest's car.

MR. MR.
Yes.

ISA
Who would have guessed it would be stolen by that band of bank robbers?

MR. MR.
And then they sold me to that bullfighter from Barcelona—Antonio. Well, I should probably go to the Drake now. Oh! How was the Plope's visit?

ISA
It was very nice. Wasn't it Sister Unction?

UNCTION
It was a very pleasant yet uneventful visit.

MR. MR.
He didn't suspect anything did he?

ISA
Not at all. You made a very convincing chair.

MR. MR.
Good. Any news on your sainthood?

ISA
He says that things look very good, but I still need to perform one more miracle. However I know that I need to be patient. After all, miracles don't just waltz in and say—

[*Messenger enters playing a banjo and singing.*]

MESSENGER
Hello, folks and how ya doing?
I'm the bringer of news and all that's ensuing.
Whether its good news or bad news, I can't decipher
I'm just an envoy, a messenger a cherubic town crier.

UNCTION
Oooh, how exciting, maybe it's news of your next miracle.

MESSENGER
Up in your driveway has just pulled a limo
A big fat mobile—well it sure ain't slim-o
Inside's a man you better not bother
The Plope, the plontif, the great holy father.

ISA
The Plope?!

MESSENGER
I'll say it again, a man not to bother
The Plope, the plontif, the great holy father.

[*Exits.*]

ISA
The Plope?!

MR. MR.
Perhaps he left something behind.

UNCTION
[*Looking out the door.*] The Cherub's right! The hydraulic lift is removing him from the car now! I can't believe it! The Plope is coming. The Plope is really coming here!

ISA
Luis, would you excuse Sister Unction and myself for a moment. [*Drops him to ground and motions Unction over to the corner of stage.*] Sister, the Plope's already been here hasn't he?

UNCTION
Oh, right.

ISA
But now the Plope is coming for the first time, isn't he?

222

UNCTION
Right.

ISA
Exactly. He's already come, and he hasn't come. It's like democracy. It exists and doesn't at the same time. And that's how everything must go. Everything is normal. No awkward silences. My brother is a chair, and the Plope is always correct, even if we have to stretch the truth.

UNCTION
What about rule 47?

[*Messenger enters.*]

MESSENGER
He's now on the sidewalk and comin' yer way
Bringing with him the end of the play
At the pace that he's walking, it'll just be a minute
'til he blesses this house and everyone in it.

[*Exits.*]

ISA
Forget about the rules. Now we've got to deal with my brother.

MR. MR.
Are you going to take out the nails now?

ISA
No time, Luis. Besides, the Plope's already seen you as a chair. Unction! Help me with this sheet.

[*They grapple with sheet.*]

ISA
Hurry!

[*A loud ripping noise comes from the sheet.*]

ISA
Unction, you ripped it!

UNCTION
I ripped it?

ISA
Yes, be more careful. [*The sheet is over Mr. Mr.*] Come on, Luis, up we go.

Help me out, Luis.

MR. MR.
Do you remember that time when—

ISA
Luis, what are you?

[*Mr. Mr. is now upright. The hole in the sheet matches the hole in the cushion, so that his face shows through.*]

MR. MR.
I'm a chair.

[*Isa does not notice that the rip has made Mr. Mr.'s face visible.*]

ISA
Very good, Luis. Unction, get the chair!

[*Unction goes to get the chair.*]

UNCTION
[*In front of Mr. Mr. sees that his face is showing. She points.*] Mother Isa!

ISA
Get the chair, Unction.

[*Messenger enters.*]

MESSENGER
My skills can't be packaged, nor bottled, nor barrelled
Cuz I'm a trumpeter of truth, a pursuivant town herald
I play the banjo, the fiddle and also the cello
But I'm gonna stop now so the Plope can say—

PLOPE
[*Enters energetically.*] Hello!

UNCTION
[*Throws herself to the ground.*] Your Plapalcy!

PLOPE
Yes, that's me. The Plope.

MESSENGER
My work is done here so off I'll be going
No tip, no thanks, no gratitude showing

But that's what you get when your labor's for hire
As a messenger, an envoy, a cherubic town crier.

[Exits.]

PLOPE
How good it is to finally visit the famous Mother Isa Home for the Wayward. I hope I haven't caught you an inappropriate time.

ISA
No, not all.

PLOPE
[To Isa, who is still wearing a black suit.] Ah, Luis you're here as well.

ISA
Yes, I am.

[They perform a secret handshake which ends with them saying in unison:]

PLOPE and ISA
Semper Ubi, Sub Ubi Huzzah!

PLOPE
You wouldn't be here to influence me on a certain matter would you now, Luis?

ISA
That wasn't my intention, sir.

PLOPE
Oh, that's too bad. Are you going to introduce me to your sister?

[He refers to Mr. Mr. who in the white sheet is now dressed as Isa was before.]

ISA
Oh yes, your Plapacy, this is Mother Isa.

PLOPE
Mother Isa, it is an honor.

MR. MR.
I'm a chair.

PLOPE
Yes of course, you are the chair upon which the world's conscience sits.

MR. MR.
No, I'm a chair.

ISA
Your Plapalcy, you'll have to excuse my sister. She's a little nervous. But you must be exhausted from that walk up the sidewalk. Let's get you off your feet and sit you down right over here.

[*He sits in the chair which is still downstage right.*]

ISA
This is one of Isa's Servants of Servitude. Why don't you two get to know each other while I go talk with my sister?

PLOPE
Hello, I'm the Plope. [*Sticks out ring to be kissed.*]

UNCTION
[*Kisses it.*] Charmed, I'm sure.

PLOPE
Gladys?

[*The Plope and Unction continue to talk in mime over the following.*]

ISA
[*To Mr. Mr.*] OK, Luis, you're not a chair anymore.

MR. MR.
Which means?

ISA
Which means that the Plope is here now and we've got to—

MR. MR.
Uh-huh. Which means?

ISA
Which means you won.

MR. MR.
I always win the chair game.

ISA
Oh that's not true.

226

MR. MR.
Think what you want. But it's true.

ISA
Anyways, the Plope is here now—

MR. MR.
So he wasn't here before?

ISA
No.

MR. MR.
Was it a bishop that came?

ISA
Yes, and now the Plope is here—

MR. MR.
Yes, I should go give my speech and—

ISA
No! You can't! The Plope is somehow convinced that you're me and that I'm you.

MR. MR.
Well, we are twins.

ISA
Exactly. So we have to pretend to be each other until he leaves.

MR. MR.
Like when we were in boarding school.

ISA
Yes, but without barricading yourself in the bathroom.

MR. MR.
Wouldn't it be easier to just tell him the truth? That you had my feet nailed to the floor and then we played the chair game?

ISA
Luis, there is a reason we keep our private lives private. Please, my sainthood is on the line here. It's the one thing I long for, now that I have a Nobel, the Presidential Medal of Freedom, and two Latin Grammys.

MR. MR.
What about a Jeff Recommendation?

ISA
I know my limits. You'll do it won't you?

MR. MR.
Of course.

ISA
Thank you, Luis. I'll make it up to you, I promise.

MR. MR.
Between breakfast and lunch?

ISA
A little something called brunch. So, your Plapalcy, are you feeling better rested?

PLOPE
Luis, why didn't you tell me that Princess Gladys was in town?

ISA
Princess Gladys?

UNCTION
Actually, I haven't been formally introduced to Mr. Mr. as I just have arrived from Monaco, where I am a Princess, in Monaco.

PLOPE
Well, allow me. Luis, may I present Princess Gladys of Monaco. Gladys, this is Mr. Mr.

ISA
A pleasure. [*Kisses her hand.*]

UNCTION
Charmed.

PLOPE
You know, Gladys, besides being the world's richest man, Luis here is also a bachelor.

MR. MR.
AHEM!

ISA
Oh, excuse me, your Plapalcy, allow me to introduce my sister, Mother Isa.

MR. MR.
[*Curtsies.*] Your Plapalcy.

PLOPE
Mother Isa, it is an honor to meet you. Why look at you. You're the very mirror image of your brother.

MR. MR.
What brings you to my humble mission?

PLOPE
I have come with not one but two very pressing issues before me. One is very happy news in which all will rejoice. The other is of the gravest seriousness. Which one would you like to hear first?

ALL
Happy news.

PLOPE
Everyone always wants to hear the happy news first. I should point out that the happy news might not turn out to be so happy after all, depending on the outcome of the grave and serious issue.

ALL
Grave and serious.

PLOPE
Good choice. It's always better to postpone one's happiness for later. That way, we can have a happy ending. We wouldn't want to end this on a serious and disturbing note, would we, [*To Isa.*] Luis?

ISA
Of course not, father.

PLOPE
That's right, Luis. See you're using your head. You're thinking about the future. I like it when you use your head, Luis. So, tell me, Luis, what's going on in that head of yours?

ISA
I'm thinking good thoughts.

PLOPE
Yes, I'm sure that you are. But you didn't answer the question, my son.

229

What in God's name are you thinking?

ISA
Uhm.

PLOPE
You know, Luis, I always enjoy the luncheons at the Drake. Especially when my favorite son of the [*Conspicuously clears his throat.*] Church delivers the keynote address. If I had known that Princess Gladys was in town, I would have been sure to invite her to join me at my table.

UNCTION
Oh, your Plapalcy.

PLOPE
But then, word got to me of what you planned to announce at your speech.

ISA
How did you hear?

PLOPE
John Ashcroft moves in mysterious ways. Suddenly my usual excitement turned into apprehension. Tell me, Luis, is it true what I hear?

ISA
I suppose that depends on what's being said. I imagine that there are a thousand things being floated about. You know how these things are.

PLOPE
No. Not a thousand things.

ISA
Yes, I exaggerate. But certainly scores of speculations, rumors and conjectures—

PLOPE
No. Just one thing. That's all that I hear. Just one thing. Is it true?

ISA
That would still depend on what that one thing being said is.

PLOPE
That's an excellent point, Luis. I always expect that from you. Now, tell me, is it true? Yes or—

[*Chauffeur enters.*]

CHAUFFEUR
No time to lose.

PLOPE
Ah look, it's one of the feeble in search of comfort at the mission.

CHAUFFEUR
Feeble, look who's talking. I'm here to take Mr. Mr. to the Drake. It's time for him to deliver his speech.

PLOPE
Did you hear that Luis?

ISA
Yes.

PLOPE
Good, now tell me what he said, because I couldn't hear a word.

ISA
[*Awkward pause.*]

UNCTION
Oh, your Plapalcy! You don't recognize Renaldo. From Monaco. He's our President there, in Monaco.

PLOPE
I didn't know that Monaco had a president.

UNCTION
He was just elected, and sometimes he even forgets himself. [*She throws the Chauffeur's hand up into a presidential pose.*]

CHAUFFEUR
[*In "Monacan" accent.*] You'd be surprised how many people don't know that we even exist at all. Who thinks about us these days? Nobody! But that's all going to change, now. I've got big plans for Monaco.

PLOPE
Oh you do?

CHAUFFEUR
Big plans!

PLOPE
Such as?

CHAUFFEUR
[*Awkward pause.*]

UNCTION
We're getting the bomb.

PLOPE
The bomb?

UNCTION
Yes, but it's going be very tasteful, very Monaco.

CHAUFFEUR
You know you're not really anybody these days if you don't have the bomb.

PLOPE
That's an expensive proposition.

CHAUFFEUR
It's worth it.

PLOPE
I hope it won't interfere with your monthly tithe to the, ahem, Church.

UNCTION
Oh no, your Plapalcy! Because Mr. Mr. is going to fund the whole thing.

PLOPE
Is that true, Luis?

ISA
It's the least I can do.

UNCTION
That's what he's going to announce today at the luncheon.

PLOPE
Is that true, Luis?

ISA
Yes.

PLOPE
You're not just saying that to please me are you?

MR. MR.
Yes, he is.

PLOPE
Oh I don't care even if you are. This is such good news. You should have heard the ridiculous rumor that Ashcroft was spreading about you. I knew that you would never, ever allow such a thing to happen. Ever. To celebrate, I now pronounce you a Knight of Templar.

ISA
Thank you, your Plapalcy.

MR. MR.
Excuse me, but Luis already is a Knight of Templar.

PLOPE
In that case, I pronounce you an Honorary Doctor of the Church.

ISA
Thank you, it is an honor for me.

MR. MR.
Actually, it's an honor that my brother received seven years ago.

PLOPE
Well then Baron of the Innocents' Blood.

MR. MR.
He's got it.

PLOPE
Protector of the Pilgrim's Patriarch?

MR. MR.
Got that too.

PLOPE
Viscount of the Virtuous Visage? [*Mr. Mr. nods head.*] Exalted Eminence of the Eternal Entity? [*Mr. Mr. nods.*] Huh. How about martyr?

MR. MR.
No, Luis is not a martyr because he's not dead.

PLOPE
Then it's decided. Mr. Mr. I hereby pronounce you a Martyr of the Church whose name shall not pass my lips. [*Performs a physical action to seal the action.*] This day shall now and forever be a feast day to celebrate your martyrdom, and at the same time the sainthood of Mother Isa. God, I love symmetry.

ISA
Sainthood?

UNCTION
What about the final miracle?

PLOPE
A miracle has occurred right here in these walls today. Luis has come to his senses and Monaco is getting the bomb! Mother Isa, by the power invested in me by me as the sole legal authority of the Church that shall remain nameless, I hereby pronounce you a Saint, with all due laudatory perquisites implied. Allow me to bestow upon you this honor with all the—

MR. MR.
I can't.

ISA
Dearest sister, this is no time for false modesty.

MR. MR.
It's not for modesty's sake, but for the truth. I'm not a member of the Church.

PLOPE
My daughter, everyone is a child of God. The Church is God's family on earth. Therefore everyone is a member of the Church, whether you like it or not.

ISA
Isa, this is what you have always worked for: to be acknowledged by the institution that you've rejected your entire life.

MR. MR.
It needs to be done in the correct way, by the rules. Before I can accept I want to convert.

PLOPE
That's wonderful. For years now I've been trying to get Luis to put in a—

ISA
You're going to what?!

MR. MR.
In troubled times like these, when things are not as they seem, and skim milk masquerades as heavy cream, one is drawn to the rock of eternal truth.

234

ISA

But, sister, you've been an atheist since you were eleven years old. Remember the night that you renounced the sovereignty of God?

MR. MR.

Yes. Mother asked me to recite a prayer for poor old Grandmama, who had been bludgeoned to death by father with a didgeridoo in one of his fits of delirium brought on by the syphilis, having confused her for the hunchbacked dwarf who tended the garden, and who had had a tempestuous affair with mother and cousin Rosario. And Antonio.

ISA

And you, Isa, refused to recite the prayer, you jumped up on the table and shouted to the heavens: If such an entity actually exists that dares to demand my submission, then I curse it with my every breath.

MR. MR.

Soon strange signs began to appear. The dogs went wild, the wind chimes began to clang incessantly and odd circular patterns appeared in the crops. Mel Gibson was unable to finish his supper.

ISA

And I cried like a snotty little kid.

PLOPE

So it's decided. Mother Isa, I welcome you into the Church whose name will not be released at this time. Come here so that I may declare you a saint with all the—

MR. MR.

I can't.

PLOPE

Isa, I thought we cleared up that technicality of your doomed soul.

MR. MR.

It's just that one can't be a saint until you're dead. That is one of the eternal truths of our church. And I am not dead.

ISA

Well, neither am I. And I'm the one that's becoming a martyr.

MR. MR.

You'll have to enjoy martyrdom without me. One can't be a saint until one is dead.

PLOPE
Why is that the converts are always the most persnickety about the rules? Isa, let me be honest with you. The Church is in trouble. On Monday, we're announcing our reconfigured accounts of the number of souls saved. I hate to say it, but we may have to declare spiritual bankruptcy. It would sure help soften the blow if we could preempt the bad news by announcing your sainthood. Not to mention bolster our souvenir income.

MR. MR.
I'd do anything for the church, that I joined three minutes ago.

PLOPE
Thank you, Isa.

MR. MR.
Renaldo, bring me the knife. Renaldo.

[*He does. Mr. Mr. sticks his hand out the side of the cushion, grabs the knife and positions himself for hara-kiri.*]

MR. MR.
Tis a far far better thing I do, than I have ever—

ISA
Isa! Wait! What are you thinking?! [*Takes the knife away from him.*] Suicide is an affront to God.

PLOPE
Your brother is correct as always. [*Takes knife and hands it to Chauffeur.*] Here, you do it.

CHAUFFEUR
Me?

PLOPE
We can't have the princess do it.

CHAUFFEUR
But I'm not a priest. I'm a ...

UNCTION
President.

CHAUFFEUR
Exactly. And presidents don't kill innocent people.

PLOPE
Actually, Congress passed that resolution a few weeks ago.

CHAUFFEUR
Well if Congress says so. In the name of the Monacan People, who for too long have been ignored, pushed aside and denied the full fruits of our labor, simply because we are—a small European kingdom.

ISA
WAIT! I want to have a word with my sister.

PLOPE
Certainly.

ISA
In private.

[*Plope, Chauffeur, and Unction turn around, cover their ears, and hum.*]

ISA
What are you doing, Luis?

MR. MR.
What do you mean, Luis?

ISA
Stop it! I'm not Luis, you are.

MR. MR.
Is the game over? Should we tell the Plope?

ISA
No.

MR. MR.
Then allow me to get my sainthood, Luis, in the only way I know how. And you can go give your important speech about Monaco's nuclear weapons program.

ISA
I'm sorry about that.

MR. MR.
Don't be. To tell you the truth, while I was in the chair, I decided to change my plan to simply offering the workers stock options in the failing industries like the airlines.

ISA
Well, I'm sorry.

MR. MR.
Hey, being in a mildly unhealthy incestuous relationship means never having to say you're sorry. That's rule number 37.

[*They embrace and kiss.*]

PLOPE
[*As all three turn back.*] Are we done yet, Luis?

ISA
[*Stops kiss.*] Yes.

PLOPE
Good, because sainthood delayed is too often sainthood denied. Renaldo.

CHAUFFEUR
As I was saying before—in the name of the Monacan People, who for too long have been ignored, pushed aside and denied—oh forget it. Glory! Ready! Go! [*Stabs Mr. Mr.*]

MR. MR.
Goodbye, Luis.

ISA
Goodbye, Isa.

MR. MR.
I win.

ISA
You always do.

[*Mr. Mr. falls.*]

PLOPE
Goodness, look at the time. We need to run if we're going to make that luncheon. Princess Gladys, will you accompany me at my table?

UNCTION
I'd love to, your Plapalcy, but I'm not sure if I should.

PLOPE
What do you mean? We'll be celebrating Mother Isa's sainthood and Mr. Mr.'s martyrdom.

UNCTION
I'm just afraid that the people there won't think that I'm—well, that they won't necessarily recognize me as Princess Gladys.

PLOPE
Pish-posh. You'll be with me, and if I say that you're Princess Gladys then you're Princess Gladys. I'm unflappable. Now let's go. We'll all ride in my car.

CHAUFFEUR
Wow! The Plope Mobile!

PLOPE
Not you killer.

ISA
Have the car waiting in front of the Drake.

[*Chauffeur exits.*]

PLOPE
Luis, you should get to know Princess Gladys.

ISA
I'm sure that I'll be seeing a lot of her. After all, now that my sister will be sleeping with the worms, Gladys is going to be taking on her work here.

UNCTION
I am?

ISA
It was always her wish.

UNCTION
Wow! Mother Gladys!

ISA
But on one condition. You must follow all the rules except rule number 99.

UNCTION
Rule number 99?!

ISA
Rule number 99.

PLOPE
Wonderful. Now tell me, Luis, what will you be speaking about today?

[*Plope and Unction exit.*]

ISA
Speeches that still need to be written ... ant bites on your eyelids ... fingers stained by cigarettes ... held on the very threshold of a swoon ... a turn in your stomach beneath a sky full of stars ... the moon rising a different hour every night ... awoken by the deathly quiet before the dawn break ... a desire to live in anguish ... finding one's words the next day ... fading bruises ... passing planets ... the horrific beauty of life.

[*Exits.*]

THE END

L TTER PURLOINED

Colm O'Reilly's graphic for the *Letter Purloined* t-shirt.

Letter Purloined
by David Isaacson

Letter Purloined was first performed by Theater Oobleck at Live Bait Theatre on January 12, 2006, with the following cast:

King Navodar. . . . . .David Isaacson
Queen Diri . . . . .Heather Riordan
Ogai. . . . . .David Kodeski
Ordina. . . . . .Kat McJimsey
Bianca . . . . .Diana Slickman
General Cassio. . . . . .Colm O'Reilly

Material for this play purloined from William Shakespeare, Edgar Allan Poe, Jacques Lacan, Jacques Derrida, Princess Marie Bonaparte, and the life and times of Radovan Karadzic.

Thanks to Ann Manikas, Jacob Isaacson, the cast, outside eyes, Theater Oobleck, Melinda Evans, Erica Erdmann, Rachel Claff, Jeff Dorchen, Eric Ziegenhagen, Neo-Futurists, Greg Allen, John Roberts, William Sanders, John Ragir, Sharon Evans, and David Bremer.

Dedicated to Joel and Helen.

242

CHARACTERS

King Navodar (Nav'-oh-dahr). Wears a crown.
Queen Diri, his wife, a psychiatrist (Deer'-ee). Wears a crown.
Minister Ogai, husband of Ordina (Oh'-gah-ee).
Ordina, his wife, Superintendent of Police (Or-dee'-nah). Very neat.
Bianca, the Special Prosecutor. Wears sunglasses.
General Cassio. He sounds like a Casio keyboard.

Note: Cassio "plays" his dialogue by pressing different imaginary "buttons" on his body that operate like the buttons on a Casio electronic keyboard, changing instruments, adjusting tempo, adding drum fills, etcetera. I have printed the lyrics only as a guide for the actor, who only sings/hums the instrumental. Where these lyrics end in an ellipsis, Cassio continues his music underneath subsequent dialogue.

A Note on the Structure of This Play

The scenes of this play are intended to be performed in a different order every night. This randomness is no mere theatrical conceit; the relationship between order and meaning is an essential theme of the play. So though the scenes here are printed alphabetically (and chronologically), please read them in random order.

The program for the play should include the following note:

"This play consists of twenty-six scenes that have a chronological order, from A to Z. We will perform thirteen scenes, have an intermission, then perform another thirteen scenes. But we will not perform the scenes chronologically. We will perform them in the order you see on the back wall of the theater.

"The play, then, will never be performed in the same order twice. That is, the odds are 400 billion zillions to one against it being performed in the same order twice. It's true. We did the math."

Here's how the mechanics of it work: The first twenty-six audience members to arrive are given a handkerchief in the lobby. The handkerchiefs are distributed in random order; each handkerchief has a large letter of the alphabet printed on it. On one side this letter is printed in red; on the other, the same letter is printed in black, backwards. The audience members are told something along the lines of, "Please bring this letter into the theater with you. It will be purloined from you in there."

As the audience takes their seats, the actors "steal" the letters from the audience—again, in random order. The handkerchiefs are then attached, in the order they are "stolen," in four rows along the back wall of the theater so the red sides are visible to both audience and cast.

The play is then performed in the order determined on the wall. After each scene, the handkerchief bearing the letter of the scene just performed is flipped, so we now see the black-backwards side of the handkerchief.

Before you read this play, cut out the letters on this page, put them in a hat, and take them out one at a time. This will determine the order you read the scenes in.

A B
C D E F
G H I J
K L M N
O P Q R
S T U V
W X Y Z

SCENE A: ALL ABOUT ANNIHILATION

Navodar and Cassio enter, clearly exhausted. They stop at edge of "river."

CASSIO
[*Hums a bit of Chopin's Sonata No. 2—The "Funeral March."*]

NAVODAR
Yes, Cassio. It's sad. Sad. The Slaughter of the Innocents ... [*Takes out handkerchief to wipe face. The handkerchief is bloody.*] Uch. Blood. [*Holds it up to Cassio.*]

CASSIO
[*Al Green's "Take Me to the River": "Take me to the river/ wash me in the water."*]

[*Navodar tries to wash out blood.*]

NAVODAR
Won't come out. Dry cleaning. Thank God for dry cleaning.

[*Cassio pulls out his bloody sword.*]

NAVODAR
Ucch. Yes, your sword, too. We wrote something once:

Keep up your bright swords,
for the dew will rust them.

A small Swedish journal published it, Cassio. "Plowshares," we don't know if you're familiar. It later merged with "Schrapnel"—that quarterly out of Sudan?—and there was quite the to-do over whether to call it "Schrapshares" or "Plowpnel"—Sad. We're sad. The Slaughter of the Innocents.

CASSIO
[*Rogers & Hammerstein's "Happy Talk," from* South Pacific: *"Happy talk, keep talkin' happy talk/ Talk about things you'd like to do."*]

NAVODAR
Oh, sure. *Intellectually* we know we should be happy. Because by slaughtering innocent people today, we preserve the ... [*He's looking for the phrase.*]

CASSIO
[*New Order's "Temptation": "Hoo-hoo-hoo-hoo-hoo/ Hoo-hoo-hoo-hoo-hoo/ Hoo-hoo-hoo/ Hoo-hoo-hoo."*]

NAVODAR
Right! The *New Order*! The new order that permits Innocence to exist! Can Innocence exist in, like, a ... [*Again, looks for the right word.*]

CASSIO
[*Neil Young's "Like A Hurricane": You are like a hurricane/ there´s calm in your eyes/ and I´m getting blown away ..."*]

NAVODAR
... in, like, a hurricane? No! Innocence requires stability. So we slaughter Innocence, Cassio, in order to preserve it.

[*Cassio stops song.*]

NAVODAR
Or that's what the Royal Air Force's website says, at any rate. [*Looks at handkerchief.*] Have you noticed, though, it's the innocent blood that's hardest to wash out? Do you want to know the—what?—the irony of it? Oh, we know you're all—what are you?—bluff, buff soldier, hiding your emotional life behind your lo-fi techno hummy-hummings, your microchip drum-fills—

CASSIO
[*Angry spasm of drumming.*]

NAVODAR
Don't bark at us like that. Yeah, we've snuck a peak at your "therapist's" file, Ogai put us up to it. ... Anyway, you can stand a little—can't you?—a little ironic something-or-other?

CASSIO
[*Elton John's "Your Song": "It's a little bit funny, this feeling inside ..."*]

NAVODAR
Yes, it *is* a little bit funny. We'll take this handkerchief to the dry cleaner, and they'll get the blood out, all right. They'll clean it in carbon tetrachloride and then that carbon tetrachloride will go directly into the River Lethe, that great river that winds through our Kingdom, and children, innocent children, children who owe their innocence to the social order we have preserved, will drink from that River, and Innocence will be slaughtered all over again.

[*Cassio ends song.*]

NAVODAR
So the clean-ness or bloodiness of our handkerchief, the whiteness or redness

246

of it, in the end, they signify the same thing. You know. That word. Death.

[*Outro Music: Rogers & Hammerstein's "Happy Talk" from* South Pacific.]

SCENE B: BEAUTIFUL BEQUEST

Navodar and Cassio. Navodar is holding bloody handkerchief. Cassio is holding bloody sword, looking offstage, playing Hilliard & Mann's "Dearie." Enter Diri, sneezing furiously.

NAVODAR
Keep up your sword, soldier.

[*Cassio puts away his bloody sword. Navodar hides handkerchief behind his back.*]

CASSIO
[*"Down by the Riverside" (traditional): "I'm gonna lay down my sword and shield/ down by the riverside."*]

NAVODAR
Hey, Diri! Sneezing furiously today?

[*Diri sneezes.*]

NAVODAR
Sneeze, sneeze, sneeze. A neurotic manifestation of ...?

DIRI
Fear of intimacy. Uh-huh. My mother would never touch me. [*Diri approaches Cassio coquettishly.*] What *was* that on your [*sneeze*] sword, Cassio? You've been engaged in some man-play?

[*Navodar takes note. Is annoyed. Takes out handkerchief, mops brow.*]

NAVODAR
Well, *wife*. Wife of ours. Let us give you a—

[*Goes to her. He is about to say "kiss." She sees handkerchief.*]

DIRI
A handkerchief! A silk handkerchief! For me?

NAVODAR
No! We mean, yes! For you!

DIRI
Because of my furious sneezing! Uh-huh. And the most beautiful design! What are these? Strawberries!

NAVODAR
Of course!

DIRI
Lovely strawberries. Uh-huh. It's been so long since ... [*Sneeze.*] since you've given me a gift. Look, Cassio. Look how lovely. [*She shows it to him.*]

CASSIO
[*Stevie Wonder's "Isn't She Lovely," in the style of a pipe organ: "Isn't she lovely/ Isn't she wonderful?..."*]

[*Diri looks in Cassio's eyes.*]

DIRI
So long since he's given me—what's that?

NAVODAR
Pipe organ, sounds like.

DIRI
Muted trumpet, please.

[*Cassio continues "Isn't She Lovely" in the style of a muted trumpet.*]

DIRI
So long—Lovely. I'll never part with it. Never. Never part with it. Never. Never ever. [*Sneeze.*]

[*Outro Music: Stevie Wonder's "Isn't She Lovely."*]

SCENE C: CASSIO'S CURSE

Cassio on a couch. Diri, in a chair, compulsively scratches herself throughout.

CASSIO

[*Makes metronome sound. For quite some time.*]

DIRI

Uh-huh. Uh-huh. Uh-huh. We don't seem to be making much progress this morning.

CASSIO

[*Carole King's "I Feel the Earth Move": "I feel the earth move under my feet."*]

DIRI

Uh-huh, you've hummed about this before—feeling unmoored, the earth seeming to move beneath your feet, vertigo—

CASSIO

[*"I feel the sky tumbling down, tumbling down."*]

DIRI

And uh-huh, it seems the sky is falling, uh-huh.

CASSIO

[*The Who's "Go to the Mirror Boy": "See me, feel me, touch me, heal me."*]

DIRI

Certainly, everyone wants to feel heard, healed, seen, and—uh—*felt*, but ... Perhaps we should—uh-huh—take a step back.

CASSIO

[*"Happy Birthday to you/ Happy Birthday to you."*]

DIRI

Uh-huh, well, that's a big step back. By all means, let's talk about the day of your birth.

CASSIO

[*Rogers & Hammerstein's, "So Long, Farewell," from* The Sound of Music: *"And up in the nursery/ An absurd little bird/ Is popping out to say 'cuckoo'/ Cuckoo, cuckoo."*]

DIRI

As you emerge, into this world, a particularly loud *cuckoo clock* strikes on the nursery wall, terrifying you, uh-huh, and sending you—

CASSIO
[*Simon & Garfunkel's "Sound of Silence": " ...into the Sound of Silence."*]

DIRI
—into a psychogenic well of silence. What did the doctor do?

CASSIO
[*Pat Benatar's "Hit Me With Your Best Shot": "Hit me with your best shot."*]

DIRI
Let's see. [*Sings:*] "Mm-mm with your best shot."

CASSIO
[*"Why don't you hit me with your best shot."*]

DIRI
Oh. He gives you a shot ...

CASSIO
[*Kiki Dee's "I've Got The Music In Me": "I got the music in me/ I got the music in me."*]

DIRI
That's right. He vaccinated you with a phonograph needle. And since then, you've just had this music in you.

CASSIO
[*"I got the music in meeee." Cassio stops music.*]

DIRI
And now you've come to me.

CASSIO
[*Robert Palmer's "Bad Case of Loving You": "Doctor, doctor, gimme the news/ I got a bad case of lovin' you."*]

DIRI
Don't you see? Your synth-pop, your bossa nova, your boom-chuckas ... they're not really from your childhood doctor's shot at all. They are your own personal, special neurotic reaction—uh-huh—to the horror of leaving the womb—a horror, in your case, you associate with the sound of a cuckoo.

CASSIO
[*"Cuckoo. Cuckoo ..."*]

[*Diri's scratching gets excessive here.*]

DIRI

And I want you to—uh-huh—to embrace the music in you, to *enjoy your symptom*. Because traumas, from beginning to end, tear us up, destroy our sense of ABC. Uh-huh. Un-moored.

[*She stops scratching. Cassio stops his "cuckoos."*]

DIRI

But our symptoms, our beautiful symptoms—our vomiting, hysterias, our "out out damned spots," pus-filled blisters—our symptoms make us whole again. They complete us.

[*Outro music: "So Long, Farewell" from* The Sound of Music.]

SCENE D: DECIPHERING

Diri at a table, she reads aloud as she writes.

DIRI
Memoir of psychosomatic phenomena, subcategory: self-induced. A) The sneeze. Uh-huh. *Check.* B) Compulsive rubbing of hands and temples. Uh-huh. *Check.* C) Echolalia. Uh-huh. *Check.* D) Echolalia. Uh-huh. *Check.* E) The "cold sweat." Ah. The cold sweat. Sudden onset of perspiration, often triggered by anxiety ... early trauma ... childhood abuse ... etcetera.

[*Pauses. Tries to make herself sweat. Feels her forehead and neck. Nothing. Writes.*]

Initial difficulties in simulating glandular symptoms.

[*Pauses. Tries again, this time discovers some sweat. Writes.*]

Cold sweat!

[*She searches about for handkerchief. Finds it. Mops brow. Looks at handkerchief.*]

Mmm. Lovely handkerchief, really. Strawberries. Lovely pattern.

[*Mops again. Looks again.*]

Are those strawberries? Odd kind of strawberries. Yugh. And the *smell.* The smell is odd. And Navodar's—the way he—his *attitude* as he gave it me. Odd, odd, odd. It smells like ... it's blood.

[*Drops it.*]

It's a bloody hanky! But how? Whose blood? Who? Cassio's sword was bloody, I remember. Is it Cassio? Cassio's blood?

[*She dances around with it, fondling and kissing it. She puts it down her panties and wipes it there. Has idea. Writes.*]

Possible hysterical-neurotic symptoms for further development and study: Compulsive handling of the genitals, uh-huh, possibly even touching *objects* to genitals.

[*Smells handkerchief. Writes.*]

Possible smelling or sniffing of genital area.

[*Wipes handkerchief again. Sniffs. Writes:*]

Or of objects held to or associated with genitals.

[*Wipes again. Stares at handkerchief.*]

If I wish—if the psychoanalyst wishes to *interpret* a symptom, to decipher a text—what happens when the *thing* is more than what you can think *about* the thing? When it says more about itself than does the deciphering?

[*Outro Music: The Moody Blues' "Come Back (I Don't Want To Go On Without You)."*]

SCENE E: EVIL AND EMERY

King's rooms. Ogai and Navodar.

OGAI
Time for your pedicure, Sire.

NAVODAR
Oh. Really? We mean, because last time you did it, and we don't mean to say—but ... it hurt.

[*Ogai begins pedicure.*]

OGAI
If you don't like my technique, Sire, may I ask you, why is it that your *wife* does not take on this particular duty—the pedicure—your wife, whose dainty fingers and natural conscientiousness regarding your illustrious person would make her the obvious candidate for all foot-care activities?

NAVODAR
Our wife, Ogai—you *know* this, sees clients during the morning, every morning.

OGAI
Oh, that's right. And I'm not trying to make trouble here—or to make more trouble than it is my nature to make—that's right. Your wife still ... *works*.

NAVODAR
Mm. Why shouldn't she?

OGAI
Shall I be blunt?

NAVODAR
No.

OGAI
Most wives, no matter their personal ambition, would give up their own thing if their husband becomes, as you have, the undisputed Sovereign of the Realm.

NAVODAR
Maybe.

[*Ogai jabs his foot.*]

NAVODAR
Ow!

OGAI
Kofi Annan, for instance.

NAVODAR
Kofi Annan?

OGAI
You know, my friend, William—

NAVODAR
William?

OGAI
The American? The painter? My American friend *William*? The one with the oh-so post-modern paintings?

NAVODAR
Not that *word*.

OGAI
American?

NAVODAR
Post-*modern*! Post-*modern*! Don't say—

OGAI
Yes, you know the one. So anyway, William, the *painter*, shared studio space in Brooklyn with Kofi *Annan's* wife.

NAVODAR
[*Looking at his foot.*] That's blood.

OGAI
But when Kofi Annan became Secretary-General of the United Nations, she—his wife—gave up the studio space.

NAVODAR
What's the deal you could utter that—*that* name to us?

OGAI
William?

NAVODAR
Kofi Annan.

OGAI
Other foot, please.

NAVODAR
Really Ogai, you know he's our—

OGAI
Our what?

NAVODAR
Not wanting to sound too dramatic here, but our *sworn enemy*. Arch—well, *arch-nemesis*. Sorry. It's what he is. Whenever we massacre, he says "No massacres." If we commit genocide, the next day there he is in the papers making some splashy speech against genocide. Ow! Less ... *ardor* around the cuticles, please. Innocents get Slaughtered—and these things happen, we're not saying we *condone*, or *bear* any—but these things do occur, as they have here, Innocents get Slaughtered—and when they do, as sure as day follows night, Kofi Annan's sure to take some oh-so-noble stand *against* that Slaughter.

OGAI
Yes. Yes. Precisely. And when Annan acts against you, he has—what?—the *full support* of his better half. When he hosts a diplomatic dinner—

NAVODAR
Are you done?

OGAI
File. [*Pulls out file.*] When he hosts a diplomatic dinner and slyly lets slip that he is considering fresh sanctions against you, and he, Annan, cannot stress enough the importance of the international community, blah blah, being brought to bear, blah blah blah, rogue nation, etcetera—

NAVODAR
Ow!

OGAI
Who, at this critical juncture, is right at his side, filling the champagne mug of the cultural attaché from Walla-Walla, Luxembourg? Why, none other than *Mrs.* Kofi Annan, his wife, who has given up a rewarding career—

NAVODAR
Really, Ogai, we're a well-read type of guy, a reader *type*, you might say, and we've spent many a day poring over the literary treasures found in the vast libraries of the great cities that our armies have so successfully seized and occupied, and yet we have never encountered in these volumes

and reams and tomes of the printed word any mention of a man with the ability to inflict such extraordinary pain with a simple emery board!

OGAI
Yes, but what of *my* pain? The pain of a servant—an *aide*, you call me, I know—who when trying to make a *point*, a point regarding the Royal Toes, is interrupted with digressions about armies and libraries?! The point being that, when your *arch-whatever you call him*—your opposite number, Kofi Annan—achieved his current exalted position, his *wife* abandoned her still-lives, her portraiture, her bucolic landscapes, in order to help *him*—Kofi Annan—achieve his ultimate goal, that being the destruction of *you*. Now you, a man who has sacrificed his *own* artistic ambitions, can surely appreciate—

NAVODAR
Well OK, admittedly ... certainly, we can't pretend there was no—that we didn't give anything up—

OGAI
Of course.

NAVODAR
Sacrifice is a strong word, but .... We wrote something once, just a little thing, about those days, those quiet Sundays with Diri, before ...

O my soul's joy!
If after every tempest come such calms,
May the winds blow till they have waken'd death!
And let the labouring bark climb hills of seas
Olympus-high and duck again as low
As hell's from heaven!

OGAI
Not bad by half. You see? Sacrifice! Your country needed you, you answered the call. Not everyone has that kind of sense of duty.

NAVODAR
Mmm. Y'mean Diri again? You know, if we didn't know better, we might think you were trying to sneakily plant the seeds of doubt in our brain, slowly poison our thoughts about our wife in such a way—in the end, after many episodes of plotting and connivance—as to undo us, our marriage, and our reign.

And now look at this. Our feet are a bloody mess. You who follow me, have walked in a trail of blood.

[*Outro Music: Tina Turner's "Stand by Your Man."*]

SCENE F: FLIP FLOP
Ordina on couch. Diri in chair.

ORDINA
I think what I've been avoiding—I think why the therapy—the therapeutic process up to now—has been so ... slow, I think ... I've been holding back, is the truth. And, the story I'm about to tell you—that I think I'm ready to tell you—is *complicated*, by the fact, that one of the principal characters in the story is—and this is awkward, *beyond* awkward, really—is ... your husband.

DIRI
Fuckin' fuckin' hell! Shit!

ORDINA
What?

DIRI
Please go on.

ORDINA
But you ... swore.

DIRI
I did? Oh, never mind that. That's the copralalia.

ORDINA
Excuse me?

DIRI
Uncontrollable outbursts of profanity. A neurotic symptom I'm developing for myself. Please disregard. Continue. My husband. Yes?

ORDINA
Right, well, I ... I don't know what he's told you, but we—he and I—I wouldn't say an *item*, but we were *involved*, I don't know what *he* would say, there was definitely ... I loved him.

DIRI
God *fucking* damn! Shit!

ORDINA
Right. Or, you know, I *thought* it was love. Because, you understand, what is love, after all?

DIRI
Hell.

ORDINA
But I was in love with *two* guys, is the thing. It was, that's what was done then—free love. I even—my name was, you won't believe this, *Orgasma* back then, there were drugs ... anyway, he was a *poet* for god's sake—I was in love with Navodar—

DIRI
Fuck!

ORDINA
Uh. *And* in love with Ogai. And I was a mess back then. Just so ... flibberty-gibberty. All over the map. A wreck. And I decided I've just got to decide—because I'm seeing *both* these guys. I mean, I don't know how much detail you want me to get into, about the "seeing"—

DIRI
Shit!

ORDINA
Skip the details, right. So I write them letters, and what I decide is, I'm going to send Ogai a "Dear John" letter—"Darling, I'm so sorry, but"—and send Navodar a—the sweetest love letter I can write—"Precious, you are my life, my rock"—

DIRI
Bitch!

ORDINA
What?

DIRI
Excuse me?

ORDINA
Nothing. Should I ...?

DIRI
Please.

ORDINA
And but here's where it starts to go bad, because I wake up the next morning, and realize I've flip-flopped 'em. I put the break-up letter in the envelope for Navodar and the "sweet nectar of your man-lust" letter is addressed to Ogai.

DIRI
Shit-licking scum-whore!

ORDINA
Well, I was—what can I say—an *extremely disorganized* person. I mean, things like that happened to me—really—*all the time.* Which is why my life since has been a concerted effort to be the most—everything structured, down to the tiniest ... So anyway—the letter—I run to Navodar, and shit—

DIRI
Shit!

ORDINA
Just as I'm dashing up the walk, there's the mailman walking away, so I run in, and of course Navodar's reading this "Dear John" thing. But the thing is, instead of being all broken up about it, he's *beaming*, just *gleaming* at me over the top of letter, the happiest goddamn guy in the world.

DIRI
Goddam!

ORDINA
Yeah! So I'm like, "Fuck you!"

DIRI
Fuck you!

ORDINA
Fuck you and go to hell!

DIRI
Fuck you!

ORDINA
And I'm outta there, thinking, so, well, I lost *one*, but I still got the other. So I run across town to Ogai. And the mail hasn't gotten there yet. So I go in, all lovey-dovey, flirty, all coy about this very *ooh-lah-lah* letter I sent him, and—*thwock!*—it comes through the mail slot, and he reads it, and looks at me kind of all funny-like, and proposes marriage. Right there on the spot.

DIRI
Shit!

ORDINA
It was only on our wedding night, he shows me the letter. And it's the break-up letter. You see, I hadn't mixed 'em up at all.

DIRI
Shit!

ORDINA
So it seems like things have gone beyond "the medium is the message," if you know what I mean. I think that, what I've come to understand, about letters, is it's like telling a joke, or pitching a baseball. It's all in the delivery.

[*Outro Music: The Carpenters' "Please Mr. Postman."*]

SCENE G: GYRATING GADGETS

King's rooms. Navodar and Ogai.

OGAI
Your crown, please.

NAVODAR
What?

OGAI
Hand over your crown.

NAVODAR
Our crown?

OGAI
Give it to me.

NAVODAR
Why—?

OGAI
It's time to dry your crown, Sire.

NAVODAR
Dry it?

OGAI
Traditionally, it is the role of the royal consort, the First Lady, but as she is—

NAVODAR
With clients.

OGAI
—the drying of the crown falls to *me*.

NAVODAR
But ... is it wet?

OGAI
It *might* be wet.

NAVODAR
But *unlikely*—

OGAI

It is the mere *chance* that the Royal Crown is wet, and therefore susceptible to rust and mildew, that necessitates the Royal Consort's ritual drying of said Crown. And as the Royal Consort is, as you said, seeing to her own needs—yes, I believe *Cassio* is her client at this hour, 10 to 10:50—so anyway, the First Minister, myself, *must* dry the crown.

NAVODAR

Here. Just to shut you up. [*Hands over crown.*] If our wife has *Cassio* as a client, we don't see how that really—she has many clients, and Cassio is just *one* of these ... What are you doing?

[*Ogai has pulled a telescoping pole out of his man-bag. He extends it, and puts the crown at the end of the pole, and is spinning it.*]

OGAI

Your Royal Corps of Engineers has determined that this is both the most efficient and hygienic method of crown-drying. Centrifugal force. Not unlike the kinetic sculptures wrought by the new studio-mate of my friend William.

NAVODAR

William?

OGAI

The American? The painter? My American friend William? The one who used to share studio space with Kofi Annan's wife?

NAVODAR

Not that *name.*

OGAI

William?

NAVODAR

Kofi *Annan*! Kofi *Annan*! Don't say—

OGAI

We'll talk about it later. My point is a sculptor—this is what I was saying—moved in. To William's studio. This sculptor used motors, large stainless steel disks, and old pole vault sticks to create mammoth, whirligig art-machines.

NAVODAR

[*Referring to the spinning crown.*] Seems dangerous.

264

OGAI

Dangerous, yeah, particularly for the delicate painted surfaces of my American friend William's canvasses. William, at this time, was working on a series of paintings in which he would paint—oh, you know— prototypical, one might even say—and some critics *did* say—stereotypical post-modern scenes.

NAVODAR

What would a—?

OGAI

Oh, I think they were, in this case, in this series, *biblical* scenes—but with cartoon characters. So, Minnie Mouse holding the head of John the Baptist, but instead of John the Baptist, Dudley DoRight. That sort of thing.

NAVODAR

Trite.

OGAI

Perhaps. But here's the thing. After he painted these scenes, very elaborate stuff, very High Renaissance/Baroque/Hannah-Barbara stuff—*detailed*— after this, he'd entirely paint over it, not leaving a trace, paint over, with very mundane stuff, but *interesting*-mundane—household objects.

NAVODAR

What? Lamps?

OGAI

And couches. And chests of drawers. CD players. Accurately, realistically rendered. Dining room chairs.

NAVODAR

Your friend is a little—

OGAI

My friend is a *lot*. But his dealer, she'd let her customers in on the secret, you know: "underneath this *oh-so-prosaic* picture of a refrigerator, there's a beautifully rendered epic: "Speed Racer and Penelope Pitstop Expelled from the Garden of Eden" or what have you. And word spreads, and suddenly William, my American friend, the painter, even though people don't really know if the scenes underneath are *there*, or if it's all rumor, or maybe *because* they don't know what's under, suddenly William's *hot*.

NAVODAR

The *artiste-du-jour*.

OGAI
Or whatever. The *sculptor*, though—his new studio mate—before he'd get the balance just right, or properly adjust the motor speed, his sculptures would bash into William's paintings, gashing and lacerating the table or lamp or couch, the *painting* of the table or lamp or couch, and inadvertently revealing the "Rape of the Sabine Flintstones"—or what have you—or perhaps the *lack* of any such scene—underneath.

NAVODAR
We begin to see. You're cooking some analogy, some fable. Mundane surfaces. Hidden texts. Some tiresome instructional fiction.

OGAI
Not at all. I merely mean to point out that if you don't *like* centrifugal force as a means of crown-drying—if you don't *approve*, you find it *dangerous*—perhaps your wife, if she wasn't with *Cassio* this morning, perhaps she could come up with a more delicate, *womanly* drying technique.

NAVODAR
Cassio. Yes. *Cassio.*

OGAI
And if the sculptor had kept his whirligigs under control, he would have left William's prosaic surfaces undisturbed. But no. The meaning of the newly pockmarked canvases was irrevocably revealed. And by revealed of course I mean changed. And by changed of course I mean destroyed.

[*The crown flies off the pole offstage.*]

OGAI
Oops.

NAVODAR
Such is the fate of a crown. Such is the fate of the thing ... the thing that is transferred.

[*Outro Music: The Rezillos' "(My Baby Does) Good Sculptures."*]

SCENE H: HELL AND NIGHT

Cassio alone on stage. Crown flies on, lies at his feet. He regards it. Looks around. Cautiously picks it up and puts it on.

CASSIO
[*Arlen/Harburg's "If I Were King of the Forest" from* The Wizard of Oz: *"If I were king of the forest/ not queen/ not duke/ not prince."*]

[*Enter Navodar and Ogai.*]

NAVODAR
Cassio. You seem to be wearing our crown.

[*Cassio hands crown to Navodar.*]

CASSIO
[*Paul McCartney's "Uncle Albert/Admiral Halsey": "We're so sorry, Uncle Albert/ We're so sorry if we caused you any pain."*]

NAVODAR
Sure. Whatever. Carry on. Go ... put down an insurgency, or something.

[*Cassio exits, humming "F-Troop" theme.*]

OGAI
A man who can only *hum* ... is a man with something to hide.

NAVODAR
He *is* a little *R2-D2*.

OGAI
You noted how he caressed that crown? Well, *I* did. I'm a very detail-oriented person, I said that on my résumé. And speaking of which—details—it's time to wash your money.

NAVODAR
Wash our money? Money *laundering*, you mean?

OGAI
Washing. It would hardly do, when you hand out alms to the poor—these alms with your very likeness engraved upon them—it would hardly do for them to be dirty. That's not the type of image—

NAVODAR
Oh, wash away. [*Hands over coins.*]

OGAI
I heard him call your wife "Dearie." [*He spits on coin. Rubs it.*]

NAVODAR
Cassio?

OGAI
The same.

NAVODAR
Ogai, that's her name. Diri. D-I-R-I.

OGAI
But Cassio wasn't D-I-R-I-ing her. He was humming—you know that tune: Ray Bolger and Ethel Merman?—D-E-A-R-I-E.

Dearie, do you remember when the Met let Caruso sing?
My, didn't the rafters ring?

NAVODAR
Alright. What of it?

OGAI
I'm just saying. Cassio's a proper man.

NAVODAR
What makes you think, Ogai, that we have not already had this precise conversation with our wife?

OGAI
Which conversation?

NAVODAR
The "Does Cassio call you 'Dearie,' you strumpet" conversation? The "Have you ever considered finding another line of work?" conversation. The "don't fuck with us, we're a very jealous kind of guy!" conversation.

OGAI
Well, if you *had* had that conversation with her—which I doubt you have, but if you have—she probably twisted the whole thing to her own benefit.

NAVODAR
What?

OGAI
She could spit in your face and convince you it was for your own good.
[*Spits on coin.*]

268

NAVODAR
Enough already! [*He snatches money from Ogai and turns to leave.*]
Rumor-mongering! Pesty pesty man! We feel like you've put us on one of
those racks your lovely wife keeps in the dungeons.

OGAI
My ... *lovely* wife?

NAVODAR
O, now, for ever
Farewell the tranquil mind! farewell content!

[*Exits.*]

OGAI
Cassio and Diri. Navodar and Ordina.

Sometimes I get tired with my own performance. Actors are a sorry bunch.
I heard an actor say something once. Actually more than once. I went
back again and again, in my student days in the States, getting student
rush tickets. James Earl Jones and Christopher Plummer. In *Othello*. On
Broadway.

And it is thought abroad, that 'twixt my sheets
He has done my office.

A sorry bunch. Christopher Plummer doesn't think that James Earl Jones
slept with his wife. And he doesn't really think *Othello* slept with *Iago's*
wife. And he doesn't really think that *Iago* really thinks that Othello slept
with his wife. And yet he says, or he says Iago says,

that 'twixt my sheets
He has done my office.

Maybe what Christopher Plummer's doing, really, is reading aloud a *letter*
he has received from Iago, an Iago who thinks he's a cuckold. Though
since Iago never existed, it is a *dead* letter Christopher Plummer reads, a
dead letter that nonetheless got delivered to Christopher Plummer, and
that Christopher Plummer nonetheless reads. A sorry bunch. Actors.

Ordina and the King.

that 'twixt my sheets
He has done my office: The thought whereof
Doth, like a poisonous mineral, gnaw my innards;
And nothing can or shall content my soul
Till I am even'd with him, wife for wife,

269

Or failing so, yet that I put Navodar
At least into a jealousy so strong
That judgment cannot cure.
I have't. It is engender'd. Hell and night
Must bring this monstrous birth to the world's light.

Mmm. That's my story and I'm sticking to it.

[*Outro Music: Guy Lombardo's "Dearie."*]

SCENE I: INTERMEZZO

CASSIO
Ray Charles, a blind man, still could, in peaceful dreams, see that the road leads back to you.

In my dreams, I speak.

I had a dream, or am having a dream, that I die, or died. It felt, or feels, like the kind of dream that is a memory, or a prediction. And when I die, or died, my life passes before my eyes. This sped-up life, though complete, does not come in chronological order—more ... cut-and-paste, random. As I experience it, or experienced it, it is, or was, or will be as real to me as the chronological life that came before, or that *seemed*, or *seems*, to come before.

The road leads back to ...

No. I cannot honestly tell which is the chronological and which the memory-life.

[*Outro music: Ray Charles' "Georgia on My Mind."*]

SCENE J: JUDICIAL JUGGERNAUT

The Throne Room. Navodar's throne has a pillow on it.

NAVODAR
Ah, Bianca. Our Special Prosecutor!

BIANCA
Sire, it is incumbent upon me to report a vile butchery, a deed of brutal ferocity.

NAVODAR
You don't say?

BIANCA
It's the Innocents, Sire. They've been Slaughtered again.

NAVODAR
Well, that hardly seems tolerable. It's *in*tolerable, is what it is!

BIANCA
It is a grotesquerie in horror absolutely alien from humanity, Sire.

NAVODAR
Not in any way tolerable! Well, now, getting to the bottom of—cutting to the chase—anything in those reports on the perpetrators? Possible perpetrators? *Alleged* perpetrators?

BIANCA
I have received no *firm* identification from any of the witnesses.

NAVODAR
Witnesses, yes. There would be. You have, of course, a witness *list* there, do you? Names? Addresses? E-mail?

BIANCA
I have interviewed *alleged* witnesses.

NAVODAR
Full reports! We want full reports on all witnesses—all statements from witnesses—on our desk—first thing. We'll crush them.

BIANCA
The perpetrators.

NAVODAR
Naturally. The perpetrators. Whom else would we crush? *Alleged* perpetrators, of course. Innocent until proven.

BIANCA
Excluding testimony of inconsequence and incoherence, the following emerges: There was a force of twenty-six armed individuals. And while the exact features of each were to a great extent obscured by the white handkerchiefs fastened over their faces, still, corroboration rises upon corroboration: the apparent leader of this assemblage of blackguards bore a remarkable resemblance ... to you.

NAVODAR
Ah, yes. Ah, hah, hah, yes. It was only a matter of time.

BIANCA
Matter of ...?

NAVODAR
Before a doppelganger showed up.

BIANCA
Your Majesty has a lookalike?

NAVODAR
Every majesty does. Read the literature, Bianca. The Prince, the pauper in the iron mask, Charlie Chaplin. Comes with the territory.

BIANCA
Since I see no cause, out of hand, to reject your thesis, I am led to the following conundrum, for which perhaps the literature to which you refer can provide some guidance: How do I know, given the situation of doubleness you find yourself in, that it is *you* that I am talking to at this moment and not this double of you?

NAVODAR
Ah, yes. Well, you don't. You don't know. It makes your job difficult, we know—

BIANCA
In some measure.

NAVODAR
But let us assure you that we have the utmost confidence in your abilities. That is, either *we* do, if we are we, or our doppelganger does, if we am he. But hey, there's no call to doubt—Here's our wife, the *King's* wife, in any—and if *she* can't tell you—

[*Diri enters, eating continually from a large tub of ice cream, followed by Cassio, who is playing Hilliard & Mann's "Dearie."*]

NAVODAR
With the King's General, Cassio, so conveniently padding in her footsteps.

Diri. Who are we?

DIRI
An imbecile.

NAVODAR
Well, there you have it. She would hardly talk to our *doppelganger* that way. So ... the counterfeit King remains at large.

BIANCA
Your husband, Doctor, was confiding that he has a double.

CASSIO
[*The Doublemint gum commercial jingle: "Double double your refreshment/ Double double your enjoyment."*]

DIRI
Uh-huh. Or fears he has one.

NAVODAR
Our wife, Bianca, practices her practice on us.

DIRI
And of course, by "fears" I mean "desires." You caught his—you know what I mean—his therapeutic neurotic manifestation?

BIANCA
I—

DIRI
"Our" wife? The royal "we?" Uh-huh? You've noticed?

BIANCA
It would be difficult indeed not to notice such a peculiar usage, which I took to signal his complete identification with the nation, and with the people of that nation.

CASSIO
[*George M. Cohan's "Yankee Doodle Dandy": "I'm a Yankee Doodle Dandy/ Yankee Doodle do or die."*]

DIRI
Uh-uh. Uh-uh. He needed—well, I prescribed it, actually. The manifestation. There was a crisis of sorts—

274

NAVODAR
We was a wreck.

DIRI
The dread of—i.e. e.g. ipso facto *longing for*—this supposed double—

NAVODAR
It was bad.

DIRI
Rather than *suppress* the neurosis—you see, the damage comes in the suppressing. The "We"—the so-called *"royal* We"—*publicizes* the neurosis, and by publicizing, neutralizes it—a neutral neurosis, or *neutered* neurosis ... I haven't decided which to use for my book—which term. Ice cream?

BIANCA
No thank you.

DIRI
Now there's side-effects here, any cure has its—you know yourself how it is—and the consequence of pulling this doppelganger here out of the unconscious—

NAVODAR
Uch. The dreams we used to have. Very Superman versus evil twin.

DIRI
—by giving the doppelganger an audible place in the very *syntax* of the patient—a doppelganger *effect*—so to speak—is that the patient—my husband—can never be "I"—the individual subject—being always "We"—himself and the imagined Other, uh-huh, the narcissistic reproduction of himself.

NAVODAR
But irony of ironies, it appears that our doppelganger exists after all, as we're sure will become clear—ah, clear as the conscience of a poet—when Bianca submits her detailed report, including any statements by witnesses, whatever witnesses, along with any distinguishing physical characteristics of those witnesses, which she will deliver to us—

BIANCA
In twenty-six days, upon completion of sundry investigations, you will receive my report in the form of a White Paper.

NAVODAR
Wonderful. That sounds immensely official.

[*Bianca exits.*]

CASSIO
[*Styx's "Renegade": "Oh Mamma, I'm in fear for my life from the long arm of the law."*]

[*Navodar hands pillow to Cassio. Aside, to Cassio.*]

NAVODAR
Cassio, kill her. [*Cassio follows Bianca, humming:*]

CASSIO
[*Bob Marley's "I Shot the Sheriff": "I shot the sheriff/ But I didn't shoot no deputy, oh no! Oh!"*]

DIRI
Look how Cassio lock-steps after her.

NAVODAR
Mmmm.

DIRI
She loves him, you know. Ice cream?

NAVODAR
Bianca loves Cassio? [*He ignores the offer of ice cream and stares after them for a long time.*]

DIRI
Uh-huh. She woos him to her.

NAVODAR
What a delicious nightmare.

DIRI
Not that love is any *simple* matter for Bianca, uh-uh: the embrace of the Other, a neurotic aversion ... It's all there in her speech, of course. Drives me crazy. Her particular chatter.

NAVODAR
Yeah, it's ... something.

DIRI
The grammar. Objects never match easily with subjects. Between them, an obstacle course of subjunctive phrases, dangling modifiers, funky participles, the gamut. And all just to avoid—uh-huh—to eliminate the possibility of that most simple of expressions, "I ... love ... you."

NAVODAR

Thy bed, lust-stain'd, shall with lust's blood be spotted.

DIRI

Poetry, darling? You're sweating. Here, let me ...

[*She puts down tub of ice cream, pulls out a red-spotted handkerchief and starts to mop his brow. Navodar finally turns to her.*]

NAVODAR

"Supposed double?" "Imagined Other?" "Narcissistic reproduction?" Yes. A lot of help you are. We could just kill you sometimes.

[*He knocks her hand away, and the handkerchief falls to the floor. Outro Music: Styx's "Renegade."*]

SCENE K: KERCHIEF
Ordina sees handkerchief on floor. Picks it up.

ORDINA
The Queen's handkerchief! Yes, I've often noticed her fondling it.

[*Enter Ogai.*]

ORDINA
I have a thing for you.

OGAI
A thing for me? It is a common thing—

ORDINA
Ha!

OGAI
To have a foolish wife.

ORDINA
O, is that all? What will you give me now for the same handkerchief?

OGAI
What handkerchief?

ORDINA
What handkerchief? Why, that Navodar first gave to Diri—that which so often you did bid me steal.

OGAI
Hast stol'n it from her?

ORDINA
No, 'faith; she let it drop by negligence. And, to the advantage, I, being here, took't up. Look, here it is.

OGAI
A good wench; give it me.

ORDINA
What will you do with 't, that you have been so earnest to have me filch it?

OGAI
Why, what's that to you?

ORDINA
Just this. I have done a thing—can we drop the talk?

OGAI
What talk, pray?

ORDINA
The "what talk, *pray*" talk. That—this formal way we get of talking when we're—when we've been fighting and are kind of walking on eggshells with each other—or your way of punishing me—the "did bid me steal"— that kind of talk. Calling me "wench."

OGAI
Sure then. Whatever. Though I don't think there's anything wrong— we're both King's ministers, after all—part of a Royal Court, for god damn—anything wrong with upholding a certain style, some *elevation*, in our discourse. So what do you want for the handkerchief?

ORDINA
I have an idea.

OGAI
Whoo-ee.

ORDINA
That I'd like you to present to the King.

OGAI
Why don't you—?

ORDINA
You have his ear. It's about Kofi Annan. It's a golf course.

OGAI
A golf course is your idea?

ORDINA
Building a golf course. An *extraordinary* golf course.

OGAI
And Kofi Annan?

ORDINA
Well, it's like China. We have a—it's a public relations problem. Well, a *routinely-commit-heinous-crimes-against-humanity* type of public relations problem. A *Kofi-Annan's-pissed-off-at-us* kind of problem. But you can do that—commit your heinous crimes—you can do that if you

have established *International Legitimacy*. Like China.

OGAI
I'm supposed to go to the King with this?

ORDINA
China with the Olympics. So that when people think of Tiananmen Square they won't think of the tanks—

OGAI
And that guy standing in front of the tanks.

ORDINA
They'll think of beach volleyball.

OGAI
So a golf course—

ORDINA
Not just *any* golf course. A golf course so special that Tiger Woods will come and play it. And once you have Tiger Woods ...

OGAI
International Legitimacy.

ORDINA
I've made some sketches. [*She pulls them out.*] Preliminary. You see what will be different—extraordinary—about this course is that the holes can be played in *any order*.

OGAI
How?

ORDINA
The player can choose, you see. It adds a level of strategy, the mental element, and you know if there's one thing that really separates Tiger from the rest of the golfers ...

OGAI
The mental element.

ORDINA
So he could choose to play all the Par Fives *first*, to create an intimidating lead, or last, to come from behind. Or anything. But the challenge is, to design it, is the tee for every hole has to be equidistant from every other green—ease of access from hole to hole—and I've used some logarithms—but you see. And then the other challenge—this is even harder, in its own

280

way—is that every hole has to be *dramatic* enough to feel like it could be an eighteenth hole, the *final* hole, you see?—with equal potential for birdies and bogies—and yet also be *welcoming* enough to have the feel of a *first* hole. There.

[*Ogai takes sketches.*]

OGAI
So I bring these sketches—

ORDINA
And you get the handkerchief.

[*Ogai snatches handkerchief from her. Enter Bianca, walking across stage lost in thought. Stops on a dime and looks at Ordina and Ogai.*]

BIANCA
Your handkerchief, Ogai? Your white handkerchief? Spotted with red?

OGAI
Mine? No. It is my wife's. She lent it to me only, to mop my brow. Here you go, my sweet plantain. [*He hands handkerchief back to Ordina.*]

ORDINA
No, bunny-wunny, don't you recall? This is your very own and personal prized hanky of yours. [*Hands it back. Bianca regards them intently.*]

BIANCA
Observation has become with me, of late, a species of necessity. [*Exits.*]

ORDINA
I don't like this. She eyed that handkerchief like ... if it be not for some purpose of import, give't me again. Poor Diri, she'll run mad when she shall lack it.

OGAI
Oh, *now* who's using a formal tone?

ORDINA
Look, I'll take it to a seamstress. I'll have a copy made, and then—

OGAI
Not a copy. Definitely not a copy! Not a duplicate, no. No.

ORDINA
What? Why? Why? Why must you always push yourself into the middle of things? Always twist, and turn, and influence, and interject, and control?

OGAI
Well now, that's a good question. Like you, Ordina, I like order. I like to *create* order.

ORDINA
What kind of *order* could possibly come from—

OGAI
Well, yes, a different *type*, you know, a different *kind* of order. *Your* order—the order you adopted for yourself when your general *disorder* started fucking you up—*your* order is very par three/ par four/ par five. Numeric. Numeric order being very based on—it's very Aristotle, really, or whoever—*empirical*. Whereas *my* order is more like the alphabet.

ORDINA
Which also, there's a set order, A, B ...

OGAI
C, D—but the *alphabetic* order is based on just the *idea* of the order, really, it could be any order at all, and yet because of *who-knows-why*, it just has this one accepted order—the alphabet does. Not based on—not Aristotle, or .... So that's my order then, the meddling, *who-knows-why* order.

ORDINA
And that makes you happy.

OGAI
Happy? No. No. Not happy. Not happy.

ORDINA
No? With your meddling, your order. Then why—?

OGAI
I create structures. I make a love triangle, for instance. You know all about love triangles. And maybe—who knows—maybe I make them to recreate that one point in my life, the point when you betrayed me, when life fell apart for me.

ORDINA
The punishment goes on.

OGAI
So I make them. For instance, I use this handkerchief, let's say, to make a love triangle. I look at it, my love triangle, and it is good. But as soon as I've created it, and looked at it, and seen it is good, I see ... something's wrong.

282

ORDINA
Yes, is that bl—

OGAI
I'm *talking. I* am talking. Something wrong. There is the triangle ... and then there is a *fourth* figure ... familiar figure ... *myself.* And it seems to me, then, that there are two of me, really, the one who *created* the little scene, the triangle, the structure, and the one who finds himself accidentally in the scene, the one who is *created.* Then it occurs to me, if I am a double, a duplicate, maybe all these other people, the three people in this triangle of my devising, are doubles as well. Double knavery. Order is not order. This is not a handkerchief. I am not what I am. I am the beast with two backs.

[*Outro Music: Jackson Five's "ABC."*]

SCENE L: LABYRINTH

Diri sits in a chair, neurotically scratching herself. This scratching starts off subtle, gets more intense throughout the scene. Bianca lies on couch.

BIANCA
Truth is not always in a well. In fact, as regards the more important knowledge, I do believe that she is invariably superficial.

It was before the first dawn of morning.

DIRI
At night. Uh-huh.

BIANCA
Indeed, the only rays of light in my time-worn establishment were the ghastly, feeble emissions from my G3 Powerbook. I was, as is my nocturnal custom, clicking through from random site to random site, when the first reverberations of horror made themselves known in the blogosphere. An odd treble of a scream heard out an open window, something bloodlike discovered on the rocks by the river, horses missing from stables, some break in protocol down at the guardhouse. I traced this nascent dread through thread after thread, through listserv and chat room, until a kind of map formed itself in my mind, the longitudes and latitudes demarked by these bits and bytes of observance, a topography of rumor and conjecture, replete with legend, sites of interest, and embellished with illustration: a ploughman on the farmland, skyscrapers rising out of cities, a sea serpent on the lake, and finally, at the center of the map, inked in the merciless style of Fra Angelica—The Slaughter of the Innocents.

DIRI
Slaughter of innocence.

BIANCA
But when I emerged from my sanctuary, following this mental map to the place I knew some atrocity had just occurred, I was met with a bizarre sight. Here, where I expected to find a mass grave, a golf course had popped up overnight.

DIRI
A grave.

BIANCA
As the dump trucks and diggers rolled off into the dawn and the last rolls of sod were tamped into place, I tried to investigate without happenstance: I would take each hole in order, plumb each water hazard, sift through each sand trap, hack through every rough.

DIRI
Digging. Digging deep.

BIANCA
But the links themselves seemed to thwart me: fairways doubled back on themselves, doglegs led nowhere, and I would find myself suddenly on the 18th hole, or back on some green I had already traversed. The sun was now high the sky and I had found no carcass, no stain, no trace.

Cadillacs and Audis started filling the freshly paved parking lot, the first golfers arriving. I went to the newly-erected clubhouse and secured some tolerable clubs, joined a threesome, and determined to play the course, letting it lead me where it would, my mind only on the game, and, most emphatically, *not looking* for clues. And that is when the labyrinth coughed up its dead.

DIRI
Labyrinth. Uh-huh.

BIANCA
On the eleventh hole—which I played immediately after the thirteenth—I nearly tripped over a mangled limb in the middle of the fairway. On the third, which followed the eighth, I glanced upward, trying to judge how the prevailing winds might affect the seven-iron I was about to strike, and saw draped over the limb of a magnolia tree, the bullet-pocked skeleton of a little girl. On the final hole, which for me was the first, I read the green perfectly and rolled my ball in from twenty feet. Retrieving the birdied putt, I saw unblinking up at me from the bottom of the cup, a solitary eyeball.

[*Diri is by now scratching furiously.*]

DIRI
Well, uh-huh, what an interesting dream, uh-huh. Golf. Uh-huh. Digging through the sand trap, uh-huh.

BIANCA
Dr. Diri, it was *not* a dream.

DIRI
Uh-huh, *right*, uh-huh. The dream that is *not* a dream. Uh-huh. *Blood*, uh-huh. The *eyeball*, uh-huh. The *labyrinth. Lab-uh-rinth. Labia-*rinth. The *hole*. What your dream means, in the clinical sense—

BIANCA
It was not a dream.

DIRI
What the dream-that-is-not-a-dream means, in the clinical sense, is the *atrocity*—so called—you *seek* for, uh-huh, try to *recall*—childhood trauma, primal scene—you don't *have* to *dig* for those things. The *dig*—as in your dream—

BIANCA
Not a dream.

DIRI
The dig itself obscures them. Because that primal scene, early trauma, it gets deferred, deflected, *differented* through our thoughts,—uh-huh—our language, the way we scratch ourselves, and—you see—it shows itself, on the *surface*—no digging necessary—in *plain sight*. Oh, I've scratched myself bloody. [*Checks around for handkerchief. Can't find it.*]
Where's my ...? Where's that handkerchief? My lovely ...? Where? [*Stops looking. Holds hand up to bloody cheek, takes hand away and looks at blood on hand.*] Don't search, don't dig, don't search for the meaning. The meaning's right here. The meaning inscribes itself—

BIANCA
—on the face of things.

[*Outro Music: John Lennon's "Mind Games."*]

SCENE M: MEDDLING MAL-INTENT
Ogai is alone in Cassio's apartment, holding the handkerchief.

OGAI
I will in Cassio's lodging lose this napkin
and let him find it. Trifles light as air
are to the jealous confirmations strong
as proofs of holy writ. This may do something.

[*Drops it. Sound from off: Cassio playing.*]

CASSIO
[*"She'll be coming 'round the mountain when she comes."*]

[*Ogai exits. Cassio enters and finds handkerchief. Picks it up. Smells it. Looks at it in horror. Buries head in it.*]

[*The Moody Blues' "Come Back (I Don't Want To Go On Without You)":* "Here in the gloom/ Of my lonely room/ I hold her handkerchief/ And smell her sweet perfume."]

[*Pulls out bloody sword. Looks at it. Gets pen and paper. Writes as he plays Queen's "Bohemian Rhapsody":* "Mama. Just killed a man/Held a gun against his head/Pulled the trigger, now he's dead./Mama. Life had just begun./And now I've gone and thrown it all away."]

[*Outro music swells as Cassio seals his letter with red wax:* "Mama, oh-oh-oh-oh/ Didn't mean to make you cry/ If I'm not back again this time tomorrow/ Carry on, carry on/ As if nothing really mattered."]

SCENE N: NOLO CONTENDERE

Bianca is sitting. Cassio comes up behind her, carrying a pillow. He is about to suffocate her.

CASSIO
[*Bob Marley's "I Shot the Sheriff": "I shot the sheriff/ But I didn't shoot no deputy, oh no! Oh!"*]

[*Bianca turns around just in time.*]

BIANCA
Ah, Cassio. This is indeed one of those occasions, the frequency of which to clouded minds verifies occult beliefs, when the thinking *of* a person seems to draw them nigh. For here you are, and in my hand, I have that which I was intending to deliver to you. [*Pulls out piece of paper.*]

CASSIO
[*Blackwell-Scott's "Return to Sender": "Return to sender, address unknown/ No such number, no such zone."*]

BIANCA
Ah, but you must accept it, though from your response I see you know well what it is: a subpoena.

CASSIO
[*Sonny Curtis's "I Fought the Law, and the Law Won": "I Fought the Law and the ... law won/ I Fought the Law and the ... law won."*]

BIANCA
It is of a standard variety. You are required—as is set forth within— to furnish me with all or any documents in your possession or from the Military Archives pertaining to or bearing on the Slaughter of the Innocents.

CASSIO
[*The Beatles' "Carry that Weight": "I never give you my pillow/ I only send you my invitations."*]

[*Cassio hands her pillow.*]

BIANCA
Oh. Well. Yes. OK. Alright. I ... this is ... it's a pillow.

[*Cassio pulls out handkerchief and hands it to her.*]

CASSIO
[*Ragavoy/Berns' "Piece of My Heart"*: *"Come on and, Take it/ Take another little piece of my heart now baby."*]

[*He exits.*]

BIANCA
Handkerchief! Handkerchief! Alright. Slow. Think! Handkerchief.

I hold in my hand a handkerchief, a handkerchief that could be *the* handkerchief—an object pertinent to my investigations—worn by the as-yet-undetermined War Criminal in the course of Slaughtering the Innocents. A handkerchief received from the hand of the subpoenaed *Cassio*, and therefore, one cannot discount the possibility, an admission of guilt?

And yet—and this is a fact that strongly militates against this possibility—the handkerchief is an item typically counted among one's most *personal* of effects. The investigator, then, must also leave open the chance—a quite distinct chance, given its pairing with that other icon of personal paraphernalia, the pillow—that this handkerchief was offered, not as artifact of guilt, but as intimate gift. ...Yes, this *pillow and handkerchief* offering seems to denote an *invitation* of most suggestive stripe.

[*Looking at handkerchief.*] Is this blood? Or ... strawberries? Love's made an idiot of me. I'm white as a ... pillow, a handkerchief, a paper. I am my own White Paper.

Sherlock Holmes, when entering a room—a crime scene—assembles a geography of clues—a saucer of milk, a severed thumb—and then, his *Sherlock Holmes* mind a time-space calculator, converts that geography into a chronology: the florid-faced man strode first here, then there, then administered the acrid cup or struck the lightning blow.

My mind is not of that stamp. I cannot, as a matter of course, organize a panoply of signs within the march of time. The truth of the scattered clues emerges, for me, not from their orderedness, but from their scatteredness.

[*Outro music: The Beatles' "Carry that Weight."*]

SCENE O: OBSERVATION

Ogai and Navodar.

OGAI
And did you see the handkerchief?

NAVODAR
Was that ours?

OGAI
Yours by this hand.

NAVODAR
Cassio had our handkerchief?

OGAI
Ay, what of that?

NAVODAR
That's not so good now.

OGAI
Oh?

NAVODAR
Because we gave it to Diri, or she took it, and now he—

OGAI
Ah.

NAVODAR
Our heart is turned to stone. [*Tentatively strikes chest.*] We strike it, and it hurts our hand. Now that's pretty—could you write that—you got a pen—write it down for us?

OGAI
Heart turned to stone, hurts our hand?

NAVODAR
Yes. So you think Diri—?

OGAI
Well ...

NAVODAR
No, really.

OGAI
If I give my wife a handkerchief—

NAVODAR
What then?

OGAI
Why, then, 'tis hers, my lord; and, being hers, She may, I think, bestow't on any man.

NAVODAR
We'll kill her.

OGAI
Do it not with poison. Strangle her in her bed, even the bed she hath contaminated.

NAVODAR
Oh please. Don't be so—Christ, now—so dramatic.

OGAI
Sorry.

NAVODAR
Really, what we should do is ask her for the handkerchief back. Come up with some story ... something poetic.

It comes o'er our memory,
As doth the raven o'er the infected house,
Boding to all—he had our handkerchief.
It is not words
that shake us thus. Pish! Noses, ears, and lips.
—Is't possible?—Confess—handkerchief!—O devil!—

Oh, that's nice. We never really lose the knack, do we?

OGAI
Hardly.

NAVODAR
Y'know why we gave up poetry?

OGAI
Ennui?

NAVODAR
Postmodernism. Those critics, theorists. "Where is the meaning?" La la

la. In the writing? In the writer? In the reading? In the reader? In the—*thumpa-whump-dump*—*text* itself? The *meaning*. Or is it somehow in that—in some *spot*—the spot where it's *transferred*, where it's the *thing* and the *writer* and the *reader* all at once. All that—the theories ... it just made it hard to sit down and—there you have it—type a poem. So we became King. Thinking, you know, when you're King, it's clear, these issues. *Meaning.* Where it is. We even wrote a poem about it.

OGAI
Quel surprise.

NAVODAR
Our parts, our title and our perfect soul
Shall manifest us rightly.

But we was wrong, it turned out. It's the same thing. The same questions. The power of the King—the meaning of the King—is it somehow in himself, or conferred, somehow, before the fact, or continually given by—oh—the people, or the military, or the High Court? So it makes it hard to—again—just sit down and—you know—sign an order of execution, or declaration of war.

OGAI
Or prohibition on smoking in taverns. What's the meaning of a handkerchief? Is its meaning there already, in the weave of it? Or is it in the *giving* of it? Or *receiving* of it? Or in the guy who sees, who watches the guy give it to the girl, and knows that nothing now can ever be the same again?

[*Outro Music: John Lennon's "Jealous Guy."*]

SCENE P: PAYBACK

Ordina is apparently violently smothering someone in bed with a pillow. Ogai enters.

OGAI
What are you doing?

ORDINA
Oh ... nothing.

[*Ordina picks up pillow and reveals that no one was there. She lays her head down on pillow. Ogai gets in bed next to her.*]

OGAI
How was your Tuesday dungeon inspection?

ORDINA
As always. The worst scum of our society: deviants, thieves, and revolutionaries living indefinitely in a sub-human state of filth, disease, and corruption.

OGAI
Yes, well, and how are the pimps doing these days?

ORDINA
In mourning.

OGAI
Oh?

ORDINA
For their castrated genitals.

OGAI
And the cutthroats?

ORDINA
Paranoid. We give them switchblades and stick'em all in a single cell.

OGAI
The forgers?

ORDINA
Them? Mmm. Our social workers who are either young, stupid, or *do-goodery* enough to work in the prisons report among the forgers a creeping dread. Perhaps related, they surmise, to the fact that we are removing their hands, one knuckle at a time.

OGAI
A shame. One must admire their craft. Artists, really.

ORDINA
Yeah, I guess I prefer them to the bludgeoners and jay-walkers of Stalag Three. There's one—a forger—who, with just a quick peek at the signature of the Royal Exchequer, bequeathed himself the entire budget of the Ministry of Streets and San.

OGAI
Any fingers left on that one?

ORDINA
He's new. Only a pinky or so gone. Oh *shit*.

OGAI
What?

ORDINA
What shit are you up to?

OGAI
I need your forger.

ORDINA
Fuck you.

OGAI
This is your husband speaking. Have you forgotten your vows? "Cherish and obey?"

ORDINA
Those were not our vows. We had a hippy wedding performed by druids atop a daisy-covered promontory. I vowed to love you "as the tree loves the western winds" or some such.

OGAI
"Cherish and obey," is, I think, implied in that. Look Ordina, you can resist, but the fact is you never deny me anything. That is the nature of our sick co-dependence. The nature of your *guilt* and my incredible ability to take *advantage* of that guilt. Perhaps, after years more work with Dr. Diri, you could feel self-actualized enough to refuse me, but for the time being we both know you will succumb and place the services of your forger at my disposal.

[*Pause.*]

294

ORDINA
What do you need written?

OGAI
A love letter to Diri.

ORDINA
You love Diri?!

OGAI
No, for God's sake! For God's sake, how could you—how could you even—your accusations—No! No! I mean, no. A love letter, the letter I need, a love letter to Diri in the hand of *Cassio*.

ORDINA
Cassio?

OGAI
Who is the one man that stands between me and the King?

ORDINA
Cassio.

OGAI
A missive, an incriminating missive from *Cassio* to our *Queen*—a *love* letter—should such a letter be discovered by our *King*, it would certainly knock Cassio off my path to power.

ORDINA
It will never end, will it?

OGAI
What?

ORDINA
The payback. The paying back to you. The endless this-for-that.

OGAI
Of course not. Don't you see?

ORDINA
See?

OGAI
That's why I married you. To make it forever. To make the this-for-that forever. So here's the text of the letter. For your forger. [*Pulls out pitch pipe and blows.*] In Cassio's vernacular.

[*Plays a few notes of Sam Cooke's "You Send Me" on pitch-pipe. Ordina recognizes tune, and sings back.*]

ORDINA
Darling you send me
I know you send me
Darling you send me
Honest you do, honest you do
Honest you do, whoa-oh-oh-oh-oh-oh

[*Ogai joins in. They duet.*]

OGAI
Darling you send me
I know you send me

ORDINA
Darling you send me

ORDINA and OGAI
Honest you do, honest you do
Honest you do, whoa-oh-oh-oh-oh-oh

[*Outro music: "You Send Me."*]

SCENE Q: QUEEN'S QUANDARY

Diri holds up letter still sealed with red seal. She sniffs it and takes in the enchanting aroma. She holds it to the light, then sideways, peering into it. She puts it down on desk. Runs a finger along it. Walks away. Hurries back to it. Holds it to cheek and stands there, spacing out. Navodar calls from offstage.

NAVODAR
Diri!

[*Diri, embarrassed, jolts out her reverie, looks at letter, looks around for a place to hide it. Indecision. Navodar enters. She calmly puts it right down in plain sight.*]

NAVODAR
Diri, we have a salt and sorry rheum offends us.

DIRI
What? A *room*?

NAVODAR
A *rheum*. A *rheum*.

DIRI
A *rheum*?

NAVODAR
Yes, a *rheumatic condition*—we have the sniffles.

DIRI
Uh-huh. Then why—?

NAVODAR
Ogai has been on us to elevate our language. More King-like. So ... we have a salt and sorry rheum offends us. Lend us thy handkerchief.

DIRI
What?

NAVODAR
That which I gave you.

DIRI
You gave me a handkerchief?

[*Ogai calls from offstage.*]

OGAI
Dr. Diri, so sorry, I know it's not my time. I'm just dropping off—[*Enters, holding a letter identical to that on the table. Sees Navodar and stops short.*] Your Highness.

NAVODAR
Ogai, did we or did we not give our wife a handkerchief?

[*He crosses and sits on desk, right on the letter. Diri makes an oh-jeez-don't-sit-on-my-letter gesture.*]

DIRI
Uh-uh!

NAVODAR
What?

DIRI
Nothing.

[*She makes an oh-well-I-better-not-say-anything gesture. Ogai is curious and wanders over to investigate.*]

OGAI
A handkerchief? Yes! Of course. You are a giver-of-hankies kind of guy. You *stand* for chivalry. [*No reaction.*] You *stand* for generosity.

NAVODAR
Yes, so *where's* our bloody hanky?!

[*Navodar stands, and Ogai gets a gander of the letter on the desk. He then pulls out HIS letter, plays with it.*]

DIRI
Bloody?

NAVODAR
It's a Britishism. A poem:

That handkerchief
Did an Egyptian to our mother give;
She was a charmer, and could almost read
The thoughts of people: she told her, while she kept it,
'Twould make her amiable and subdue our father
Entirely to her love—

Are you listening to us?

298

DIRI
Uh-huh.

NAVODAR
But if she lost it,
Or made gift of it, our father's eye
Should hold her loathed and his spirits should hunt
After new fancies: she, dying, gave it us;
And bid us, when our fate would have us wive,
To give it her. I did so.

DIRI
A handkerchief, you say?

NAVODAR
To lose't or give't away were such perdition
As nothing else could match!

OGAI
Well put. "Perdition." Nice.

NAVODAR
We thought so.

DIRI
Is't possible?

[*During following, Ogai places his letter next to the one on the table. Diri looks at them both, does a doubletake.*]

NAVODAR
'Tis true: there's magic in the web of it:
A sibyl, that had number'd in the world
The sun to course two hundred compasses,
In her prophetic fury sew'd the work;
The worms were hallow'd that did breed the silk;
And it was dyed in mummy which the skilful
Conserved of maidens' hearts.

Will you pay attention and look at us?!

[*Diri looks back at Navodar. Ogai circles back to desk, picks up HER letter, continues to play with it as he was formerly playing with HIS.*]

DIRI
I *am* looking at you.

NAVODAR
No, you're—

DIRI
I'm just working to perfect my lazy eye. A neurotic manifestation of an inner—[*Turns back to desk.*] Gone!

NAVODAR
Our mother's handkerchief?

DIRI
Uh-uh, the ... [*Sees Ogai smiling with letter.*]

OGAI
Oh, look at the time, I must be on my way.

DIRI
But—

OGAI
Yes?

DIRI
Nothing. I'll see you for your regular appointment.

[*Ogai exits.*]

NAVODAR
Didn't he say he had something for you?

DIRI
Uh-huh. We are all messengers, really, you know, Navodar. Couriers. Mail carriers. Carrying—what to call them, the things we carry? The letters, the hankies, the scrap-paper remembrances of dreams. ... Uh-huh. Carrying stories for each other, through rain, snow—what is it?—sleet, and the kind of fog that, professionally speaking, I'd have to call a psychoneurotic amnesia. Only the problem is, the mail system fails. Postage is due. Insufficient address. Uh-huh. The dead letter office fills, stacked high to every corner. Or the message just remains in our pouch, we carry it forever, and never drop it off.

[*Outro Music: Bing Crosby's' "Sit Right Down And Write Myself A Letter."*]

Letter Purloined

SCENE R: RHAPSODY
Ogai opens envelope, sealed with red wax. Reads:

OGAI
What the—? Zounds, Cassio's notation. OK.

[*Tries to hum out musical content of letter. Navodar enters.*]

OGAI
Ah, Your Highness. Good. Name this tune.

[*Pulls out melodica. Plays Queen's "Bohemian Rhapsody," sight-reading, but hiding the letter behind him.*]

NAVODAR
Oooh. Easy. [*Sings:*]

Mama. Just killed a man
Held a gun against his head –

"Bohemian Rhapsody," Queen.

OGAI
Oh right.

NAVODAR
Pulled the trigger, now he's dead.

OGAI
"Pulled the trigger." Thanks.

NAVODAR
No problem. Though now the fucker'll be buzzing 'round all day. [*Taps his skull.*]

OGAI
Please. We've talked about this—couldn't you—if you don't talk in a more *kingly* fashion—

NAVODAR
Oh, yeah.

OGAI
In a manner more behooving your socio-political status—

NAVODAR
Quite right.

OGAI
It's just that it makes it hard—

NAVODAR
I understand.

OGAI
Makes it difficult to get excited about being a servant—

NAVODAR
An *aide*.

OGAI
Makes it difficult to get into all the "Yes, sire. Whatever you desire, sire" routine, the servile *language*—

NAVODAR
Certainly. Aide-like language.

OGAI
If you're not holding up your end, *language-wise*.

NAVODAR
Right. OK. How about this? "That song to-night will not go from my mind." [*Taps his skull, and sings as he exits:*]

Mama. Life had just begun.
And now I've gone and thrown it all away.

OGAI
Ah. "Beelzebub has a devil set aside for me. For me. For me." [*Looks at letter.*] Just a piece of paper. But ... If fortune ever turns against me, and I don't see why it should, this little white paper will undo Cassio, and assure my ascendancy. But for now, it needs proper camouflage.

[*Ogai quickly takes off red wax. Reseals letter with black wax. Unseals it. Crumples it. Uncrumples it. Spills coffee on it. Rips it, almost across. Regards it.*]

OGAI
All that's spoke is marr'd. All that's spoke is marr'd.

[*Outro Music: "Bohemian Rhapsody."*]

SCENE S: STRUMPET OF SUBSTITUTION

Navodar is apparently violently smothering someone in bed with a pillow. Diri enters.

DIRI
What are you doing?

NAVODAR
Oh ... nothing.

[*Navodar picks up pillow and reveals that no one was there. Navodar lays his head down on pillow. Diri gets in bed next to him. He turns, his back to her. Diri pulls out letter with red seal on it. Unseals. Makes a ripping noise.*]

NAVODAR
What?

DIRI
Nothing.

NAVODAR
We heard—

DIRI
I'm working on my rending.

NAVODAR
Your—?

DIRI
A hysterical symptom I'm developing. Tearing at one's clothes or person. Very *Bacchae*. Very Britney.

NAVODAR
Mmm.

[*Navodar turns back. Diri starts to read letter, hums Sam Cooke song, "You Send Me." Navodar turns back.*]

NAVODAR
What?

DIRI
I didn't say anything. [*Tucks letter under pillow.*]

NAVODAR
How was work today?

DIRI
Mmm. The usual. Clients.

NAVODAR
Cassio?

DIRI
What about him?

NAVODAR
Do you love him, Diri? Are you leaving us? What are you rending under there?

DIRI
Under where?

NAVODAR
Under *there*.

DIRI
No, I said *underwear*. I am rending my under*wear*. Love *Cassio*?

NAVODAR
Just a question.

DIRI
Uh-huh. You don't love me anymore.

NAVODAR
How can you say that?

DIRI
You never call me "Dearie" anymore.

NAVODAR
We do. We're sure we do. We think we just did. "Do you love him, *Diri*."

DIRI
Uh-huh. You see?

NAVODAR
No, we don't.

DIRI
You don't call me "Dearie."

NAVODAR
We just—

DIRI
Yes, called me *"Diri,"* called me D-I-R-I, called me by my *name*. You don't call me—

NAVODAR
No, we said "Dearie," D-E-A—

DIRI
No. It's a substitution.

NAVODAR
And Cassio?

DIRI
What of him?

NAVODAR
Does he call you Dearie?

DIRI
It's my name.

NAVODAR
Dearie as in:

[*Sings from Hilliard & Mann's "Dearie":*]

Dearie, do you remember Man O' War winning every race?
He ran at a record pace ...

DIRI
If he does call me "Dearie," it simply proves I'm doing my job.

NAVODAR
The job of court strumpet?

DIRI
Strumpet? What kind of—?

NAVODAR
Ogai has been on us to elevate our language.

DIRI
Elevate?

NAVODAR
More king-like. And we thought "strumpet," that kind of phrasing ... "job of court strumpet"—

DIRI
By "doing my job", of course, I meant doing my job as a *therapist*. *Transference*, Navodar. Uh-huh. *Substitution*. The patient—Cassio—substitutes the psychiatrist—me—for powerful figures in his life—parental figures, romantic figures ... usually parental figures.

NAVODAR
Mmm. Strumpet!

DIRI
So the *substitute*—me—becomes the object of all the resentment, malice, desire, hate, lust, and, invariably, *love* formerly directed at the parent, or whoever.

NAVODAR
So if Cassio calls you [*Singing.*] *Dearie*—

DIRI
Then the therapy is going well.

NAVODAR
Have you ever considered finding another line of work?

DIRI
I would never do that to you.

NAVODAR
To *us*?

DIRI
Desert you like that. Without my techniques, uh-huh—what I mean to say is transference ain't just for therapy anymore. It's the whole show.

NAVODAR
What show?

DIRI
The whole *despot-tyrant-keep-'em-under-y'r-thumb* show. Our show. Uh-huh. I got the whole thing published.

[*She reaches for a journal by the bed. Hands it to Navodar. He reads cover.*]

NAVODAR
"Therapeuta-Praxis."

DIRI
Very respected journal, very big in the psy-ops community. I'm right after the article by Rumsfeld.

[*Navodar flips through and finds the article.*]

NAVODAR
"Transcendent Transference: The Use of Common Therapeutic Practice in the Oppression of the Masses." By Queen Diri, M.D.

DIRI
Nice, huh? Start there. [*She points to page.*]

NAVODAR
"In the classic Oedipal situation—the child wishes to kill the father. Guilt ensues; the child represses his urges and transfers his hostile feelings onto the *mother*."

DIRI
Uh-huh.

NAVODAR
"Flashing forward some twenty-odd years, these feelings may be resurrected *vis à vis* the Royal Couple."

DIRI
That's us.

NAVODAR
"The desire to kill the *father* is replaced by the desire—sanctioned by the propaganda of generations of revolutionaries—to kill the *tyrant*. Fear and guilt cause the subject to once again transfer hostile feelings onto the *queen* or consort." [*He looks up from journal and comments.*] Mmm. Hillary Clinton.

DIRI
Well, she's the classic case of course. In the literature. So …

NAVODAR
[*Reading.*] "The relation between the citizenry as a whole and the Royal Couple, then, is fraught with transferred feelings of love, hate, etcetera. The Royal Couple, in turn, must manipulate these feelings in the same manner as the therapist manipulates the transference during analysis."

DIRI
There. Uh-huh. There you have it. That's my job, Navodar. Managing the transference of the populace. And you are damn lucky to have a wife who can perfect her craft—*my* craft—within the crucible of the analytic experience, with Cassio or whoever.

NAVODAR
Yes? Yes? Well ... What *were* you rending under there?

DIRI
A substitute.

NAVODAR
What?

DIRI
Substitute. Just more substitution. Navodar?

NAVODAR
Yes Dearie?

DIRI
Was that—?

NAVODAR
D-E-A-R-I-E. [*Sings.*]

Dearie, do you remember when we waltzed to the Sousa band?
My wasn't the music grand?

DIRI
Navodar?

NAVODAR
Yes?

DIRI
What's *this* tune? [*She hums a couple lines of Sam Cooke's "You Send Me."*]

NAVODAR
That's easy. [*Sings.*]

Darling you send us
I know you send us

DIRI
Darling you send me

BOTH
Honest you do, honest you do
Honest you do.

[*Outro Music: "You Send Me."*]

SCENE T: TWO TRIFLES

Bianca comes from behind Cassio with pillow, looking like she is going to smother him with it. Cassio is humming Eric Carmen's "All By Myself." Cassio looks up just in time.

BIANCA
I am returning these articles to you.

CASSIO
[*Blackwell-Scott's "Return to Sender"*: "Return to sender. Address unknown/ No such number/ No such zone."]

BIANCA
I cannot accept—the pillow, the handkerchief, that which they might portend—I return them to you as one might return for proper recompense a negligee, purchased dearly and with delight, but which, upon long consideration in a bedroom lookingglass, is deemed too revealing to retain. I don't want—I'm giving them back.

[*Cassio ties handkerchief over his mouth.*]

BIANCA
Observation has been with me always a species of necessity, but now at last, I can't, I don't *want* to see.

[*Cassio embraces Bianca and gives her a passionate kiss through the bloody handkerchief. Bianca responds, but pulls herself away.*]

BIANCA
No, I ...

CASSIO
[*Rogers & Hammerstein's "So Long, Farewell"*: "So long, farewell, auf Wiedersehen, goodbye/ Goodbye, goodbye, goodbye."]

[*He exits.*]

BIANCA
The handkerchief is always both contested site and negotiated settlement. A negotiation between nose and nasal putrescence and person and society or—when we talk of lovers—a set of erotic signs dependent for their interpretation on the codes of the court or else some other, some charged hormonal calculus. The handkerchief held between newlyweds in a marriage dance. The handkerchief that dabs the brow. The handkerchief as pocket ornament. Handkerchief as veil. Or tied to a stick and waved in desperate surrender. The handkerchief on the head in deference to

310

God. The handkerchief falling to signal the start of a duel, or dropped as coquette's gambit. The handkerchief soaked in the blood of a handsome guillotined criminal who has captured the imagination of the populace. Handkerchief as magician's prop. Now you see it. Now you don't.

[*Outro Music: Elvis Presley's "Return to Sender."*]

SCENE U: UNAMBIGUOUS UTTERANCE
Ordina's offices.

DIRI
Ah. 'uperintendent.

ORDINA
*Super*intendent. Superintendent of Police.

DIRI
Uh-huh. 'omeone 'tole a letter of mine.

ORDINA
Of ... what? No, I'm not getting it.

DIRI
Ah, becau' of my verbal affliction.

ORDINA
No ...

DIRI
My inability to pronounce the letter "eh." An hy'terical 'ymptom relating to—

ORDINA
The letter "eh?"

DIRI
Uh-huh. Like in 'nake. Or 'ex.

ORDINA
Ah, ah-hah, aaah. *Some*one *stole* the letter "S" from you.

DIRI
Uh-uh. I mean, I don't *have* it, the letter "eh," but it wa'n't *'tolen*. It ju't a manife'tation of an inner neuro'i'.

ORDINA
Well, that clears things up. But what was—?

DIRI
'tolen? A letter. Like "mail a letter" or "The Collected Letter' Of?" I had a letter. It wa' taken. I want it back.

ORDINA
Forgive me. As a Queen, you know the Force—Police Force—it's a matter

of language. We require acute—it's *precision* that we need, precision of expression, in depositions, in anything. You know, and as my analyst, you know also my *personal* requirements, Doctor, mired as I am— as we discovered yet again last week in the dream-work, my dream about being devoured by the porcelain leprechaun, the howling of the blood-red toads, etcetera—being mired in the anal-sexual phase, my personal requirements, then, for just this kind—this level—of accuracy and precision. Police-work—and my own psychic needs—must, really, *shun*—absolutely—all ambiguities, paradoxes, half-meanings.

DIRI
But ambiguou' *how*?

ORDINA
"Letter of mine." "Had a letter." Our law books—have you read them?

DIRI
'Cour' not.

ORDINA
Well, they're excellent, developed by consultants from Harvard, Princeton, the best. And they're chiefly devoted—you won't be surprised—to matters of *ownership*—the definition and protection of property. However—and here's the catch—neither the *letter* of the law nor any precedent I know of provides us a definitive take on who *owns* a letter. That is to say, is it the *sender* or the *sendee*? And you know—oh you know better than anyone else—that I have some personal history with letters ... and the sending of them.

DIRI
Uh-huh. I'm the "'endee," if you mu't know.

ORDINA
Very well, the sendee. And as possession is nine-tenths of the law, you, as the receiver of the document, would be the "owner."

DIRI
Good.

ORDINA
Nine-tenths of the law. But the law, it seems to me, always works best when it is ten-tenths.

DIRI
Nine-tenth' 'eem to *me* more than 'ufficient.

ORDINA
Efficient?

DIRI
'Ufficient. Like in, "'uffice it to 'ay."

ORDINA
But what of the claims of the sender—who did you say that was again?

DIRI
I didn't 'ay.

ORDINA
Quite right. Well, then what of the claims of this unidentified someone? For were he—can I assume it is a he? Never mind. Were he—feel free to contradict me if he is not a "he"—Were he to inquire as to the status of *his* text—I use the term "his," "his text" provisionally here of course—he might ask you, might *already* have asked you, "Did you get *my* letter?"

DIRI
He ha' not a'ked.

ORDINA
No. "He" has not a'ked. Asked. But if he *had*—"Did you get my letter?" You see, "*my* letter." My. Not in his *possession* any more, certainly, but still: "My" letter. You see, I'm trying to determine *ownership* here, not a trivial issue in a case of alleged pilfering.

DIRI
Not alleged.

ORDINA
Or let's imagine—may we imagine?—a squabble—a love spat, say—between the sender and sendee, can we imagine such a thing? Hypothetically?

DIRI
Uh-uh.

ORDINA
Well hypothetically, then. A love spat. In such a case, with such a spat, the sender might appear at midnight in the sendee's antechamber, demanding "my" letters back—you see, again indicating that ownership was never really ceded to the addressee.

DIRI
'hit!

ORDINA
By "hit" you mean "shit?"

DIRI
Uh-huh.

ORDINA
But that's really only the beginning of those who might have some claim on the letter. Marxist theorists—some of the more ineffectual of whom have managed to maintain places in your husband's cabinet—believing that a worker's contribution to the means of production should guarantee him a stake in the produced product or a share in the surplus value he has created, might say that the mailman *himself* has a claim to the letter, the meaning—the *ever-shifting* meaning—of which was dependent on his successful delivery of it. So as you can see, the phrase "my letter" is far too ambiguous to serve as the basis of any official police action.

DIRI
Alright. It was General Ca'io. General Ca'io. If you mu't know. He 'ent the letter. And Ogai who took it.

ORDINA
Ogai!

DIRI
Now I'm not telling you to arre't your hu'band. Ju't get the letter.

ORDINA
On what basis?

DIRI
On the ba'i'—the letter belong' to me.

ORDINA
Because possession is—

DIRI
In this ca'e, ten-tenth' of the law!

ORDINA
Then it belongs now—I'm sorry—to my husband.

DIRI
Uh-huh. Uh-huh. I get it. Uh-huh. Ownership is slippery, it slides and slips along—

ORDINA
Don't you mean, it's *lippery*? It *lides* and *lips* along?

DIRI
Uh-uh. I've worked through my missing letter neurosis. Isn't that *wonderful*? I'm very, very *happy*. Now what will make you stop your slippy-sliding and get the damn letter for me?

ORDINA
It is the nature of any police force, particularly one in a monarchy, where civil servants are notoriously underpaid.

[*Diri turns slightly away and pulls out a coin. Hands it to Ordina.*]

DIRI
One hundred navodollars?

ORDINA
One hundred navodollars.

[*Diri turns to go. Turns back.*]

DIRI
Which is exactly what you owe me for your last session.

[*Ordina hands coin back to Diri.*]

ORDINA
Round and round and round it goes. And where it stops ...?

[*Outro Music: From* Cabaret, *Kander & Ebb's "Money."*]

SCENE V: VOICES FROM A VALISE

Ogai asleep in bed. Ordina enters and pries his man-bag from his sleeping grasp.

ORDINA

May your pernicious soul, Ogai, rot one half a grain a day.

[*She is looking for letter in the man-bag. Removes contents, and lays them out in neat, ordered way, as she names the objects. She can take the objects out in any order, so the order below is just an example:*]

ORDINA

One: Pedicure kit. Two: One *navodollar*. Three: Telescoping pole. Four: Binoculars. Five: Black sealing wax.

[*Looks thoroughly through bag for letter. Not there. Regards objects. Rearranges them. Lists off items in re-arranged order.*]

ORDINA

One: Black sealing wax. Two: Telescoping pole. Three: Navodollar. Four: Binoculars. Five: Pedicure kit.

Objects. Material evidence. Empirical. Solid. [*Pause.*] Speak to me! Talk! Speak to me! What's your story? Objects! What story do you tell?

[*Outro Music: The Who's "The Seeker."*]

SCENE W: WHERE OH WHERE

Bianca's office. Enter Ordina.

ORDINA
Bianca, hi, look, you've got this ... well, intuitive-inductive style—if not, maybe the thoroughness and attention to detail that *I*—anyway, hi, I'm here for help.

BIANCA
I am only too happy to assist the police, particularly because I expect any service I render will be returned with your full cooperation in *my* investigations.

ORDINA
Your ...?

BIANCA
The Slaughter of the Innocents.

ORDINA
Oh. Right. That. Of course. Well. It's a simple thing, really, my problem. Which is why the Force is so—because it's so simple, and yet we've totally got our heads up our assholes about it.

BIANCA
Perhaps it is the very simplicity of the thing which puts you at fault.

ORDINA
You're funny.

BIANCA
Perhaps the mystery is a little *too* plain.

ORDINA
Sure. Whatever.

BIANCA
A little too self-evident.

ORDINA
That's the kind of thing you always say, which I don't really *get*, and ... it's just so annoying.

BIANCA
Well, what is this matter?

318

ORDINA
OK. Between you and me, a certain *text*—very important—has been purloined from an illustrious person. The individual who purloined it is known—beyond a doubt. And he's still got it.

BIANCA
How is this known?

ORDINA
Well, it's—there's some potentially racy material in the letter—the text is a letter, OK?—and if the thief didn't have it anymore—if he'd passed it on to a certain someone ... well, there'd be some repercussions which haven't happened yet.

BIANCA
Be a little more explicit.

ORDINA
By holding onto the letter, he's like *Mister Yo-I've-Got-Some-Power-Over-You*. Over the illustrious person, you know.

BIANCA
Still I do not quite understand.

ORDINA
No? Well, if he passed the letter on to the King—that's the "certain someone," OK?—there'd be some serious *reputation-impugning*, so by *holding* on to the letter he's got a—whatchamacallit—*ascendancy* over the—you know—illustrious personage—the *Queen*, actually. He stole the letter from the Queen, is the thing.

BIANCA
But this ascendancy would depend upon the robber's knowledge of the Queen's knowledge of the robber. Who would dare—

ORDINA
The thief, I'm afraid, is my husband, who really doesn't give a shit about anything except his little plottings and—So here's how he does it, right? The Queen's alone in the royal boudoir, OK, with the letter. Then in comes the King and the Queen doesn't want the King to see it. The letter. So she *lah-de-dah* tosses it on the table, and *well-well-well* in walks my husband.

BIANCA
Ah, I think I can surmise what then must have taken place. Ogai's lynx eye perceives the paper, recognizes the handwriting of the address, observes the confusion of the personage addressed, and fathoms that person's secret.

319

ORDINA
Well, yeah, like I was saying—your intuitive-inductive style, *voila.*

BIANCA
But to just purloin the article, so openly ...

ORDINA
Yes, well the *odd* thing is, Ogai happens to have, in his pocket, a letter remarkably similar to the one sitting there ... I mean, crazy, right? But with my husband ... so he's chatting, affairs of state, puts the forged—that is, the—*his* letter on the table next to the Queen's letter, and, more chatting, "oh, look at the time, bye-bye" ...

BIANCA
And he takes from the table the letter to which he had no claim. Its rightful owner saw, but, of course, dared not call attention to the act, in the presence of the third personage who stood right there.

ORDINA
Right, the King. So Ogai's out of there, leaving Cassio's—that is, Ogai's lett—a letter of no importance—upon the table.

BIANCA
Well, then. Obtaining the original letter should not pose any great difficulty. I imagine you are able to exert some degree of influence over your husband.

ORDINA
Oh god, don't even—My only leg up, really, is some sense—I *thought*—of where he hides stuff—I know where he keeps the porno, for instance.

BIANCA
But it wasn't there, of course.

ORDINA
No. I had to call in the whole damn Force to search the premises—meaning, I mean, *my* premises.

BIANCA
Couldn't the document have been elsewhere—his wallet?

ORDINA
I check his wallet and pants pockets after he goes to sleep, shirt, vest, jacket, coat pockets, and socks, shoes, hatbands, his man-bag.

BIANCA
Your husband carries a purse?

ORDINA
It's a man-bag.

BIANCA
Very well, then. Describe your search of the house.

ORDINA
OK, we go room by room, furniture first, opening every drawer. After the cabinets, the chairs. We have this technique, we probe the cushions with those long needles you're always on my case about.

BIANCA
The same needles you employ on the criminal classes?

ORDINA
Right. Now, we removed the tops from the tables.

BIANCA
Why?

ORDINA
Sometimes tabletops are taken off by thieves, the leg excavated, the stolen article stuffed in there, and the top replaced.

BIANCA
The books of your library?

ORDINA
Opened every book, turned over every page, not just—you know—giving the book a quick *shake* like they do over at Internal Affairs.

BIANCA
I presume you looked to your mirrors, between the boards and the plates? You checked your bed and bed-clothes, the curtains, the carpets?

ORDINA
Oh yeah. And then the walls, floors, ceilings. This part, I gotta say, I *loved*. We divided all the surfaces into twenty-six compartments, assigning a letter to each compartment, so we wouldn't miss any; then we checked out each individual square inch of each compartment throughout the house. But nothing.

BIANCA
Then I accept. If the police find themselves at a loss, I will take it upon myself to provide you with some aid in this matter.

ORDINA

Thanks. I ... owe you one. Or whatever. [*Exits.*]

BIANCA

This undertaking may well serve coincident ends. For Ogai's mal-intent exceeds this minor pilfering.

ORDINA

[*Re-enters.*] Oh, I nearly forgot to mention. The letter was sealed with red wax. [*Exits.*]

BIANCA

Perhaps these scrambled letters touch the very matter which must remain the foremost object of my every action—the Slaughter of the Innocents. For every misdemeanor leaves a paper trail. The excess—the excessiveness of any crime—finds its remainder in writing, which is itself excessive, like crime. Like love.

ORDINA

[*Re-enters.*] Yeah, and one more thing. This might help. The letter's from Cassio. [*Exits.*]

BIANCA

Son of Sam had his parking ticket. Leopold and Loeb? An eye-glass prescription. The Vietnam War had its Pentagon Papers. Enron? Cartons of shredded memoranda, the content obliterated. Their only message now?—their shreddedness, their paperness. That they are a trail. A trailing trail of trailing papers trailing ... no end.

[*Outro Music: The Who's "The Seeker."*]

SCENE X: 'EX

Diri's office. Bianca is on the couch. During opening lines, Diri dresses in leather jacket, pulls off skirt to reveal leather bikini bottom, and pulls on leather boots.

BIANCA
I wish to relate a valuable breakthrough I made—one quite above the plane of the ordinary.

DIRI
What? A tic? Hiccups? The stutters?

BIANCA
Nothing of that stripe at all. I went to their apartments last night.

DIRI
Their?

BIANCA
The apartments of "O" and "O."

DIRI
Uh-huh. [*Picks up leather whip. Fingers it. To self.*] A dream. They always want me to interpret their dreams.

BIANCA
On entering the room—[*She turns to look at Diri, sees her get-up for the first time.*] Ah. Confronted as I am, by such a spectacle, I find my speech arrested, as it defers to my blush.

DIRI
You don't like what I am wearing? If I don't model good therapeutic behavior for my patients, what kind of doctor—?

BIANCA
Your attire, then, and accouterments, are the model of—?

DIRI
The public cowhide fetish—very International Mr. Leather, very *Annie Get Your Gun*—that I have been developing all morning, is a neurotic manifestation—the *perfect* neurotic manifestation—to overcome an intensely withdrawn personality brought on, of course, by my parents' forcing me to wear a training bra at a ridiculously early and physically inappropriate age. Uh-huh. If *you*, Bianca, if you could only develop your own symptoms ... but you said you had some breakthrough. You entered the room of "O" and "O?"

BIANCA
And that is the narrative I shall impart, though, to preserve my own modesty, I will look somewhat askance as I proceed. [*Reclines again on couch.*] I enter the room of "O" and "O," wearing, of course, my green spectacles.

DIRI
Uh-huh. So that the room to you seemed darkened. A darkened room.

BIANCA
I wear these spectacles so no one might suspect I am cautiously, thoroughly *surveying* the room. At length my eyes, in going the circuit of the room, fall upon a card-rack, hung dangling from a little brass knob just beneath the middle of the mantelpiece.

DIRI
Mantelpiece? Hmmm. The chimney. The fireplace.

BIANCA
That's where it hung.

DIRI
The fireplace. [*Cracks whip.*] The *desire*-place. [*Again.*] The *hole.* [*Again.*] The gaping hole at the center of the room. Uh-huh. The fallopian chimney. [*Again.*]

BIANCA
[*Referring to the whip.*] Do you *have* to do that?

DIRI
Little brass knob equals clitoris. Proceed.

BIANCA
I'll make every effort. In this rack, below the mantel, sits a solitary letter.

DIRI
A letter?

BIANCA
Yes.

DIRI
It is a *letter* you are looking for.

BIANCA
It is thrust carelessly into the rack.

324

DIRI
Thrust there? [*Crack.*]

BIANCA
It was much soiled and crumpled—

DIRI
Soiled? [*Crack.*]

BIANCA
—torn nearly in two, across the middle—

DIRI
Uh-huh, it would be. The message's clear, I hope?

BIANCA
Clear? Later, when I had leisure to read it, it was mortally clear. But you? Do you know the message?

DIRI
Uh-huh. What you're looking for, and last night you "found," is what—well—what *everyone* looks for.

BIANCA
What *you* are looking for.

DIRI
Everyone. Do you remember ever catching your parents—you know—doing it? [*Crack.*]

BIANCA
Might I enquire as to the pertinacity of—

DIRI
Pertinacity? [*Crack.*] What is the sound of sex?

[*Pause.*]

BIANCA
Squish?

DIRI
How about, "OH! OH! OOH! OOOOOH!" ... You see, Bianca? "O" and "O?" You enter the room of "O" and "O," the room where your parents pant and moan—getting it on—what those in my profession call—uh-huh—the *primal scene*! [*Crack.*]

It is dark, represented of course by the *sunglasses*—see, I am so proud of you! You've had your own neurotic manifestation all along: the sunglasses! I missed that entirely ... Dark so that *you* can see, but believe you yourself are *not* seen, which is—now, come on—the totally classic situation for the child in the primal scene.

BIANCA

Doctor, I would be remiss if I failed to inform you, there is no primal scene!

DIRI

Uh-huh. Denial. Denial of ... of *what*? What was your *eureka* moment, seeing that primal scene? You saw ... *what*?

BIANCA

I would have no idea!

DIRI

Dad has a penis! [*Crack.*] Mom does not! [*Crack.*]

BIANCA

And yet in my narrative, this "dad," to whom you attach such import, does not exist! No mom! No penis!

DIRI

Uh-huh. No penis *on* the mom. [*Crack. Accidentally catches herself with the whip.*] Ouch!—"Clearly," you say, speaking to yourself from within the pregenital stage of the libido, "my father"—uh-huh—"is *castrating* my mother." I mean, maybe you didn't use those *exact words*, but—

BIANCA

And how does this concern—

DIRI

In this way, actually, in this way: the child—*you*—feels—what? regret? longing?—for the thing that's been stolen from your mother, and—ipso presto—from you: the *missing maternal penis*. [*Crack.*]

BIANCA

Missing maternal ...? It is a purloined *letter*.

DIRI

Uh-huh. The "*letter*." Which hangs *over* the *fireplace*, just like ...? Just like what?

BIANCA

Just like a *letter*.

326

DIRI
Just like a *female penis*, if it existed, you know, would hang over the vagina. [*She uses the whip to illustrate where the penis would be on Bianca.*] So in your dream you find—

BIANCA
What dream?

DIRI
The dream you've been telling me. The ... the dream. The *dream* of the darkened room. The *dream* of the torn and soiled letter-penis.

BIANCA
Dr. Diri. That was no dream. And there was no primal scene. Every time I cross your threshold, giving myself over to your care and guidance, you pursue these fancies with an incomprehensible zeal, and every session I respond in kind: I never had a father. Never had a mother. I was a hospital mix-up. A test-tube baby, mislabeled and dumped in the incubator by accident. I was brought up, like all such cases, in the Holy Mother Mary Convent for Scientific Aberrations. The novices all followed the example of their august Mother Superior in sewing up their every orifice and breathing through special valved tubes inserted directly into the trachea. So you see, *Madame*, there *was no primal scene*!

DIRI
But "Oh" and "Oh"?

BIANCA
Ordina and *Ogai*.

DIRI
And the letter?

BIANCA
Is the letter purloined.

DIRI
And what ... what's in the letter?

BIANCA
The solution to the mystery. The end of my investigations. That letter ... that letter, Diri, *is my White Paper*.

[*Outro Music: Cheap Trick's "Surrender."*]

SCENE Y: YIN FOR YANG

Bianca's office.

ORDINA
Here it is. I have a thing for you.

BIANCA
A thing for me?

ORDINA
The letter.

[*Hands a letter to Bianca. Bianca peruses it.*]

BIANCA
Knowing your husband's script—his looping r's, his fallen s—from various edicts and official memoranda, I can ascertain at once his hand is here within faithfully reproduced.

ORDINA
Yes, well, my forger friend does good work. I mean, considering he's short—God—pinky, index, and ring finger now.

BIANCA
[*Holding up letter.*] And you are quite resigned, our plot shall proceed?

ORDINA
If you are right, and Ogai is guilty—

BIANCA
I have reason to say so.

ORDINA
The Slaughter of the Innocents, the purloined letter, of course ... And beyond that my own reasons, reasons of my own, our marriage ... so yes, yes, *alright* already.

[*Exits. Music starts: Queen's "Bohemian Rhapsody" (instrumental). Bianca reads.*]

BIANCA
I, Ogai, being of sound mind and body, and under no duress from any agent of the State, do hereby make the following confession, to which I swear on the proverbial grave of my mother: I have just killed a man. I placed the muzzle of a standard-issue army revolver against the head of said man, and pulled the trigger. Now, as far as I can discern, he is dead. On a purely personal note, let me state that this tragedy affects

328

me dearly. I felt, really, that my own life had—in a spiritual sense—"just begun." And now, for all intents and purposes, I have gone and thrown it all away. I apologize to you, the reader of this text, and to the memory of my mother's tears. Words fail. Now I can only say, "Carry on. Carry on."

[*Bianca seals letter with black wax. Unseals it. Crumples it. Uncrumples it. Spills coffee on it. Rips it, almost across. Music swells.*]

SCENE Z: ZED

Bianca and Cassio lie in bed.

CASSIO

[*The Turtles' "So Happy Together": "Me and you and you and me/ No matter how they toss the dice, it has to be/ The only one for me is you, and you for me/ So happy together ..."*]

BIANCA

I visited Ogai at home, on the convenient pretext of questioning him for my White Paper. I complained of my weak eyes, and lamented the necessity of these spectacles, under cover of which I cautiously and thoroughly surveyed the apartment, while seemingly intent only upon the conversation of my host. I was looking, of course, for the purloined letter.

CASSIO

[*The Who's "The Seeker": "I've looked under chairs/ I've looked under tables/ I've tried to find the key/ To fifty million fables ..."*]

BIANCA

At length my eyes, in going the circuit of the room, fell upon a card-rack, hung dangling from a little brass knob just beneath the middle of the mantelpiece. In this rack, below the mantel, sits a solitary letter. This last was much soiled and crumpled. It was torn nearly in two, across the middle—as if a design, in the first instance, to tear it entirely up as worthless, had been altered, or stayed, in the second.

What is that? Oh, right. The Who. [*Sings.*]

I've looked under chairs
I've looked under tables
I've tried to find the key
To fifty million fables
They call me The Seeker
I've been searching low and high
I won't get to get what I'm after
Till the day I die

Nice.

To recommence, the letter had a large black seal. It was thrust carelessly, and even, as it seemed, contemptuously, into one of the upper divisions of the rack. No sooner had I glanced at this letter, than I concluded it to be that of which I was in search.

CASSIO

[*Lewis/Stock/Rose's "Blueberry Hill": "I found my thrills/On Blueberry*

Hill/On Blueberry Hill/Where I found you ..."]

BIANCA
To be sure, it was, in appearance, different from the one Ordina had described. Here the seal was black; there it was red. But, then, this very difference, and the soiled and torn condition of the paper, so inconsistent with the true methodical habits of Ogai and Ordina, and so suggestive of a design to delude the beholder into an idea of the worthlessness of the document; these things, together with the hyperobtrusive situation of this document, full in the view of every visitor; these things, I say, were strongly corroborative of suspicion, in one who came with the intention to suspect.

I returned the next day with a feigned desire for just one more query on a subject—the Slaughter of the Innocents—of which I knew him to be wholly ignorant.

It was at this juncture when you yourself, stationed in the street below and operating at my behest, started to play a high-volume pizzicato polka in "fuzz guitar" mode.

[*Cassio does so.*]

BIANCA
Ogai rushed to the window, threw it open, and looked out. In the meantime, I stepped to the card-rack, took the letter, put it in my pocket, and substituted the facsimile Ordina had devised for me.

Ogai believes he holds the cards. And when he resolves to lay down his tricks, to divulge among the populace the contents of his secret purloined letter, he expects trump to prevail. You, Cassio, overthrown. But—if I do not extend the metaphor of bridge too far—he's miscounted, and he's quite set already. The letter he has is mine, and I—

[*From under her pillow, Bianca pulls out a crumpled, coffee-stained letter with a black seal on it. Cassio stops playing.*]

BIANCA
—have his. [*She opens it.*] It's in your notation, I believe.

[*She hands it to Cassio who "reads" out loud.*]

CASSIO
[*"Mama. Just killed a man*
Held a gun against his head
Pulled the trigger, now he's dead.

Mama. Life had just begun.
And now I've gone and thrown it all away."]

BIANCA
Life had just begun. And now I've gone and thrown it all away.

[*Bianca takes pillow, and smothers Cassio. Bianca sings, as he resists and she overpowers him. He moves no more. She removes pillow.*]

BIANCA
And now I've gone and thrown it all away.

[*Outro music: Queen's "Bohemian Rhapsody."*]

Colm O'Reilly's poster design for *There Is a Happiness That Morning Is*

There Is a Happiness That Morning Is
by Mickle Maher

There Is a Happiness That Morning Is was first produced by Theater Oobleck at the Chicago DCA Storefront Theater in April, 2011, with the following cast:

Bernard........................Colm O'Reilly

Ellen..........................Diana Slickman

Dean ....Kirk Anderson

Music for "Fall Down" composed by Chris Schoen

For making this play's rehearsals and premier an easy dream, let me thank Diana, Colm, and Kirk.

And for making so much so very real, I thank, again, always, Jean.

CHARACTERS

Bernard
Ellen
Dean

A classroom with a large chalkboard along the back wall. Two lecterns sit left and right on a green rug. Bernard enters, looking like he's spent the night walking a forest. He writes SONGS OF INNOCENCE on one side of the board; addresses us, his class, from the lectern, left.

BERNARD
There is a happiness that morning is.
Just is, just on its own. Outside the hiss
and song of whatever serpents and larks
are playing throughout the chambers of our hearts.
The morning doesn't care. It doesn't care.
Look out that window, there.
The fact is I could slit my wrist
up here, that sun would still persist.
The birds would still pick seeds out of their feathers,
and sip the dew blown from those mountains whether
I cry or dance or die. Be assured
the morning will not be in the least disturbed.
Out there's a joy that will remain no matter
what the result of our dramas and chatter.
If you learn one thing from me let that be it.

Okay, if any of you still need to get
your yellow forms to me, please do. Please.
By end of class, or you'll incur the fees.
The yellow forms. All right? All right.

Now some of you might know I spent the night
out in the forest—after what happened—alone.
Not so fun. But this morning to be shown
these faces—all of them—you're all here,
even you! You've never come all year!

You're like a hundred suns who've risen
to un-ink the gloom of my night's prison.
Means more to me than I could ever say
to you, on this, perhaps my final day.

All right. Let's get this done.

I'll begin by saying that, one:
I have a special happiness this day.
As the result of last night's ... passion play.

The morning's joy has nothing on mine.
The morning's joy is well and fine,
but I've got a happiness that's like ... it's weird:

it rings me like a cylinder that's mirrored
on both its inside and its out, and so
reflects exterior fears, all doubts and low
esteem of self, deflects all that away.
While I, here snug within, as safe as clay
within my shining tube of happiness
immune to all life's crappiness
can look hard into the inside mirror
and see into myself and know no fear.
I look inside myself, today,
I look within and do not turn away
from anything: the webs, the salted snow
in there ... my usual happiness, you know,
is very spirited—like a jumpy gas
whose bubbles I amass
to lift me out of my inner grindings and goth,
to carry me away on a spastic froth.
While this is more ... it's more like breath. A calm
that lets me face all troubles with aplomb.

That's number one. Now, number two.
I am so sorry if any of you
were made distracted or upset
by hearing tell or witnessing, yet,
what I and Professor Parker did last night
out by the hedge and oak, there in plain sight.
But if it makes a difference, and it should—
it should just flip this matter to the good—
Look. We love each other very much.
Ellen and I. And the thing that's been such
a central point all term
if there's one thing that you've learned
from the poetry of William Blake
—and, really, what convincing does this take?—
is Love makes all the difference. Just because.
It does. It does. It does. It does.
With love all things are better, not worse.
As love, in fact, is real and does immerse
us all, like morning, in its reality,
and gives a certain luminosity
to everything it comes to brush against.
It's just common sense.
Two people in love committing a murder
seems a better thing to us than were there
only one committing the same. And why?
Because a single person's just some guy,
alone. A lonely person. And all he's done

as a single, lonely person killing someone
is make himself—that's right—just more alone.
But love, we know, creates a magic zone.
Lovers make assassination
seem more a tender assignation.
It highlights their togetherness.
But Ellen and I, our crime, of course, was less,
much less than murder, yes? What did we do?
We read an old poem, out loud, to you.
And while reading—sure, it now sounds somewhat crass—
had intimate relations on the grass.
In twilight's blue.
In front of all of you.

And now, for this, we would be finished here.
We would be finished after fifteen years.
And not just us. The regents say that they
might have to close the school. What with the way
the papers picked the story up so fast—
I guess the pictures that you took got passed
along.

[*Approximately here, Ellen enters and writes SONGS OF EXPERIENCE on the chalkboard opposite INNOCENCE, pointedly drawing a line between the two halves of the board. She's not noticed by Bernard, as the idea here is that she's in the same classroom, but we're seeing her some hours later, in her class after lunch.*]

       The money thing was bad before
all this. Enrollment now will hit the floor,
they say. Unless, I'm told, we apologize.
For this public showing of our dew-dipped thighs.
Say we're sorry. Me, this morning, to you,
And Ellen after lunch to her class at two.

ELLEN
[*At her lectern.*] I'm sorry.

BERNARD
And, yes, I'm happy to. My mood being such
this morning—happy!—there's just not too much
that I'd refuse. And it will be sincere.
Above all, though, I'd like to make things clear.
I'll show that what we did beneath that tree
relates directly to Blake's poetry.
That what we did out on that lawn makes sense
of every line in Songs of Innocence.

338

ELLEN
I'm sorry.

BERNARD
We'll finally see what words can really mean.
And then I think that you, and President Dean,
the board, and all your parents'll understand.
And Ellen, too, as she extends a hand
this afternoon, she will explain as well.
And better than me. She always did excel
at what we need a lover most to do:
make sane the madness that love brings us to.

ELLEN
I'm sorry.

BERNARD
We're not the first to play at Eden, are we?
But here I'll say it truly: I am sorry.

[*During Ellen's next speech, Bernard writes out the text of William Blake's "Infant Joy" on the board.*]

ELLEN
I'm sorry. But I want this day set free.
Our last afternoon with William Blake to be
a celebration. Just as I aspire
to join to every day its dance, its choir.
I want of every day a fatted bliss.
And let me tell you: I succeed in this.
I am at war with sorrow and distress
and have no heart for grey-lipped confessing
of—of what? I'm like Baryshnikov.
Each day: a dance. A joy. So fuck off.

I'm sorry to take that tone. But on this campus
there's one who'd use last night's rumpus
—what happened between myself and Mr. Barrow
out by the hedge—would use that event to narrow
my sluices; dam and perplex life's sea.
He'll fail. This day will find its ecstasy.

He thinks last night was a scandal? Yawn.
One cock in a pussy on the lawn.
This day will bloom a thousand rosewood trees
to pleasure its aching vulva, if need be.

339

He thinks that happiness is outside somewhere.
Outside of us, out in the dirt or air.
Something that by his devious fuckery
can be kept out by idiotic decree
and his dung-packed battlements of woe.
But Happiness has its Kingdom here, you know.
It lives and shouts and rules inside of us.
Inside, and thus
it's not a thing to try to worm or wind
its way into the dark cage of our mind;
it's born there, it's always been a part
of each of us, inside our skull, our heart.
Inside but never hidden, no, it hovers
patiently ... as nerves that swell the lover's
lip are always there, just waiting to be asked,
"Come on, come up." No magic need be tasked,
it's all inevitable and only he—
the dry-humping, rot-minded flea
who's proud to be called President of this dump—
he believes that he has got the jump
on happiness, and that his shaming calls
for me to say that I regret—it galls!—
regret my night, he thinks that this will block
my ease of heart and so unwind the clock
of joy. But, ah, regrets, no, I have none.
I'm sad my time with all of you is done.
And I'll not be here in the Fall.
But I have taught you all, or almost all,
what I believe and know.
Just one more poem to go ...
This afternoon here I'll say all I mean.

But first, a final word on President Dean.
He is a detriment to your education
and he is a fucker. His administration's
spray of piss-ideas and policies
has moistened all the cobbles, bricks, and ivies
in this place. He's made it his latrine,
this once-proud school. Conditions are obscene.

The mold's enough to induce toxic shock.
The ceiling drips, there's never any chalk.
I've loved this place, but please: this rug. This smell
that lingers ... oh. He's let it go to hell.
And as his flaccid soul is best expressed
by the laying of rotten eggs in lovely nests,
he thrills that mountains and lush wood surround

340

his dilapidated compound.

He likes when ugly things invade the Good.
Last night was case in point, So, if I could
now parse that episode, just for the books:
Our President was on the porch. He looks
upon the lawn and squints. The twilight irks
and puzzles him. Is't that evening lurks
within the day, or day is crawling, creeping
into night? Not right. Disrupts the bleeping
dried and cut of things. Creates unease.
Then ... by the hedge ... what's that? Big ... bunnies?
Oh, no. Ohhhhh no. How quickly dawns the light.
Nothing crepusculine 'bout this—it's night
and day again, thank God. And so like that
he leaps upon the sward, dragging that mat
—that mat!
—that mud mat from the commons room—
across the lawn, vaulting the daisies, fuming,
all his infant-anger gurgling out,
pink-faced and shrieking, the mat about
his shoulders now, like a blankie flapping
there behind, but not for baby's napping,
no. He throws it over us, we rutting
swine. Its rubber backing burned my butt.
He would've buried us if he'd had a shovel.
But now he wants us well in view to grovel.
As this is just his nature, his abject game:
hide away all love, make public, shame.

I found his note inside my box at dawn.
A tersely squirted jizz: my job is gone
unless I made amends. Permission—permission!—
granted then to offer my submission
here. Here. In my own class.
Where the lesson today is Kiss My Ass.
Kiss my ass, Dean.
'Cuz my and Mr. Barrow's little scene
was all higher education should aspire to be:
a fuck in the grass under the old, oak tree.

BERNARD
... for sure ...

ELLEN
And if the poetry of William Blake
says anything, if it can manage to wake

a single thought in us across the run
of centuries it's that: Fuck someone.

BERNARD
... for sure ...

ELLEN
Fuck someone hard on the echoing green.
Beneath the stars and their spears, slip low between
the roots of the dew and draw breath only to drown
in a love so true it's scandal.

BERNARD
... for sure ...

ELLEN
Write that down.

[*During Bernard's next speech, Ellen writes out the text of Blake's "The Sick Rose" on the board.*]

BERNARD
... for sure, if push is coming now to shove,
yes, William Blake was a fan of free love.
It's said his wife and he would welcome guests
while in the garden, totally undressed.
Completely nekkid. Reading *Paradise Lost*
and sipping tea. No doubt but he'd be tossed
out of this school. And in the London of
two hundred years ago? Good Lord, above.
Of last night's scene he'd certainly approve.
Paint a picture of it for the Louvre.
But the point I need to make is this:
yes, his poems, they trumpet risk,
and freedom, passion on the fly—
but always they seek to clarify.
Yes, it's good, Blake says, yes, yes,
to startle the timid world from its nest.
But equally we need to calm it down,
and clarify what we have done.
No mysteries, and nothing hid.
Illuminate, is what he did.

Once again, from *Songs of Innocence,*
sweet and short, yet so immense:

"Infant Joy"

342

I have no name;
I am but two days old
What shall I call thee?
I happy am,
Joy is my name.
Sweet joy befall thee!

Pretty joy!
Sweet joy, but two days old.
Sweet Joy I call thee:
Thou dost smile
I sing the while
Sweet joy befall thee!

I've said this now a thousand times, maybe.
What's this poem about? A talking baby.
A baby that talks, and its ... Mother, let's say;
they talk, it's like a little play,
with Baby saying, out of the blue:
I have no name, I am but two
days old. And it's a startling thing,
of course, that a baby should bring
these words or words of any kind
to a poem, or that a poem should find
that it has chosen a baby's voice
—a really quite remarkable choice—
just as what happened on the lawn last night
was a remarkable choice—but all right.
Poems and life are made up of surprise,
and this poor Mother, you can see her eyes,
she must be so alarmed! I'd be, too.
But see what Blake here has her do:
Seek clarity:
What shall I call thee?
Despite alarm or fear she wants to know.
She's open to all this slant world can throw
but needs some clarity:
What shall I call thee?
And then it's on Blake's baby to figure it out.
It has to, right? 'Cuz what's this poem about?
A talking baby! Bam!
I happy am.
Note "happy" comes before the "am's" deployed,
as existence is preceded here by joy.
I happy am. These three words.
In all the western canon there's never been heard
an affirmation of innocence as bold.

I happy am. And from this mold,
this simple frame:
Joy is my name
is the conclusion that it draws.
And that's all it says. Or needs to say. Because
it's clear now to its mom.
Though it was startling, almost, as a bomb
being talked at by a two-day-old.
This Mother, now, she is completely sold,
and takes the poem from there ... rocking, at rest:
Thou dost smile, I sing the while ...
Stillness, and peace, and happiness.
She knows now what she has there in her arms.
The name of it: it's Joy. Cease all alarms.
Its name is Joy. As Joy has taught.

Now why do we read poems? Here's a thought.
We read poems so we can repeat them.
We read poems so we can repeat them.
Either alone (out loud or in our head),
or to others. We like to say what has been said.
We read poems so we can repeat them.
For ourselves and others, we collect—assemble—
lines of poetry to throw at life.
In special situations that feel ... "ripe."
A wedding, say. Events that strive to be real.
That is, to be poetic. For these we wheel
out our tub of poems to try and boost
reality, repeating lines loosed
upon a thousand weddings before.
But here's what I think this repeating's mostly for:
mostly we read poems and repeat them
with the childlike wish we might become them.
And "Infant Joy," I think you know by now
it's just my favorite, evidenced by how
it's always central in my talks on Blake
and all I talk about is Blake, so make
of that just what you will. But outside class
I'm just as bad. Or worse. You cannot pass
me by and stay quote free, no ma'am.
"How are you, Bernard?" "I HAPPY AM!"
Trying to shore up, first, my personal sense
of my own personal innocence.
Attempting, second, to create a guise,
that shows myself as innocently wise
and full of wonder, right? The blossom-haired
professor of poems that no small college is spared.

344

The infantlike eccentric, yes, that's me,
with my eccentric repeating with giggling glee
these lines of "Infant Joy." And passively
I'd watch myself put on this massively
ridiculous and phony act. You know,
like you watch a rerun of a TV show
you hate, because there's nothing else that's on.
Or how I'd watch my shadow, at sunset drawn
across a wall, lengthen, fade, then pass ...
with more life than its originating mass.

And I would have myself repeat these lines,
but never, never once, I made them mine.
Could never join them to myself. No part.
Dissected them, and never brushed the heart.
Until last night. I read them on the lawn.
And that, it did the trick. All along
I thought I was in love. And yes, I was,
for twenty years, have been, but now because
I've been out on that grass and read them there
these lines remade my love, they've stripped it bare.
Now at last I am this poem. I'm Joy.

ELLEN
Does thy life destroy ...

BERNARD
We had our picnic in the woods: bok choy
with almonds, chardonnay, and roasted lamb.
And then she led me up. I happy am,
I said. She took me by the smallest finger
and she led me up the hill to linger
at the forest's edge a moment more.
And then she kissed me and the dress she wore
just seemed to fall away. Joy is my name.
Our public reading had begun. We came
out of the branches then. The dew cold
on my shoeless socks. I am but two days old!
And then I'm on my knees, she scratches my thigh,
draws a gentle drop of red and starts to cry
and laugh, and then we just go at it hard.
Well, you saw. Saw Heaven drop its guard.
Joy and Happy, we were the words of this baby.
And it, it was ... was Innocence, truly.

ELLEN
In the howling storm ...

BERNARD
And Ellen, today, will back me up on this.
With each caress out there, with every kiss,
these baby's words became our words.
It's not like we remembered them, or heard
them on the wind. It's like they found a door
that opened into us, into our core.
I happy am.
And all my flim-flam,
my falseness, all, all that was like I dreamed
it, even as our President screamed
and sprinted from the porch, just Happy Joy
was all I knew, I was a little boy!
Albeit one who wanted to have sex.
In no other way was this remotely complex.
Joy is my name! I cried; the President hopped
the daisies, and when his mud mat dropped:
I HAPPY AM I sang from underneath,
even with its rubber in my teeth.
I was newborn there in the tacky black,
HAPPY, HAPPY AM, no turning back.
It's with me still, the whole of it, just look:
these pants were round my knees last night. They took
up all the leaves and twigs and moist clover,
look, like they were sucked up with a Hoover.

[*From inside his pants and pockets Bernard hauls an almost unrealistically
large amount of flora—twigs, leaves, moss, petals, etc. Scatters them over the
floor and audience.*]

Swept up in Love's wild roundelay.
Here's some for you, so glad you came today.
You know that this is what you took a class in?
This stuff right here, it's night-blooming jasmine.
Its flower only opens in the dark,
so for its pollinators to find the mark
its scent is potent past belief. Here, smell.
I want you all to smell. It's how you'll tell
that all I say is true. Here, take some, yes.

ELLEN
[*Referring to the twigs and leaves, etc., which were not, apparently, cleaned
up after Bernard's class.*]

What is this goddamn mess?

BERNARD
Fragile, almost nothing, but so strong.
It's like our heart, our heart whose quiet song
won't quit transmitting til it has Love's ear.
It is all true. Just wait til Ellen gets here,
at two. She'll say this all much better than me.

I think, though, I'll come back. It's just ... you see,
we haven't seen each other since last night.
I came from under that mat just so excited,
ready, I could feel my chest ballooning
with that love that comes from assuming
command of things. I'd shake our president's hand,
apologize right there. Then zip up, and
arrange a meeting for the morning to
just clear the air of all the ballyhoo.
And Ellen and I would go straight home to drink
a calming tea and talk and cry, then sink
down on the bed to finish making love.
With candles all around, the sheet above
our heads pitched like a tent. It wouldn't be
the same as being in front of you, but we
would make it work. I'm sure of that.

But when I came from underneath the mat,
Ellen was gone. The President was there,
all out of breath and giving me a stare,
a stare that crawled beneath my face. But she
had disappeared, away into the trees.
And Dean, he wouldn't shake my hand. He spat.
I think. Could that be true? I tried to chat
but he just backed away. And now what light
there'd been was gone. I turned and walked all night,
all through the woods. Calling, calling her ...

But I am sure
she'll teach her class this afternoon, right here.
And I will come. Together we'll make this clear.
And things'll be back to the norm.
Now, please—I need that yellow form.
I do. You say you want a grade—OK.
Then get it to me by the end of the day.
OK ... sorry, I'm a tiny bit hoarse.
Again, apologies for any shock ...
for those of you in Ellen's course,
I'll see you here at two o'clock.

[*Exit Bernard.*]

ELLEN
Now. Take a breath.
I needn't work to death
a topic that is death itself.
Enough of Dean, of President Elf.
Of every goblin, every troll.
I'm here this afternoon with you to foal
a final lecture on the songs of Blake.
I'm here to cry for love, to sing, to wake.
And not spin discourse on pathetic frauds,
on sorry motherfuckers and dickwads.
I'm here to find my joy in thought, the thought
that's spoke aloud. Revealed. Deftly caught.
But in these *Songs of Experience*, yes, we find
one poem not spoke of yet. One left behind
til now, inside its dark. This rose. "Sick Rose."
In 1793, we think, composed.
Is usually ninth in the twenty-five or so
"experienced" poems—a modest spot to grow.
So slight, one might just overlook this flower;
but in its coyness is its horror:

O Rose, thou art sick!
The invisible worm
That flies in the night,
In the howling storm,

Has found out thy bed
Of crimson joy:
And his dark secret love
Does thy life destroy.

Blake here has not so much a poem to give,
more a prognosis—shockingly negative.
This rose's life—a life of crimson joy,
will not just end, or fade, the word's *destroy*.
Destroyed by this, this worm, all wrapped in night—
invisible—invisible—its flight.
An agent of all that which Blake called ill:
the Secret and the Dark. Invisible.
All things shrouded, undisclosed,
every covering, he opposed.
It's what I've been at all this term,
the sickness here is not this worm,
invisibility itself

348

undermines these petals' health.
Every mystery that we please
to clench within, becomes disease:
"I was angry with my foe
I told it not, my wrath did grow."
It is the theme that runs throughout the Songs:
The hidden, all, are all the world's wrongs.
But only here would William have you see
an image of invisibility.

An aim of every poet, Blake as well,
is to, most times, show as much as tell.
That is, place fleshed and concrete things before
the reader's eye. In this, Blake sets great store.
His poems desire first to offer us
a world we feel, a world we almost touch.
But here we find that desire overturned
in service of this less-than-knowable worm.
This worm. You cannot see, or sense it.
As William Blake prevents it.
First, he tells you it's invisible.
"OK," you think. "All right, all right, but, well,
I certainly still can picture it: a worm."
But, ah, how to keep that picture firm
in mind when it is one that "flies at night"?
An invisible worm at night. Does that invite
to your inner eye a crystal visualization?
No? Well, let's advance the obfuscation
and throw our blank, benighted grub
into a "howling storm." Then further rub
it from the page by using this word "worm."
Much like the things it means, a word that squirms.
It's Beowulf's dragon, or one of old France,
or the worm of earth who is a friend to plants.
Or Shakespeare's "worm i' th' bud"—pestilent larvae—
which, yes, would fit except they do not fly
and aren't invisible. It's just—just uhg.
And even if you could perceive this bug,
there is one last invisibility
tucked within its unseen cavity:
this "dark, secret love." That's the killer.
The love that hides itself. The love that fills your
rosy heart with a love no one can know;
just as this poem can never itself show.
All this poem shows is that which Blake most hates:
A shroud, a failure to illuminate.
This nothing-worm, it's like a mud mat.

That like some furious fuck he rushes at
his page with, splat. So, yes, he's just like Dean.
I'm sorry, yes, I really didn't mean
to bring it back to that but there it is.
Even here. In Blake. My mind is his.

I fear my mind he's overthrown.

I hate this poem.

We read poems so to live as poems.
To build from thought and song a home.
We read poems so to live as poems.
And this last night was to be a poem
sprung out from all I've known. With liquid moans
from throat like milk and stones,
the sloshing glint from the wine
of the bottle, fading behind
as we went up the hill, my dress it fell
like water, and Bernard—you could tell,
I think—he was, we were, composing then.
And what we'd be tomorrow or have been
meant nothing there. I know he seems a fool
at times. But he can love. Could run a school
for love. It should, it should be easy, joy.
It should come when we call. When we deploy
such artful forces to draw and coax and flush
it out, we should need just lay down and brush
the flies away and open up.
But Dean, he came. With his holler and jump,
his mat, his shroud, to make my poem this Rose.
Sick Rose. And so, I suppose,
he wins. Has won.
It's done.

For, having sex in public, let me say,
it's different, really, yes it is, 'cuz hey,
imagine, please, the most amazing sex
behind closed doors, the kind you feel connects
you to the universe and everyone
and where your "self" just melts and you're undone
inside the world and all seems vast expanse,
well, imagine that same tantric trance
of openness when you're out in the open.
The actual world is there for you to flow in.
The humankind whose soul you'd be immersed in,
well, it happens that they're there in person.

350

You find a skin you never knew was there.
And this is happiness and this is rare,
but, too, it puts you in a delicate state.
You're open to love, not braced for shrieking hate.
Not braced for swaddling in a sticky mat.
And it breaks you, bad. Apparently that
is all it takes. That single, little shove.
For in that moment, there, encased, the love
I've felt for my one man, for twenty years,
that love I've known was strong as halted tears,
I felt it curl away, just sigh and go ...
decline its leading role in our small show.

That's fascinating, isn't it?
That love can die in just a flit?
Like anything else, not always slow ...

I'm dying. Did you know?
I have a tumor, here, the size of, well,
"potato" is the word I use, I spell
it out because I like to spell, you know.
The doctor, though, just held his hands like so ...
the doctor—just last week—he did a mime,
as if he feared to waste our quality time
with talk. So like a street clown thought to busk,
letting me unwrap his meaning's husk.
A cryptic diagnosis, much like Blake's
for his doomed rose. The kind that makes
it difficult to see just what's inside
of me. It's cancer, sure. But, look, aside
from gestures and that word, what have I got?
Please say. Most cancer's named for the part it rots:
brain, breast, mouth, liver, lung ...
but my potato's made its home among
so many, with such tendrils that, indeed,
if they should try to pick it I would bleed
to death—the point being, though, that it's so ample,
it's name cannot be simple.
And so it's nameless ... like a newborn babe.
"Potato." That will have to—I'm afraid—
will have to do. It's shocking, you agree?
That people die? Especially ones like me.
I keep forgetting that it's true. It's real.
Which should, you'd think, give it some appeal.
I'm going to lose my life. I've lost my heart ...
it has on me a small head start
off of this chain-ed Earth ... but focus, now:

I'm going to lose my life. I wonder how
repeating that improves my readiness.

[*Referring to the twigs and leaves.*]

What is this goddamn mess?

I was all night in the forest. Comfortably trapped
behind that stand of maples that they've tapped.
Avoiding Mr. Barrow. Sometime late
I heard him walking by. He was elated,
or, that's how he sounded. Called my name,
so cheerfully. But it seemed all the same
to me if I called back or not. A wash.
If I came out and there were hugs and sloshy
kisses and we went back to our place
drank tea and fell to bed to interlace
again with candles, incense, and concertos,
moaning, sighing "come on, come up" to Eros,
what would be the difference? Couldn't say.
Between me staying in the woods til day
alone or going with Bernard ... I couldn't ...
couldn't say. And so til dawn I wouldn't
leave my crouching spot. I crouched the night
away, and gnawed around this grim insight:
if love can die, how then can it be true?
So frail! What, can it also catch the flu?
A proper God's immortal, that's his job.
I think we were just two quite desperate slobs.
Desperation is so easy to
confuse with love: both make you queasy through
the hollow in your throat; both make you tremble,
bulge your eyes, and cause you to resemble
most a kitten in a bear trap,
who's undergone a spinal tap.
Both make your heart go pitter-pat, yes,
and drop a pond of sweat on your mattress.
So easy to confuse one's panic for passion.
For twenty years—really? Just desperation?
Each kiss, and pinch, and brush aside of bangs.
The sleepy scoldings, breakfast nods, harangues
against each other's taste in mustard.
All those jokes and laundry. Standing, flustered,
by a broken van, trying to bicker
in the mountain wind. The poems. The sex. His snicker
when he pitched a thumb-smudged magazine
across the room, and said, "There's what I mean,

in there, I circled it. With arrows, too."
The songs, the hairs in the mouth, the swatch of blue
we came to agree on once ... I can't renew
these now. As memories they sidle through
my days and nights like drab, exhausted strangers—
how? How? Did I, each moment, perjure
myself? I guess. With every pinch and kiss.
I've wanted of each day a fatted bliss.
So how could it possibly come down to this
absurd defeat? Love's memory pressed flat
as a discarded scab by a man with a mat?
Love's memory is hid, or dead, and so
love never was, it never—no, no,
no. No. These are just sulking words.
Dull messengers of thoughts stirred
from some infected puddle of my mind.
I'm just unhinged by death and Dean. Behind
these sodden clouds there is a lamp, I know.
A light. My love was real.

BERNARD
[*Calling off, from a distance.*]

> Hel ... hello!

ELLEN
I have to fight. Against this sorry, sorry state.
Today, this hour, I'll resuscitate
one thing, one thing at least.

BERNARD
[*Off, getting closer.*]

> Here I come!

ELLEN
If not the whole of love, I'll dig a crumb
out of this Hubbard's cupboard.

BERNARD
[*Off, closer.*]

> It's all right!

ELLEN
Here comes Bernard. I thought he might.
And that's all I should need: to see his face,
here, with all of you, in light. A trace,
at least, of what I felt will not have perished.
I'll find it here, among these things I've cherished

353

always: students, Blake, Bernard, this room,
and here, in the shine and breeze of this afternoon
I'll give the lesson of this final day:
how to seek that bit of love that stays
around. Whatever that might be. The thing
that hooks itself inside the heart and clings
there past all craziness. Some brief candle
in his face, his voice, will prove I did not stand
alone along this road. I walked with him.

[*Bernard enters, running, out of breath.*]

BERNARD
Hi ... hi ... here I am.
I'm here. I'm here. I ran.
... sorry ... I ... some of you
I told I'd be here right at two ...
meant to be on time ... excuse me ...
out of ... up all night ... you see ...
I took a nap. At one.
And overslept. I wish you hadn't begun ...
But that's OK ... I'm here.
I'm here. I ran ... oh, God. Oh, dear.

[*Goes to Ellen, hugs her.*]

I missed you. Where were you?

ELLEN
Just ...

BERNARD
            ... just out there, thinking through
all this?

ELLEN
            Just in the woods.

BERNARD
                        All night?
I looked there—where? I—

ELLEN
                        Yes. All night.

BERNARD
OK. OK. Well, anyway ...

354

[Goes to lectern, addresses class.]

It was the nap I blame for my delay.
It was a nap that had no care for clocks.
You know of what I speak: it's like there's rocks
behind your eyes; some ancient, weight-drunk stones,
that by their brutish density alone
squeeze out your cognizance of Time and crush
all your alarms and urgencies to mush.
Turn consciousness to punctured bubble wrap.
I'm sorry I'm late. I had that kind of nap.

I wanted both of us together here,
this afternoon, with all of you this near.
In light. As I believe proximity
might help you all to see—quite literally—
with clearer sight just what love is.
It's this. And when Blake speaks of his,
his love, it is the same.
And it's the same
as last night's effort to express.
The vital difference here is that we're dressed.
And not pumping away in distant shrubbery,
in what, perhaps, seemed shadowed mummery.
And when we say we're sorry here, together,
for this thing we did that caused displeasure
and distress, such an apology,
by dint of being from two, will be more lovely,
yes? We've said we're sorry on our own,
but now, relax, and see how we atone
in unison, I think, to make it fun.

[To Ellen.]

On three. Is that all right? And then we're done.
On three we'll say, "We're sorry for the fuss."
One, two three. "We're sorry..."

[Realizes Ellen hasn't gone along.]

Uh, what's ...
... what's wrong?

ELLEN

What's wrong. Oh, Mr. Barrow ...

BERNARD
                                          What?
[*Pause.*]
You haven't, have you. Said you're sorry. But ...
but that's ... it's just not that big of a deal—

ELLEN
No. I suppose. If that's ... that's how you feel?

BERNARD
I do. Don't you?

ELLEN
                    Well, I ...
[*Pause.*]   Apparently,
the world's made mad by sex and poetry.
That you should ask me to apologize
to Dean, that you should ask that I chastise
myself so you might be forgiven, anon,
for the fucking you received upon the lawn
last night—

BERNARD
                    —that's not—

ELLEN
                              A QUITE REMARKABLE
REQUEST. To think I'd be amenable—
me, who has perhaps two months to live—
to think it'd sit just fine with me to give
that self-important stump his satisfaction.
And why? As part of a ritual preparation
for death perhaps? Before my flesh is dressed
with herbs and oil, before a coin is pressed
beneath my tongue to pay the ferryman,
I am to kneel before the very man
responsible for—

BERNARD
                         For what? For what? Just what's
Dean done, exactly, that's so wrong?

ELLEN
                              The cuts
he's made to arts, to science—

356

BERNARD
                    Yes, to each
department save our own. He's let us teach
exactly what and as we please. For sure,
the budget moves he had to make, they were
perhaps—

ELLEN
                    It's been a relished happiness
for me and Mr. Barrow to express
for fifteen years our laughing, joyful disdain
of that so temptingly mock-able drip, that stain
on this secluded glade, our home—right?
Right? Or is my mind a ghost, a flight
of creaking stairs in place of memory?
For shite's sake, he stands there asking me
what Dean has done! Assault and battery
with a muddy rug!

BERNARD
                    It doesn't matter. Please,
how could it? How could anything? Ever.

ELLEN
Ah.

BERNARD
                    We had our moment, nothing can sever
us from that. Not campus politics,
not death. Not even death. Not all the sickness
this earth can vent. As I was saying this morning,
certain joys are safe; able to ignore the implorings
of misery, the seductions of despair.
Professor Parker and I were blessed to share
in an invulnerable ecstasy. The kind
that's like the sun, the cauldron of space, the wind:
it insists. Insists that it is sovereign,
free from human time and the sucking, soft fen
of doubt and mortal ends.

ELLEN
                    If that were true
then, really, what's the reason for me or you
to bother with apologies? Why say
we're sorry for realizing an unassailable
bliss?

BERNARD
Because—

ELLEN
Just wait. Before you strain
yourself with more of this.

BERNARD
Ellen—

ELLEN
Wait.
I didn't feel ... I'm sorry. I have to confess.
I didn't feel it. Your moment.

BERNARD
Yes.
I know that's what you think.

ELLEN
Oh, God.

BERNARD
Last night,
this morning, too, I know I couldn't quite
admit that you had had a different response
—or it appeared, at least, your needs and wants
were not fulfilled—

ELLEN
I ran away and hid.

BERNARD
Because you were embarrassed. What we did
was stark, and strange, and yes, ridiculous.
As that's what happens when love uses us
to show itself down here. Love lumbers to
this low dimension, awkwardly, and pins you
like a flinching moth against its page.
Rarely is there elegance or grace,
especially if your flesh is of a certain
age. It's why we tend to draw a curtain
over the slobbering, the moistened jiggle,
and the muh huh huh. Passion's wriggle,
its clumsy, sweat-caked absurdity
most times eclipses its sublimity,
as was the case last night with us out there.

358

And, now I've had my nap, it's so clear.
You think you felt nothing but shame, embarrassment.
Embarrassment, though, is just love's surface tint,
its light veneer, a taint that will be rinsed
away so easily when we've convinced
this college that we're sorry for the flap
we caused. And then both they and you will tap
into the deeper truth of what was done.
Please.

ELLEN

      Where have you gone? My only one.

[*To the class.*]

He was a poet, once. No more, it appears.
A poet would never fret about "veneers"
or "taints" of embarrassment. It was his boast
that poetry is famously the most
embarrassing of literary endeavors.
And he well knows, the muse bestows no favors
on the easily humiliated.
But there he is: stuffed, bloated, weighted
down with shame, inventing fancy reasons
for the both of us to crawl. Treason
to the poet's creed.

BERNARD

           You're really twisting—

ELLEN

Why, though? What is to be gained, assisting
degradation?

BERNARD

        I've explained—

ELLEN

            EXPLAINED?
No, you've dodged. Last week, were those tears feigned?
When I got my diagnosis, he was there.
And he was desperate, and he wept. So wherefore
now all this goddamned good cheer?
Because of one "ridiculous" appearance
on that muddy turf? Well, then, I'm glad.
Because this happy turnabout you've had
just illustrates so well a thought I touched

on earlier: how death at times is clutched
so tightly to our mind, and then so coolly
skims away to seem a fiction. Truly—

BERNARD
Ellen, I—

ELLEN
    I'm trying to explain your newly-
minted callousness, Bernard.

[*To class.*]
      Truly
this, to all Blake's Songs, this is the key:
we play too much within Death's mystery.
We swear that Death's by every measure true
one day, and next it's just the somewhat blue
and misty end to some odd fairy tale.
And from these two extremes we build a jail
in our mind. With Innocence we fling
Death off and make a talking baby King.
A chatty tot sets all the terms. And with
Experience, this worm is what doth writhe
in every fucking thing, coiling its curse
inside each molecule of the universe.
Now, both these views are false in large degree,
and twitching back and forth between them, we
depart that slow sea and shore inside
of us: that strand forever calm and wide
where we might wade, breathe, and linger, fusing
life with The Real. But, strangely, oft, when choosing
neither view, we're choosing one too much.
As Mr. Barrow has done here, with such
evangelistic vigor—full of praise,
full of bright boasts and huzzahs for the ways
of The Innocent. Believing more than ever
now in babies that converse in clever
meter and endearing rhyme.
Dragging out this poem for the hundredth time:
"Infant Joy"! Again! But now because
of our fair sport upon the sod, what was
just charming verse is now his gospel text.
Good Lord. A talking baby, please—what next?

[*To Bernard.*]

There's no such thing.

360

BERNARD
Don't listen to her.

Last night there was. Last night we were.
This poem is true. Our joy is always there.
All it asks is that we let it share
its name with us—

ELLEN
You do not understand

this poem. You've got it wrong.

BERNARD
—its sole demand—

ELLEN
This poem's a poem of nagging, small sorrow.
The melancholy of one who has to borrow
happiness, receive it secondhand
from her own nattering child, whose "sole demand"
is that she recognize that it is Joy,
not her. No, she remains unnamed.

BERNARD
Oh, boy ...

ELLEN
Thou dost smile
I sing the while

Do you not hear the sad sigh there?
The sigh that surely every parent shares,
sensing what joy they feel is rather shoddy—
a shadow of the Joy their kids embody.
What's feeling joy compared to being Joy?
Blake's thought has more savor than this cloying
treacle you've been spooning out for years
and passing off as scholarship. See, here's—

BERNARD
Now, wait a—

ELLEN
—here's the—

BERNARD
Treacle?

ELLEN
                                        —here's the thing:
He was a folk singer. Yeah. "The Ring
of Promised Wonder" being the wet-eared name
of his quartet. A name, these days, he blames
on me.

BERNARD
        I credit you. She wrote it on
my chest. In gouache diluted with Ceylon
silver-tips tea and burgundy.
That night, remember?

ELLEN
                        No. [*To class.*] This balladry
was all some time ago—we were in school.
Bernard a third-year freshman—

BERNARD
                        This is cruel.

ELLEN
—I, a fourth-year grad. The point is, though:
a folk singer. Fine, as far as that goes,
but he just couldn't find the time to read
or study. God forbid something impede
the composing of his whole-grained odes
to truth and flowers. He ignored my goads
that he gain some acquaintance with the craft
and history of the poets, and he laughed
at the idea of earning a degree
of any sort.

BERNARD
                This isn't you.

ELLEN
                        When he,
in time, saw that his Ring of Promised Wonder
had—no wonder—little promise, under
imprimatur of some humble press
he published his lyrics as poems. These found success,
though slight, in a few overnice reviews.
And this, alone, along with my good word, he used
to get a job here teaching this one class
on Songs of Innocence. The years have passed,

fifteen. And through these years, with every Song,
he's just made it up as he goes along.
And most times, like I say, he gets it wrong.

BERNARD
[*On "it wrong."*]
Stop. Stop. You loved my music—my songs.
She drove a thousand miles with my band.
Wrote her dissertation in the back of the van,
wrapped up in a speaker blanket—

ELLEN

                                        He—

BERNARD
YOU LOVED THE RING OF PROMISED WONDER. She
was there at every gig. What is this now?
What are you saying? What? Tell me how
it is you're out there soaking up the moon
with me last night and here this afternoon
I'm just a dope, a hack, a fraud, a—look,
the truth is, back then, she's the one who took
my lyrics to her friends at that small press,
and bared her fangs at them 'til they said yes
and hired her to edit the damn thing.
You loved my songs.

ELLEN
                              I did. I did. But sing
one now, today, I don't think I would know it.
Something's happened. That mat, last night, below it,
something happened. The whole world was drained
out of itself, and in a rush seemed feigned
and hollow. Love, our woods, your songs went grey
inside my head, and turned then to display
their backs of plaster. All is parody.
A parody of things my memory
can't dimly recognize. That mat was bad.
It somehow falsified this life we've had,
and yes, I didn't want that to be true.
Spent all night in the woods avoiding you,
wanting it to not be true. And when
I got Dean's pissy note this morning, then
I really didn't want it to be true, and came
to class this day determined to reclaim
my life and passion, and I said: Bernard.
Bernard will come. I'll see him and be jarred

out of this funk. I told them all that you
with William Blake inside this room ... I knew
of nothing I've loved more, and I would strive
to find that bit of love still left alive.
A shard of The Real. But then you trotted in,
demanding we do penance for our sins,
absolving Dean of his, and being a dick
just generally. I don't know how the trick
was done, Bernard. But our love is a rose.
This rose. Sick Rose. Or worse: the love we chose
did not choose us. Not sick—it never was.

BERNARD
I take it back then, no apologies.
And Dean, Dean—forget about him, he's
a Nothing. No one. It just can't be that ...
that we're undone by him. Or by his mat.
Oh God I don't want you to die. And leave
me thinking we were, both of us, deceived—

ELLEN
I don't know what has done it, but it's done.
I'm sorry. And if I could find just one
thought in this dying mind, one memory
that told me we were real, then believe me
I would ask you now to stick around.
But just as I will drop down to the ground
alone, alone I'll teach my final class.
Please go.

BERNARD
              I won't.

ELLEN
                   Bernard ...

BERNARD
                          I won't.

ELLEN
[*To class.*]
                                  An impasse!

And a question for the ages, yes?
A lover's spurned and feels he must address
The Problem in a very public place,
there with his victim/partner face-to-face.
This makes, in movies, for sweet comedy.

364

In life, it's like uninvited sodomy.
A sort of public shit-taking, I think,
creating awkward tension and a stink.
So what to do? Well, I could slit my throat,
or summon the palace guard. But, here, take notes:
we'll see what this might—

[*She throws the contents of her mug into his face.*]

BERNARD
[*Cued off "uninvited sodomy."*]
Stop it! Stop! Don't talk to me like this!
Our love is like the Joy that morning is.
It is not born, it does not die or fail,
the poets haven't just been telling tales
all these years—

[*Getting the contents of Ellen's mug in his face.*]

OW! OWWW! OWWWWW!

[*Pause. To class.*]

It's all right, I'm OK. I thought—it's not—
I thought it was ... it's just a little ... hot.

ELLEN
It's warm milk. [*Pause.*] I'm sorry. Really, I ...
Bernard, I'm sorry but I'm lost. I look
at us and only see a mock-up.
A sort of sketch. At best a brittle crust
beneath which there is nothing but a thread
of vapor maybe, or a puff from trod-
upon fungus. Nothing life or love
could hold to.

[*Somewhere during the above, Bernard has reached into his pants or taken from the floor a bit of wilted flora. He holds it out to her. She slaps it down.*]

I don't want your litter, your mess!
I've got one thing to hold to now, it's this:
That we were *almost not nothing*.
Almost not nothing. But nothing nonetheless.
As there was nothing—

DEAN
[*Standing up from the seat he's been in in the audience, unnoticed, throughout the play.*] Stop! Stop it! Stop it! Stop it!

ELLEN
What!

BERNARD
President Dean?

DEAN
[*To Ellen.*] Despicable! Despicable!

ELLEN
Get out of my classroom.

DEAN
This is my classroom. Every classroom on this campus is my classroom.

BERNARD
Is it really you?

DEAN
What, you're not sure? I'm right here. I've been here all day.

ELLEN
Get out.

DEAN
Be quiet.

ELLEN
Get out you shit-sucking fuck.

DEAN
You will stop. You will stop with that language. I have listened to it all hour, I have suffered it, waiting, in hopes you might work out these problems.

ELLEN
Suck it, you fucking—

DEAN
I WILL PROSECUTE. I will have you arrested for last night's dalliance. You will spend the last months of your life wrapped up in court proceedings.

BERNARD
Now, you hold it—

DEAN
Quiet. Quiet. I'm so tired. I've been up all night, too, you know. Thinking this out. Up all night walking the forest, walking the campus then to sit there in that seat for the morning class and again for this one. How could you not see me? I've come throughout the years, for fifteen years, to both your classes. Never have you acknowledged me. Never have our eyes met. I have raised my hand, even, on occasion. I have stood, even, and raised my hand. And never, never. [*To the class.*] You—have you noticed me? No. It's madness.

I'm sorry, can I ...? [*Leaning against one of the lecterns.*] I'm really feeling a little—I mean, you had a nap, at least. I have not slept. And both your lectures!

BERNARD
Sure.

DEAN
Which seemed very good. Language aside. Still over my head, I have to admit. I'll never understand William Blake, though I've strained and strained to for fifteen years now, morning and afternoon at your lectures. A good effort on my part. I can tell you're on to something. I feel so close to it. Just a hair beyond my grasp.

ELLEN
I'm sorry to hear that. [*To class.*]
Well. Our time is up this afternoon.
But, please, those yellow forms, I need them soon,
so if—

DEAN
No, no! I want them to stay. [*To class.*] Please stay. Of course, if you have a final or something else pressing go ahead. Go ahead. But I have something to say and I'd like people to stay.

ELLEN
[*Gathering her things.*] Well, I'm leaving. You can arrest me, you can clap me in irons, or toss me in your lowest dungeon, but—

DEAN
[*Speaking over, Ellen continues through.*] I love you.

ELLEN
—I have to get to bed, I'm out of my mind with exhaustion.

DEAN
I LOVE YOU.

ELLEN
What? WHAT?

DEAN
I love you. I love the both of you. In my tiny, invisible way. All these years you've lectured here, and for years before. [*To Bernard.*] I have all of your albums.

BERNARD
Both of them?

DEAN
All of them yes. I play them as I go to bed and right when I get up. I came to all your concerts. Twenty years ago, like you, I drove that thousand miles. Cambridge, Ithaca, through the White Mountains and Green, every show. Right up front.

ELLEN
You are lying.

DEAN
No. You will not cancel this out. You will not brush this away. I mean something.

ELLEN
I'm saying it's impossible.

DEAN
What do you know? I'm the one who knows. The concealed love is the love that knows. Because it is the love that is truly undemanding. It is not muddled by demands, its sight is clear. And it can not be doubted because who would doubt it? Nobody knows it is there.

ELLEN
I would have seen you.

DEAN
But you didn't see me. I was right there in that seat this entire time. You see only yourself, your big ideas, your passions, your catastrophes. And you see nothing. You say your love is delusion. It is not delusion. I am witness to its truth. I am a product of it. All my adult heart is the result of it. And I made it possible.

ELLEN
[*Suspecting the truth.*] Oh. Oh, no ...

368

BERNARD
Excuse me?

DEAN
I made it possible. I have stayed on as President of this "dilapidated compound" to make it possible. I hired you both fifteen years ago to make it possible. Of course Bernard isn't qualified to lecture at any institution of higher learning, even with your recommendation. He's a folk singer.

BERNARD
Right.

DEAN
I shuffled the papers to make it possible. I am a terrible administrator, I know this. I have only stayed on so the both of you might stay on and so I might live close by your love. My personal funds—a good portion of my salary, all my inheritance—I've sunk into this dump. So we could stay in this dump, together, the three of us, in this dump surrounded by these wonderful mountains and forests, nestled here in this garden, this fresh air, the stars so clear at night, I have made all of that possible for you.

BERNARD
This is obscene.

DEAN
Obscene? Obscene? What you say William Blake would have us do I have done: envisioned and actualized a paradise, a garden of love here on earth. For you. I have given and given all for you, so you might love and play and talk and talk of rhyme and meter and grand, good ideas in a garden. And for fifteen years as the endowment has dried up, and enrollment plummeted, I have thrilled to see you holding hands at lunch or stealing a kiss behind the library, thrilled to be so near true tenderness, genuine love. Genuine. Would I have done all that I have done if it was not genuine? But now you've taken an axe to the whole thing.

BERNARD
You watched us behind the library?

DEAN
It is wrong to have sex in front of other people. Always wrong. [*To class.*] Am I right? [*Back to Bernard and Ellen.*] Always wrong. Even though, yes, yes, of course, it was so beautiful, so exciting. I lost my mind it was so exciting. Seeing the two of you, I have never felt so alive, so excited. Like a blister finally popped in my heart, I was free, so out of my self, spirited away, that's why I rushed out, my body was so suddenly so alive, I had to run and jump and play. I grabbed the mat because it was just there, it was an impulse. It had no meaning, you've given it all this meaning. For me it

369

was just the thing to grab and run with, like a child grabs a towel and plays it behind him like a hero's cape, just to sail in the wind. All of a sudden I didn't want to watch from the sidelines, I wanted to be with you, join with you. But that was wrong. And you were wrong. To do this. Just look what's happened: you think you're not in love, that you've never been in love.

BERNARD
Unbelievable. We've been on display? For fifteen, twenty years? How far did you take this, exactly? Cameras in our bedroom?

DEAN
No. Oh, no.

BERNARD
What then?

DEAN
I don't like cameras.

BERNARD
What then? What then? WHAT THEN?

DEAN
I've looked in your window. I've been in your closet.

BERNARD
While we were—

DEAN
It does not matter. It does not matter, now. What matters is you have to apologize.

ELLEN
I felt this. This is what I knew
beneath that mat. That something false—you—
had always been there. Behind the shadows.

DEAN
Maybe we should take a break. Go back to my office and talk. In private. Then call a school assembly for after dinner and you can do it there.

BERNARD
Do what there?

DEAN
Fix this. Please, please, please fix this. Apologize. Say you didn't mean it. That it was a mistake. You didn't mean for them to see anything, didn't

mean for it to be in public. That it was done in innocence. That's all the parents and the board need to hear, I think. I hope. That's all I need to hear. Bernard is right, you have to calm the waters. So things can return for the both of you to how they were. So you can stay on, here, in this place. And, yes, of course, I will leave. I can understand that you might not want me around. It will be more than enough for me to know that the two of you are here, safe and in love, for these last days of Ellen's life. And, too, when you're gone, I want Bernard to stay on. We'll bury you by the hedge. A proper place to grieve. Please, please.

BERNARD
What is this? I'm not going to stay on. I'm not going to do anything you say. We're not going to apologize, or have an assembly. I'm not qualified to speak to these young people. I thought that I was, in part, qualified, and especially after last night I've been saying "oh yes, I'm more than qualified" to speak on love and William Blake. But it's a joke. You've said it. I have no business here. And Ellen's right, all these years have been a show. A display. A show for you, you ... you fuck. You FUCK. Fuck you, you demented fucker!

DEAN
Bernard, you will not use that language with—

BERNARD
You perverted shit! You sick, shitty shit-fucking bastard!

DEAN
[*On "sick."*] Stop it! Stop it! Stop! Of course there's something wrong with me! Do you think I'm insane? That I have no perspective of any kind? Of course I'm not entirely decent or healthy. But this is not about me. This is about you and the poetry. How do you think poetry and love ever come to exist, ever come to be real? It happens when it happens because somewhere someone gives love and poetry a helping hand. A hand up into a quiet peaceful place. The forest, the mountains.

BERNARD
Well, you have failed. There is no love here in these forests, these mountains. There's no poetry. Only phoniness, self-delusion, and cancer-death. And a perverted fuck. A worm.

DEAN
I am not the issue!

BERNARD
If you had not given me this job fifteen years ago, Ellen and I would have gone our separate ways. Happily or not, that's how it would've been. But you coaxed me in to this charade. This Potemkin village. God fuck it!

371

DEAN

No, God, please, please. It's all coming undone. This set-up, my trickery, it has no bearing on your love being real or not. Your love, your happiness, is real. You're both confused because you had sex in public. You had sex in public and now she's calling you names and saying terrible things. [*To Ellen.*] You don't mean those things you said. You don't.

BERNARD

Of course she means them! She's the only one who's had the right idea all day long. [*To Ellen.*] You are right. It was all ... almost not nothing. You are right.

DEAN

No, please, stop. I'm so turned around, so exhausted, it's all crashing to dust and I'm no good with words. And I am a worm and those other things you said, and I've foisted a false thing upon you, but you have to believe me. I have been with you all along, I've seen it all, and I know. Twenty years, I know. I was there at the start when she sat in the front row at the Egg and Kettle, as close as there, and you sang "Fall Down" to her—the rest of us, the audience, meant nothing—it was all to her. I felt myself turn invisible then, that moment. And I've been invisible ever since. How could I be made invisible by something false? You sang to her and she heard, and knew, no other voice, no other poem but yours.

[*Sings.*]

Come fall down on this bed just once
And all but once, this once—

BERNARD

[*On "bed."*] Stop. STOP. STOP IT GOD DAMN IT.

DEAN

Just sing it. Sing it.

BERNARD

Shut up.

ELLEN

Let him sing it, Bernard.

BERNARD

What?

DEAN

No, no. You sing, you sing it.

BERNARD
There's not going to be any—

ELLEN
I want to hear him.

BERNARD
Why?

DEAN
Not me, no—

ELLEN
Shut up. I want to hear this. Sing it.

DEAN
Why?

ELLEN
I need to see you sing the goddamn song.

DEAN
But—

ELLEN
SING IT. Sing "Fall Down." SING IT.

BERNARD
[*Starts to go.*] I don't need any of this.

ELLEN
Stay where you are, Barrow. [*He does. To Dean.*] Go. Sing it. Crawl out of your hole and sing it.

DEAN
Come fall down on—

ELLEN
Louder. So the back row can hear. But to me. To me. SELL IT.

DEAN
Come fall down on this bed—

ELLEN
TO ME.

DEAN
Come fall down on this bed just once
And all but once, this once, my heart will die
Come on, come on, you'll make me cry enough
in days to come, just fall now once, just once,
down on this bed of mine ...

Come and dig ...

[*Pause.*]

ELLEN
All right. [*Pause.*] All right. [*To class.*] So there you are. The thing
that hooks itself inside the heart and clings
there past all craziness. Why does love die?
To resurrect and prove its magic. That's why.
It's not concerned with what is false or real.
With worms or roses, what's seen or what's concealed.
It dies to live to die to live again.
Anciently new, its now is made of then.

I forgot, yet knew this all along.

BERNARD
[*Who hasn't been listening.*]
God, that really is a crappy song.

DEAN
No ... no ... no ...

BERNARD
Crappy song.

ELLEN
No. It's not. It wasn't.

DEAN
You see? She says so. She says so. She says it's not a bad song. And it's her
opinion that counts. You just have to sing it to her again. You just have
to stand right here and make the rest of us disappear and sing it to her
again. And then she'll know. And then she'll know why she and you have
to apologize, to quiet things down, because love needs a quiet place. Sing
it. Sing it. Please. Please. Just ... oh, God, I'm so ...

ELLEN
James?

374

DEAN
... oh ... oh no ....

[*He collapses to the floor. They rush to him.*]

BERNARD
Christ, what are you doing? Get up, get up.

ELLEN
Is he breathing?

BERNARD
Come on, get up. Get up!

ELLEN
I don't think he's breathing.

BERNARD
What is wrong with you? Get up. [*Suddenly frenzied, shaking Dean by the lapels.*] GET UP! GET UP!

ELLEN
Stop it! What are you doing?

BERNARD
GET UP! [*Tries to drag him to his feet. Dean's eyes are closed.*]

ELLEN
What are you doing? Put him down!

BERNARD
[*Holding Dean up, shaking him.*] WAKE UP! WAKE UP! WAKE UP YOU FUCK!

ELLEN
[*On the first "UP."*] Stop! [*To class.*] Is there a doctor in the—no, of course not. Bernard, put him down!

BERNARD
WAKE ... UP! [*He throws Dean across the stage.*]

ELLEN
BERNARD!

BERNARD
[*Throws him again.*] WAKE ... UP!

ELLEN
Stop it! You'll kill him! [*To class.*] Somebody help me!

BERNARD
[*Throwing him again.*] WHAT ... IS ... THE ... MATTER WITH YOU?
WAKE UP!

ELLEN
[*Grabbing Bernard by the hair and dragging him away from Dean.*] GET
AWAY FROM HIM! GET AWAY!

BERNARD
OW!

ELLEN
[*Attending to Dean.*] I think he's dead. I think you killed him. Oh God.

BERNARD
I'm sorry.

ELLEN
Oh God. [*Slapping him gently.*] Wake up. Wake up.

BERNARD
Please, wake up.

ELLEN
Wake up.

BERNARD
[*Gathering up some of the Night Jasmine and putting it under Dean's nose.*]
Jasmine ... jasmine ...

[*Dean coughs and splutters and wakes up.*]

DEAN
Oh ... oh ... dear ...

ELLEN
Thank God.

BERNARD
Do you want some water? Does anyone have any water?

DEAN
No, no. No water. Just need to sit. Up.

[*They help him sit.*]

BERNARD
Put him against here.

ELLEN
Right.

[*They drag him over to a lectern and prop him up.*]

DEAN
Did I faint?

BERNARD
It's OK. You're going to be OK.

DEAN
You have to sing to her.

ELLEN
We should get a doctor.

DEAN
No! No more attention on me. You have to sing to her.

BERNARD
Just relax. Be quiet.

ELLEN
Are you sure you're all right? I can get some water.

DEAN
You have to apologize.

ELLEN
[*Going to lectern.*] There's a little bottle in here ...

BERNARD
You know, I wanted to ask: did you spit at me?

DEAN
What?

BERNARD
Last night. After I came out from under the mat. You spit on me.

DEAN
I what? No.

BERNARD
They all saw you.

DEAN
No.

ELLEN
Drink this.

BERNARD
Why would you do that?

DEAN
I ... don't know. I was just so excited. It was very exciting. I'm sorry. It didn't mean anything. You shouldn't really attach any meaning to anything I do. I'm nothing. It's the two of you who ... you have to fix things. It is wrong to do what you did in front of other people.

ELLEN
Yes. All right, I will.

DEAN
You will? Fix it?

ELLEN
I'll fix it.

BERNARD
You will?

DEAN
Thank you.

ELLEN
[*To class.*]
All right. I'm sorry we've run a bit over today.
But, please, before you go, I need to say
that I am proud—so happy—to have been
your teacher here. Outside Earth's limping spin.
Now get those yellow forms to me tomorrow.
There is just one last thing, though. Mr. Barrow.

[*She takes Bernard by the hand and leads him center. To class.*]

378

I now elevate this class above
the question of what's genuine in love,
as love itself obscures what's genuine
from lovers' love-pocked minds. What's false therein,
however, we can hope to find. This school,
it seems, is false. And now that its misrule,
deceit, and craven head have been unveiled,
I think it would be best this college failed.
So towards that end, I offer this reprise:

[*To Bernard.*]

Will you have sex with me in public, please?

BERNARD
What, here?

ELLEN
                    Let's try again without the mat.

[*She kisses him, long.*]

DEAN
[*Very weak, but explosive.*]
No! No! No! Stop! That! [*Falls back.*]

ELLEN
I think this time our President's too frail
to join the dance.

DEAN
                    Please, God ...

ELLEN
[*To class.*]
                                        Your parents: They'll
be interested to know what goes on here.
Be sure you tell them. Make it graphically clear.

DEAN
No, don't!

ELLEN
[*To Bernard.*]
                    Forgot how much I like that song.

BERNARD
I'll sing it for you if you—

DEAN
                    This is wrong!

ELLEN
No, that's all right. Undo this button, pray.

BERNARD
[*Unbuttoning and taking off his pants.*]
But do you ... do you love me?

ELLEN
                    Hearts can't say
what's in their Now when dizzied by their future.
This heart knows one thought: our coming suture.
Delay no more.

[*Kisses again.*]

DEAN
              How is it you don't care?

BERNARD
[*To Ellen.*]
I don't want you to die.

ELLEN
              Can't help you there.

DEAN
Don't watch this ... don't watch this ... I won't.
I won't watch ... stop ... I won't watch ...

[*He watches as Bernard and Ellen go at it, hard. Lights fade. Bernard's song, "Fall Down," plays as we go to black.*]

Come fall down on this bed just once
And all but once, this once, my heart will die
Come on, come on, you'll make me cry enough
in days to come, just fall now once, just once,
down on this bed of mine

Come and dig this grave with me
And be the life, this life, and death of me
Come on, come on, you'll make me cry enough

in days to come, just come down once, just once,
and dig this grave of mine
Come and wake me from this dream
and have me think it's you that's real
Come on, come on, you'll make me cry enough
in days to come, just draw me now, this once,
out of this dream of mine.

THE END

WHO ARE THESE PEOPLE?
NOTES ON THE CONTRIBUTORS

Dave Buchen has been a member of Theater Oobleck since its inception. He is also the author of *Antistasia, Pinochet: A Carnival,* and *Spukt,* among other plays. As a printmaker, he has made numerous posters for Oobleck shows as well as several books and an annual calendar. He is the co-curator of the Banners & Cranks festival of cantastoria, and is currently working on *Baudelaire in a Box,* a seven-year project creating cantastoria from all of the poems in *Les fleurs du mal.* He lives in Puerto Rico, where he plays in the island's oldest klezmer band.

Jeff Dorchen was born in Detroit in 1962. In high school he and Danny Thompson discussed forming a theater company. A few years later, at the University of Michigan, they and several other students organized a production of original plays around which accrued the company that would move to Chicago and become Theater Oobleck. Dorchen wrote *The Slow and Painful Death of Sam Shepard, Ugly's First World,* and *The Mysticeti and the Mandelbrot Set* for Oobleck. In 1992 he formed Theater for the Age of Gold to produce his own work (*Birth of a Frenchman, The Life and Times of Jewboy Cain, The Problematic Cartoonist,* and *Geek Love, the Opera,* among others). In 2000 he left Chicago for Los Angeles, dissolving Age of Gold, though he periodically returned to work with Oobleck (in Dave Buchen's *Spukt,* with Thompson in *Oobleck Election Play 2008: The Trojan Candidate,* and on Oobleck's mounting of his *Strauss at Midnight*). He now lives in Los Angeles.

Terri Kapsalis is a writer, performer, and cultural critic whose work appears in such publications as *Short Fiction, Denver Quarterly, Parakeet, The Baffler, New Formations,* and *Public.* She is the author of *Jane Addams' Travel Medicine Kit* (Hull-House Museum), *The Hysterical Alphabet* (WhiteWalls), and *Public Privates: Performing Gynecology from Both Ends of the Speculum* (Duke University Press), and the co-editor of two books related to the musician Sun Ra. She is a founding member of Theater Oobleck and has performed in fifteen productions, seven of which she wrote. She teaches at the School of the Art Institute of Chicago.

Greg Kotis is the author of many plays and musicals including *Michael von Siebenburg Melts Through the Floorboards, The Boring-est Poem in the World, Yeast Nation* (book/lyrics), *The Truth About Santa, Pig Farm, Eat the Taste, Urinetown* (book/lyrics, for which he won an Obie Award and two Tony® Awards), and *Jobey and Katherine.* His work has been produced and developed in theaters across the country and around the world, including Actors Theatre of Louisville, American Conservatory Theater, American Theater Company, Henry Miller's Theatre (Broadway), Manhattan Theatre Club, New York Stage and Film, Perseverance Theatre,

Roundabout Theatre Company, Soho Rep, South Coast Rep, and The Old Globe, among others. Greg is a member of the Neo-Futurists, the Cardiff Giant Theater Company, ASCAP, the Dramatists Guild, and was a 2010-11 Lark Play Development Center Playwrights Workshop Fellow. He grew up in Wellfleet, Massachusetts, and now lives in Brooklyn with his wife Ayun Halliday, their daughter India, and their son Milo.

The Chicago *Reader* once said, "Give Noam Chomsky a speedball, a sense of humor, and a penchant for the absurd and you'd have **David Isaacson**." He is a founding member of Theater Oobleck, for which he has written fifteen plays, including *The Spy Threw His Voice, Isak Dinesen's Babette's Feast, The Making of Freud,* and *Casanova Takes a Bath.* He has appeared in more than thirty Oobleck shows, most recently as Casanova in *Casanova Takes a Bath,* as Saul Bellow in Jeff Dorchen's *Strauss at Midnight,* and improvising as John Wilkes Booth, Marie Curie, and Genghis Khan in *6X6* at Links Hall. His work has been published by *The Louisville Review* and has been featured on Public Radio International's *This American Life.*

Mickle Maher is a cofounder of Theater Oobleck and the author of numerous plays, which have appeared Off-Broadway and in theaters in the U.S and Europe. These include *An Apology for the Course and Outcome of Certain Events Delivered by Doctor John Faustus on This His Final Evening, The Hunchback Variations, The Strangerer, Spirits to Enforce, Cyrano* (translator), *The Cabinet, Lady Madeline,* and an adaptation of Stanislavski's *An Actor Prepares.* With composer Mark Messing, his *Hunchback Variations* has been adapted into an opera. He teaches play writing and related subjects at the University of Chicago and Columbia College.

Danny Thompson is a founding member of Theater Oobleck. He is also a proud member of Danny & His Things, an animate-inanimate ensemble comprised of dozens of household objects and a human (Danny). They have created ten different precariously improvised works, including *R.I.P.R.M.N.U.S.O.B.: Nixon's Last Night in Gethsemane, Newt On A Hot Copper Roof,* and *Big Tooth High-Tech Megatron vs. the Sockpuppet of Procrastination.* In several pending lawsuits he is named as a "co-discoverer" of *The Complete Lost Works of Samuel Beckett as Found in an Envelope (Partially Burned) in a Dustbin in Paris Labeled "Never to be Performed. Never. Ever. Ever. Or I'll Sue! I'll Sue from the Grave."*

THEATER OOBLECK PRODUCTION HISTORY

1988

Godzilla vs. Lent (short plays)
    The Ghost of Electricity   John Shaw
    Walt Disney's Castle is Burning Down   Jeff Dorchen
    The Imp of the Perverse   Jeff Dorchen
    Graciousness and Profundity from Deepest Space   Mickle Maher
    Thumbelina   Helen Michaelson
    Mom Returns from the Horse Races   Bob Jacobson
    Curse of the Bohemian   Dave Buchen
Three Who Dared: A Play on the Movies   David Isaacson
Cud (short plays)
    The Dogs of Constantinople   Todd Toussaint
    The Hyena Wears a Face   Lisa Black
    Morsel in the Muck   Sarah Brown
The Pope is not a Eunuch   Mickle Maher
The Slow and Painful Death of Sam Shepard   Jeff Dorchen

1989

In Cheap Shoes   Robin Harutunian
Laugh, Red Medusa! Laugh, Laugh ... a period piece   Rachel X. Weissman
Somalia, Etcetera   David Isaacson
A Body Can Be a Worry to Anyone; or,
  A Box to Contain our Solutions   Terri Kapsalis & Jane Richlovsky
Ugly's First World   Jeff Dorchen
Green Thick & Hot (short plays)
    Tomorrow the World   Dave Bompland
    His Own Business   Annette Jagner
    Technology, Terrorism, Cops   David Isaacson
    The Ungrounding of Molly Bond   Elliot Jackson
    Excerpts from "An Evening with
      Eugene O'Neill"   Danny Thompson & Ted de Moniak

1990

When Will the Rats Come to Chew Through Your Anus?   Mickle Maher

1991

The Spy Threw His Voice: A Plagiarism in Two Acts   David Isaacson
The Mysticeti and the Mandelbrot Set   Jeff Dorchen
Rhino Fest (short plays)
    Narrenschiff   Wylie Goodman
    Birds and the Bees Without the Bees   Terri Kapsalis
    Readings   Ted deMoniak
a lot of fish there are (short plays)
    Remorse   Angela Woodward & Lisa Black
    Buck & Town   Dave Bompland
    Somebody Gets Hit in the Head   Martin Greiner
    Mallet   Ted deMoniak
    VauDeViLLe WarS: Kierkegaard
      on the Patio   Danny Thompson & Ted deMoniak

"Off the Wagon" at Free Street (short plays)
    Footnote to the Persian Boomerang   David Isaacson
    Girls Who Didn't Like Horses   Terri Kapsalis & Wylie Goodman
    Tender   Jeff Dorchen
Gone   Mickle Maher

1992

Embrace the Serpent by Marilyn Quayle
    and her Sister and Theater Oobleck   Ensemble
Radio Free Oobleck (Live Radio Plays)   Danny Thompson
                                     Terri Kapsalis
                                     Ted deMoniak

1993

The Making of Freud   David Isaacson
Rhino Fest (short plays)
    Danny and his Things in: Yugoslavia:
        A Scholarly Explanation   Danny Thompson
        A big show that is actually not "Ceremony for Broken
        Hearts" because it was not really possible to do it. Sorry.   Ted deMoniak

1994

Service Sector   Dave Boo-Khaloom
Danny & His Things in: If God Were Too Involved   Danny Thompson
Foot Notes Boot Licks Toe Jams   David Isaacson

1995

Danny & His Things in: Big Tooth High-Tech
    Megatron vs. the Sockpuppet of Procrastination   Danny Thompson
The Spy Was in Stitches: The Further Adventures
    of Secret Agent Man   David Isaacson
Anywhere Else Than Here Today   Dave B'ent

1996

Danny & His Things: In a Box   Danny Thompson
Danny & His Things in: The History of Theater in America   Danny Thompson
The Campaign by Marilyn Quayle and her Sister
    and Theater Oobleck   Ensemble

1997

Isak Dinesen's "Babette's Feast"   David Isaacson
Antistasia   Dave Barnstraw
Necessity   Danny Thompson

1999

An Apology for the Course and Outcome of Certain
    Events Delivered by Doctor John Faustus on This His
    Final Evening   Mickle Maher
Pinochet: A Carnival   Dave Bye-Bye
Necessity (revival)

The Complete Lost Works of Samuel Beckett as Found
  in an Envelope (Partially Burned) in a Dustbin in Paris
  Labeled "Never to be Performed. Never. Ever. Ever!
  Or I'll Sue! I'll Sue from the Grave!!!"   Danny Thompson & Greg Allen

2000
An Apology … (revival)
The Complete Lost Works … (revival, Vermont & New York)
An Apology … (revival)
The Golden Election by Marilyn Quayle and her Sister
  and Theater Oobleck   Ensemble
Moofy Defka! (short plays)
    A Moth   Ewa Boryczko
    The Diabolical Clocks of the Old Regime   David Isaacson
    Winston Churchill: One Night Only   Sarah Weidmann
    Ugly Friend   Dan Telfer
    The Man of June 18th   Brian Berta
    Six Seconds Ago   Reed Meschefske

2001
An Immense World of Delight at Times Most
  Unlovely and Bullocky (short plays)
    Hello   Eric Ziegenhagen & Geoff Buesing
    Dead Level   Terri Kapsalis & John Corbett
    #36 Buster Keaton and the Buddha   Blair Thomas & Michael Zerang
    Svejk the Stone Listener   Jeff Dorchen & Michael Zerang
    The Hunchback Variations   Mickle Maher & Colm O'Reilly
Tedium   Mickle Maher
An Apology … (revival, Vermont & New York)
Tedium and The Hunchback Variations (revivals)

2002
Innocence and Other Vices   Dave Bucachon

2003
Spirits to Enforce   Mickle Maher
Known Unknowns (short plays)
    The Party   Friese Undine
    Rumsfeld's Attic: On the Verification of
      Weapons of Mass Destruction in Iraq   David Isaacson
    A Carcass   Baudelaire & Dave Bicharraco
    My Life in Law Enforcement   Friese Undine
    WorkWagesWar: Original Rejected Title   Dave Bicharraco
    Scythian Sky Poetry: Oral Epics of
      Nephology, Vol. 1   Dave Bicharraco
Medicine Show   Jeff Dorchen & David Isaacson
Known Unknowns (revival)
Spirits to Enforce (revival)

2004
The Passion of the Bush: An Election Play   Dave K. Barbaridad

2005
Natural History — Dave Bluestate & Sebastian Paz
The Hunchback Variations (revival)
The Book of Grendel — Dan Telfer
The Life and Times of Jewboy Cain: Jewboy Rejux — Jeff Dorchen

2006
Letter Purloined — David Isaacson
Natural History (revival)
Natural History (English version) — Dave Buchen & Chris Schoen
The Hysterical Alphabet (A-L) — Terri Kapsalis, Danny Thompson & John Corbett
Rhymes for a Long War — Dave Buchen & Chris Schoen
Letter Purloined (revival, New York)

2007
The Strangerer — Mickle Maher
The Hysterical Alphabet (Full Version) — Terri Kapsalis, Danny Thompson & John Corbett
Spukt — Dave Buchen

2008
The Strangerer (revival)
The Hysterical Alphabet (revival)
The Strangerer (Off-Broadway)
Oobleck Election Play 2008:
    The Trojan Candidate — Jeff Dorchen & Danny Thompson

2009
Strauss at Midnight — Jeff Dorchen
An Apology... (revival)

2010
6X6 — Various
Baudelaire in a Box, Episode 1: The Wine Cycle — Dave Buchen & Chris Schoen
Casanova Takes a Bath — David Isaacson

2011
There Is a Happiness That Morning Is — Mickle Maher
Baudelaire in a Box, Episode 2: Consolations
    of the Moon, The Voyage, The Giantess — Dave Buchen & Chris Schoen
Baudelaire in a Box, Episode 3: Death
    and Other Excitements — Dave Buchen & Chris Schoen
The Hysterical Alphabet (revival)

2012
The Hunchback Variations Opera — Mark Messing & Mickle Maher

ACKNOWLEDGMENTS

Every Oobleck production is the work of many hands and this book is no exception. Martha Bayne put her editorial skills to work; Kristin Basta, Rachel Hinton, Meredith Neuman, David Schlesinger, Chris Schoen, and Bob Stockfish served as outside eyes in proofreading the manuscripts; Diana Slickman laid out the pages with some invaluable counsel from Morgan Krehbiel; Danny Thompson attacked the cover design with his usual enthusiasm and creativity, and Colm O'Reilly helped put it together. Thompson, O'Reilly, David Isaacson, and Dave Buchen supplied graphics from the archives. Terri Kapsalis and Greg Kotis graciously revisited the past to bring back Oobleck lore. John Pierson of Hope and Nonthings gave us the green light. The Oobleck ensemble (as of this writing Basta, Bayne, Buchen, Jeff Dorchen, Isaacson, Kapsalis, Mickle Maher, Guy Massey, Kat McJimsey, O'Reilly, Schoen, Slickman, and Thompson) and our board of directors (Brian Azzarello, Ann Cibulskis, Kristin Espinosa, Dennis Huston, Dan Montgomery, Greg Sendi, and Stockfish) supported the project with patience, indulgence, advice, and passion. To all: thanks, and thanks, and thanks.

And to all the countless individuals who've ever read a script, sat through a reading, gave a note at a rehearsal, countered someone else's note, exercised actor's prerogative to change a line, stayed late to sew a costume, arrived at the box office broke, applauded, heckled, wrote an angry letter after the show, praised or panned our work in the press, sent a donation, or bought us a round of drinks at the bar down the street: this work is yours as much as ours. We couldn't have done it without you.